Telephone: MOUntview 3343.   *Reserve Collection*

HIGHGATE LITERARY & SCIENTIFIC INSTITUTION

920
VAU

11, SOUTH GROVE, N.6   12843

Time allowed FOURTEEN Days

Date Issued	Date Issued	Date Issued
2 0 APR 1968	- 8 MAR 1969	
2 7 APR 1968	1 4 JUL 1969	
1 MAY 1968	- 6 JUN 1970	
2 5 MAY 1968	2 8 SEP 1970	
- 1 JUN 1968	0 OCT 1970	
1 2 JUN 1968	1 4 NOV 1970	
1 6 JUL 1968	- 9 MAR 1982	
2 3 JUL 1968	1 MAY 1983	
3 1 JUL 1968	1 7 NOV 1986	
- 6 SEP 1968	- 2 SEP 1993	
5 OCT 1968		
- 1 NOV 1968	0 7 OCT 1993	
3 0 NOV 1968		
3 1 DEC 1968		
2 5 JAN 1969		
1 MAR 1969		2000-11-65

Madly in All Directions

By the same author

ANZIO

Madly in All Directions

Wynford Vaughan-Thomas

Illustrated by Andrew Dodds

Longmans

LONGMANS, GREEN AND CO LTD

48 Grosvenor Street London W1
Associated companies, branches and representatives
throughout the world

© *Wynford Vaughan-Thomas 1967*
First Published 1967

We are indebted to the Trustees of the Dylan Thomas
Estate for permission to quote from a letter of Dylan
Thomas to the author and from the poem 'In Country
Heaven'.

Printed in Great Britain by
W & J Mackay & Co Ltd, Chatham, Kent

'[He] flung himself upon his horse and rode madly off in all directions.'

Stephen Leacock

Saddling Up

Something happened to me recently which I had been trying to dodge throughout my adult life—I collided with the Horse. Not just physically, although that occurred in plenty, but morally and socially. I don't know what the particular horse felt about it, but the event made a powerful impact on me. The collision has given rise to this book.

The horse that altered my life was no splendid animal of ancient pedigree, a Derby winner or a Foxhunter. Her name was Tika, a quiet Welsh cob, who had spent the last twelve years of her life in carrying typists trekking up and down the steep slopes of the Epynt in the valley of the Wye in Central Wales. I climbed on to her back with some difficulty outside a stable in a side-street at Builth Wells. The onlookers found something to chuckle at; for me it was the beginning of a revelation. Tika was the first animal I had really ridden in my life.

I know that thousands of people ride horses, but I am one of the few who got horse-borne for the first time in the middle of my Middle Age. Prudence cried out against the dangerous experiment.

'Your bones are getting brittle,' kind friends warned me, 'the first time you fall off—and you're bound to—you'll crack your head or break your arm and you'll be sitting up in hospital a week later wondering why they call the horse the friend of man. You might as well take up ski-ing at sixty.'

But I suddenly remembered certain splendid figures I had known in their late sixties and early seventies who could have taken up ski-ing, or anything else, without turning a hair.

1

General Smuts was one of them. I was invited to have breakfast with him in 1947 during the Royal Tour of South Africa. His A.D.C. told me, 'If you come at 6.30, you can accompany the General on his morning stroll.' I turned up at the appointed place to discover that the General's idea of a morning stroll at the age of seventy-two was a brisk climb up the 4,000-foot Table Mountain behind Cape Town. I arrived panting on to the summit ten minutes behind schedule. 'Young man,' he said to me with a smile, 'at my age I haven't as much time as you for loitering.'

I also remembered the example of that incredibly spry octogenarian, the great American architect, Frank Lloyd Wright. He came over to receive an honorary degree from the University of Wales and also the homage of the younger architects of Britain. He looked immeasurably old, with that tanned, wrinkled hide that all men over seventy acquire in the dry, merciless air of the Middle West. But he had a wit like the crack of a revolver shot in a Colorado hold-up. They showed him the Cardiff Civic Centre with its sugar icing architecture, vintage 1900, and its town hall crowned with a writhing Welsh dragon in stone.

His comment: 'The guy who designed that must have lived a hundred years behind a lighthouse.'

We interviewed him in front of our Outside Broadcast cameras set up in an improvised studio in Rhyl. The Master gazed with saturnine resignation at the sea-front hotels of North Wales, which look as if they have been made with a fretwork saw out of miles of papiermâché. He seemed so old, so ready to move immediately towards another and better-designed world, that our interviewer was bold enough to express the hope that this greatest of modern architects was now handing on the torch to younger disciples. The Master looked at and through the camera.

'Yes, I reckon I am,' he said slowly. 'I've a group of very fine youngsters around me, and we've got a whole lot of projects and commissions, the new state capital at Baton Rouge, the new museum in Detroit, the Mile High project. If the Lord spares me a few more years, as I devoutly hope He will— if the Lord

2

spares me, I say—I reckon we will clean up a cool three million!'

After that, who was I to feel too old at fifty-four to tackle such a simple—or seemingly simple—operation as riding a horse through the countryside, especially as the horse turned out to be the wisest and most amenable of quadrupeds, old Tika. This book will go at her pace, trotting for preference with an occasional gallop, but with plenty of pauses for refreshment.

My original purpose in getting up on to Tika's back was to ride through an unknown land, the Wales that lies still unspoilt beyond the arterial roads, the pylons and the television aerials. I intended this book to be a true and faithful account of all that I saw and heard on that journey, but Tika decided otherwise. Her pace was so soothing, the clip-clop of her hoofs made such a friendly music to my musings that every time I saw something notable I found myself being reminded of something else—and then on to something else again. I may have begun my ride at St David's in the Lands' End of South Wales and ended it two-hundred miles to the north at Point of Air on the mouth of the River Dee, but in between I seem to have ridden through the whole of my past life.

Now that I look back on it, I don't really mind the transformation that old Tika wrought in my carefully worked-out writing plan. I've emerged at journey's end with a book that may meander half-way around the world as it wanders slowly through Wales, but of one thing you can be certain—it's a book solely concerned with giving pleasure.

So, now, to horse!

But, wait a moment, that's a little reckless for such an inexperienced rider as myself! Before we set off I had better explain exactly why my meeting with Tika marked such an epoch in my life.

1

LET me admit that, in the past, the Horse and I have never been on what you might call intimate and chatty terms. Of course, I have nothing against the noble animal. I rather enjoy looking at him—but from a safe distance.

Racehorses in training, parading along the skyline of the Downs like long-legged, elegant mannequins; Welsh ponies tossing their wild bardic hair as they raced across the damp mountainsides; even the rare farmhorse plodding like a middle-aged civil servant over the ploughlands—all gave me pleasure to behold. But again from a distance!

For nothing in my early upbringing had prepared me for a close approach to the Horse without fear and trembling. Looking back on it, I realise that I was born into a completely non-equine world.

My native town of Swansea was on the edge of the sea in South Wales; the rambling, unplanned, smokily romantic Swansea of the early Dylan Thomas period. 'This town,' said Dylan to me in our sardonic twenties, 'has got as many layers as an onion and each one reduces you to tears.' There was a deep Welsh layer, a bewildering English one, an industrial layer, a musical layer full of choirs singing the test pieces for the National Eisteddfod, a furious sporting layer of rugby teams and boxers from the Valleys, but no horse layer. Swansea's architecture, such as it was, seemed to be designed to eliminate the Horse as a factor in the life of the citizens.

But perhaps it is wrong to talk of design when discussing old Swansea. Our town was never planned, it was sprayed over the landscape with a Flit gun. From the top-story bedroom of our tall Victorian house on the lower slopes of Town Hill my brothers and I could look out over the wondrous architectural mix-up spread below. The builders of Swansea were masters of the art of surrealist juxtaposition. The enormous back-side of the Plaza cinema flaunted itself in shameless splendour over the centre of the town. The town hall hid from the citizens amongst the docks. The local museum, a fine early Victorian dream of culture, was tangled up with overhead railway arches. It contained a choice collection of dusty bones from the Gower caves, strange fossils from the local coalpits and, marvel of marvels, a gigantic stuffed elephant which filled the entrance hall.

Looming over Swansea and dominating it, as the Duomo dominates Florence, was the market. Under the great glass dome they sold everything, from herbal remedies to Welsh flannel shirts for colliers. The Penclawdd cockle women marched through the market crowds with their wooden pails balanced on their heads. Here you could buy the black treacly laverbread, made from seaweed, and test the quality of the farm butter by the infallibly hygienic method of slicing off a small piece with a silver coin.

The Art Gallery stood next to the Working Men's Club, Lucanias jostled the chapels and pubs were sandwiched in between draper's shops. Outside the centre of the town the streets shot up the hills at alarming angles. The school I attended was carved out of the rock face like the temples of Abu Simbel. Untidy architectural chaos, but always dear to me, for it was full of the most wonderful escape-hatches from convention. Swansea was the perfect place in which to grow up as the happy Unconforming Man.

But there wasn't a horse in sight, at least not a horse as Colonel Llewelyn, Pat Smythe and the Duke of Beaufort understand the term.

Naturally there was horse-flesh of a sort ambling around. But my early youth coincided with the tail end of humanity's 10,000-year-long dependence on horse-muscle for transport; buses and bull-nosed Morrises were coming in and the van-horse was on his way out. Dust-carts still lumbered about the streets, but polite people turned their heads the other way as they passed. The milk-carts were still horse-drawn, but the milkmen's animals were the only horses I've seen that wore a hang-dog expression.

With one splendid exception! This was Mr Samuel's cob, Blodwen. Mr Samuel was our milkman, an artist at pouring milk into the milk-jug in the splendidly unhygienic manner of the pre-bottling era. Horses were his passion and Blodwen his especial pride. She was dock-tailed and dappled, and high-stepped along Calvert Terrace as if she were on her way to a dance. The brightly polished milk-churn swayed and glittered in the cart behind. Its sides were ornamented with the proud boast 'Purest Gower Milk Alone Sold', and Mr Samuel dispensed the creamy liquid as if he were handing you your winnings on the pools.

Blodwen, he told us, was a show horse. On some days she would appear decorated with rosettes and Mr Samuel would call out from the cart as he arrived with the milk, 'Whoa, Blodwen fach, let the boys look at you. Feast your eyes on those trophies, lads; they are a sign of triumph. Blodwen has been Highly Commended at the Gower Show for the second time running.'

Blodwen was my first intimation that the Horse could be a thing of beauty, but I never dared mount into the milk-cart and ride behind this bold snorting monster.

Even when we went to the country for our holidays, we never seemed to meet the Horse socially.

On Swansea's doorstep lay the enchanted peninsula of Gower with limestone cliffs, golden sands, the surf thundering in to Rhossili Bay and rock pools where, at low tide, lobsters of fragile blue with tremulous antennae could be prodded with a hook to come floating up through the delicate fronds of seaweed to triumphant capture. What chance had a horse against delights like these? If it rained and bathing was out of the question, there was no point in going to look at the farm stables. We knew that Phil Tanner, Gower's last folk singer, would be waiting for us on his bench before the King's Head at Llangenith.

Phil's beard was patriarchal, his sheep-dog always at his side and his ale in his hand as he burst into song. 'Order first, gentlemen, order. Music is a serious thing.'

Then his voice, firm as a rock at the age of sixty, warbled clearly in the sun.

I must go down to some lonely valley . . . Down, bitch!
Where no man on earth there may me find,
Where the pretty little song-birds . . . Down bitch!

'Drat the dog, what's the matter with her. She was musical enough as a puppy.'

. . . sit tuning their voices,
And always blows there a most healing wind.

Phil never sang about horses, but concentrated on Love in its many country manifestations, from the adventures of the Pretty Little Oystermaid to the goings on of Morriston Moll on Rhosilli Downs:

Where a halt was made and a game was played,
And Moll a shilling took!

So our holidays passed happily and horseless away. The University brought me no contact with the animal. Rock climbing and mountaineering gave me my thrills of adventure, and for years I only saw the Horse as a foreshortened object far away down the valley at the foot of some great precipice soaring out of the peat bogs of Wales and Scotland.

The Second World War found me cowering amidst the clash of machines. I scurried across Europe dodging tanks, shells and bombers. I came into contact with the Horse on one occasion only and then under circumstances which would not commend me to horse-lovers.

During the liberation of Lyons my Colonel and I sat down to one of the most splendid feasts that I have ever been offered in France. We ate our way manfully through three enormous courses until we came to the meat. The Colonel, who had no foreign language at his command and therefore operated on the old principle that if you shout hard enough the natives will always understand, bellowed 'This looks good', and tucked in. The proprietor beamed at me, *'J'éspère que votre ami est hippophage, monsieur.'*

'What's he saying?' shouted the Colonel.

'He asks if you are a keen horse-flesh eater.'

The Colonel reacted as if he had been caught shooting a fox: 'Good God! I'll never live this down.' And he fled the table. It has counted against me ever since in horsy circles that I stayed on and finished the meal.

That, then, is the True and Faithful Account of my dealings with the Horse up to the moment when I walked into the office of the late Hywel Davies, then the BBC's Programme Director in Wales. It was a deceptively calm day in early spring and the animal was very far from my thoughts as I sat down at Hywel's desk and began to discuss with him how I was going to explore Wales during the coming summer.

Some years ago I was rash enough to declare that I would walk the mountain watershed of Wales from south to north. Hywel immediately inserted the walk into his programme schedule, for programme directors, like newspaper editors, must give their contributors no time for second thoughts. They have to be pleasantly ruthless to succeed!

I set off from Port Talbot, where the hills come nearest to the shore in the south. I followed the dividing line between the rivers of Wales, broadcasting as I went. It was a 220-mile steeplechase over moorlands, bogs and rocky summits, never once falling below 700 feet and mostly at the 1,500-foot level. I walked the range of the Carmarthen Vans, the Epynt, the wilds of Plynlimon and the Arans. By the time I reached Snowdonia I was so fighting fit that I swept across the 3,000-foot Glyders and Carnedds in half a morning. Nine days after leaving Port Talbot I came down to the sea again in the north over Penmaenmawr.

My little stroll over the Roof of Wales started a tradition which is now dearly cherished by me. Every year Hywel invited me to talk myself through Wales in a new way. We both agreed—and in this listeners seemed to support us—that we must never travel by car: you cannot see Wild Wales through a windscreen. Our journeys had to have some sense of physical challenge about them.

Thus I have sailed around the coastline of Wales by lifeboat, jogged over the now abandoned branch railway lines of mid-Wales and marched around the country in the formidable footsteps of George Borrow.

This exercise became an important part of my life. It was my annual escape from the great Slab World that is slowly closing in on us all. Escape used to be a dirty word in my youth, but as the shape of the future becomes clearer escapism becomes respectable. Very few people indeed can master the techniques required for living the happy life in our fully mechanised, air-conditioned, noise-pervaded, mind-controlled society. I know that I am not among these happy few. The huge office slabs, the middle-aged skyscrapers which now float like antiseptic icebergs above the old, warm chaos of our cities, frighten me stiff. They are the ideal solution to the administrators problem. I remember the gleam in the eyes of one expert with whom I was surveying the swarms of workers leaving a slab at five o'clock. He announced—and he was half serious, I'm sure, 'There's only one way to deal with this lot: deep freeze them and stack them in heaps.' I knew then that I would never be a natural Slab Man. I'm happier living down in the cracks in between.

Wales has never been viable Slab Country and rural Wales is one of the few surviving cracks on a big scale in these islands I make a bee-line for it whenever I can and regarded Hywel's office as my private Davies Escape Apparatus. I feel a great sense of empty loss to know that this Welshman of energy and vision no longer sits there waiting for me.

On this occasion he gave me the smile of a man who has solved all your problems before you even put them to him.

'There's one very obvious means of progress,' he said, 'which we've completely neglected and which we ought to have thought of at the very beginning. You must ride!'

'But we've always agreed that a car is right out,' I protested.

'I wasn't thinking about a car. I'm talking about a horse.'

I could have backed out there and then and declared that I had no knowledge of the Horse and not the remotest desire to acquire it. But I went on listening, Hywel went on talking and in ten minutes' time he had convinced me that I was the direct heir of all the illustrious horsemen, from Wesley to Dr Johnson, who had ridden through Wales in the old days. 'You must revive their glories,' Hywel ended. 'I can see you happy on your horse!'

Happy on my horse! Doubts crept back as Hywel ended, but were swept away again as Rowland Lucas began to expound the details of the scheme. Rowland, I must explain, has been my travelling companion on nearly all my journeys in the past. He is the BBC's Publicity Officer in Wales and also that remarkable phenomenon, an Englishman born and bred, who has mastered the Welsh language so thoroughly that no Welshman would take him for other than a lineal descendant of Owain Glyndwr. Come to think of it, Rowland does have the air of some splendid Welsh prince pictured in an eighteenth-century engraving of Gray's 'Bard'. Unkind observers, when they see us together, have compared us to Sancho Panza and Don Quixote. We might certainly live up to the comparison if we took to the Horse!

But Rowland, I reflected, would be in a strong position, since tall men seem to be tailor-made for horse riding. Like Bronco Lane and the other TV heroes of horse opera, he would simply coil his long legs around his horse's middle and ride the Welsh ranges with ease. Smaller and rounder men such as myself can only be saddle-bouncers. Still, it was too late to back out, for Rowland had already gone into action and had done a good deal of important spade-work.

Clearly a couple of rank beginners like ourselves would have no hope of riding two-hundred miles across the mountains of Wales without the help of experts. Rowland had therefore enlisted the aid of Dick and Biddy Williams of the Duhonw Pony Trekking Centre at Builth Wells in Brecknockshire. They would supply our horses and organise stabling and fodder *en route*. In addition Biddy and her friend, Felicity Maitland-Jones, were prepared to ride with us and nurse two complete novices over all the difficulties.

Dick Williams has farming in his blood, for his forefathers have settled for centuries on the lonely lands at the foot of the Epynt. He is a man of eloquent silence on most subjects, but once you start him talking about his farm he takes you into a world of excitement and adventure. He is the only farmer I have met who can turn the growing of a field of potatoes into high-scale drama.

Biddy, like Rowland Lucas, is English-born, but has married into Wales and lost her heart to it. She was brought up in that inner sanctum of the cult of the horse, the show-jumping world. Today, in the quiet farm of Dolynwyd, three miles outside Builth, she has built up a popular pony-trekking centre and also breeds horses and ponies.

The Duhonw stream runs down through the fields of the farm. Behind rise the gaunt, bracken-covered slopes of the Epynt moorlands, but not close enough to shut off the farm from the warmth of the sun through any part of the working day. Seventeen horses ponies and young foals graze in the valley meadows along the river. On hot days they stand twitching their brown flanks against the flies under the tall trees that line the banks, or clatter slowly through the shallows to frighten the swift-moving trout. When dawn comes in late August the young foals run wild among the huge mushrooms with white velvet skins that carpet the fields overnight.

This farm of Dolynwyd, where Dick and Biddy run their trekking school, is a pleasant place. No strings of bumper-to-bumper cars, jammed behind diesel-fuming lorries or giant caravans, will ever find their way to it. The Duhonw valley is the secret, inner defence line for the Cause of the Horse.

Biddy Williams

'Come down for a week-end,' Dick Williams had reassured Rowland, 'and we'll make certain that, at least, you can sit on a horse.'

But clearly, under modern conditions, we could not simply sit blithely on our horses and set off to the north. Sixty years ago it would have been easy to saddle up and ride out into the countryside confident that we would find pubs and hotels with stables attached, grooms ready to rub down our tired mounts, fodder to feed them and soft bridle-paths along which they could trot. Today these things have vanished as if they had never been. The stables have been converted into garages, the bridle-paths covered with asphalt and the groom, if he exists at all, has retired with his old age pension to watch motor-racing on the telly. Modern horses are transported in trailers to specially selected parts of the country and let loose for a few hours to run after a fox or jump a fence or two at a show. Then they are herded back into nature reserves in some of the few areas left in this country unscheduled for 'development'. No one except mountain shepherds uses horses seriously as a means of locomotion over long distances.

Therefore, if we were going to ride two-hundred odd miles across Wales we had to treat the country as Dr Fuchs tackled Antarctica, laying an elaborate system of food dumps along the selected route. Dick Williams volunteered to be our Ed Hillary, going on ahead to set up caches of fodder and making certain that there was somewhere at each hotel where our horses could be turned out for the night. Today, even in the countryside, there is no guaranteed place for the Horse. Sheep, potatoes, grain crops, caravans, have a prior claim to land space and the poor old Horse is left looking wistfully over the hedge at most of rural Wales. But luckily the friends of the Horse are devoted and determined. The local pony clubs, hunts and trekking groups rushed to our rescue and made certain that we had a field handy at every resting place.

With our lines of communication thus secured we turned to look with confidence at the big map on the wall of Hywel's room, and planned our route. Our starting-point readily chose itself; it had to be St David's, that magic and minuscule cathedral city lost on the very westernmost tip of Wales. From the most south-westerly point of the country we would obviously have to ride to the most north-easterly, the Point of Air in Flintshire, where the Dee winds out between its vast sandbanks to the St George's Channel and the English border is only a few miles down the road. In between lay the whole of lonely and industrialised Wales, the sea cliffs of Pembrokeshire, the hills of Preselly, the uplands of Cardigan, Plynlimon, the lost lanes of Montgomeryshire and the mountains of Berwyn and the Clwyd. Together we

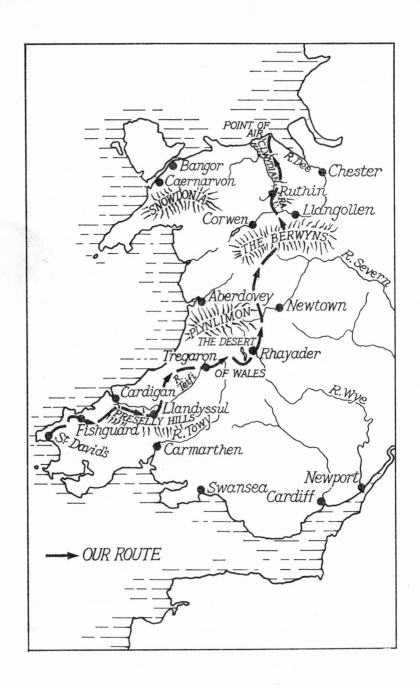

POINT OF
AIR

R. Dee

Chester

Bangor

Caernarvon

SNOWDONIA

Ruthin

Llangollen

Corwen

THE BERWYNS

R. Severn

Aberdovey

Newtown

PLYNLIMON

THE DESERT

Tregaron

Rhayader

R. Teifi

OF WALES

Cardigan

R. Wye

Llandyssul

PRESELLY HILLS

Fishguard

R. Towy

St. David's

Carmarthen

Newport

Swansea

Cardiff

⟶ OUR ROUTE

traced a track that would keep us free of towns and pylons and main roads. In my mind I could already see our cavalcade trotting between the tall hedges around the middle valley of the Wye or breasting some splendidly unkempt hillside to get our first view of the wilderness of Snowdonia on the western horizon. This was Escape at its best!

And then I came back to reality with a rush as I heard Rowland firmly outlining the arrangements: 'Dick and Biddy will be expecting you down at Builth Wells for your preliminary try-out. You can put up at the Lion and wear anything suitable—I've got some riding breeches-myself and one of those thick raincoats that reach below the knees. They saddle up in the lane near the church round about ten o'clock—you'll find the usual lot of trekkers there. If you get the same weather as I had, you'll revel in it.'

I noted the time and date of my trial in my diary. There was no turning back. The event which I had subconsciously been dodging all my life had caught up with me at last. I was face to face with the Horse.

Tika at Dolynwyd

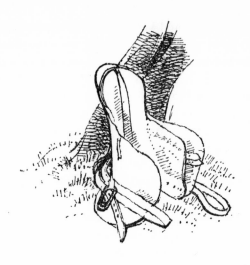

2

I did not approach this turning point-in my life totally unpre-
pared. As soon as I knew that I had to face the horse seriously I
rushed to the local library and collected an armful of books.
Frankly I had no idea, until I saw the long vista of shelves loaded
with horsy literature, that horsemen were so articulate. The only
sounds that I had ever heard them utter were nondescript noises
like 'hurrup' or 'heay' or 'eeesee gurl', plus an occasional swear
word as their mount went backwards into a hedge. I soon found
that the horse rivals wine, cooking and small-boat sailing as
Publishers' Delight Number One.

I decided to plunge in boldly at the deep end. I swept the
flimsier books aside and concentrated on a mighty tome, edited
by Brian Vezey-Fitzgerald, entitled with all-embracing simplicity *The Book of the Horse*. It was a mistake—not, I must add, in
any way the fault of the book.

The volume was too good, far too fascinating to be placed in
the hands of someone like myself who for years has been forced
to cultivate what old Horace Walpole would have described as

professional serendipity! A radio and TV commentator must go through life picking up pointless and intriguing bits of information. He makes himself a one-day expert on everything from Trooping the Colour to glass blowing. Long years of this sort of thing have given me a magpie mind—I pick up any brightly coloured item and hop away with it, irrespective of my chances of using it. *The Book of the Horse* was a magnificent gathering-ground for these deliciously irrelevant facts.

The very names of the contributors transported me into a wonderful Never-Never Land. Sir Beauvoir de Lisle, Aelfric A. Leonard, Brennan De Vine, Sylvia Calmady-Hamlyn, and the lady with the charming nom-de-plume of Golden Gorse—they lured me to tackle such subjects as The Horse in War, The Development of the Hunter in America, The Percheron in Great Britain, and Horse Harness Ornaments. I discovered the furious passions that rage over the origins of *Equus Caballus Frigidus*: the dangers of pontificating about the early days of the Welsh cob: and the complexities of training a Lippizaner stallion in the movements of the Haute École—the Piaffe, the Levade and the incredibly difficult Capriole.

By 1 June I knew the pedigree of Dyoll Starlight, I could tell you that there was no mention of the chariot in the *Odyssey* and I was a mine of information about the history of the Godolphin Arabian. But I was still uncertain at which end the horse I would find his withers.

I entered that memorable lane opposite St Mary's Church at Builth as ignorant of the animal's anatomy as when I started my researches. Again the fault was mine. I had been so carried away by that fascinating volume that I had, as it were, tackled the fences in the Grand National before I had learnt the difference between a pastern and a cannon-bone. In all my dealings with the horse I always seem to start at the wrong end.

I even went slightly astray in the matter of dress. I decided early on that I would not dare equip myself with The Complete Riding Outfit, as pictured in all the best magazines. I did not feel that I was naturally suited to jodhpurs, hunting-bowler and hacking-jacket. And yet I had received a series of dismal warnings about what would happen to me if I went riding for eight days and failed to clothe my legs and especially my rather pronounced rear quarters in the correct garb.

'You'll not sit down for weeks after' was the usual forecast, varied with 'I went pony trekking once and felt as if I'd been flayed alive after the first day; take my tip and put great big pads on your thighs.'

I did take the precaution of surreptitiously bathing my inner thighs with surgical spirit for weeks before, as I'd been assured, by those who knew, that this would 'make your skin like rhinoceros hide'. But I was darned if I was going to encase myself in an expensive pair of cavalry-twill jodhpurs. In any case, apart from the expense, it would give a totally wrong idea of my professional competence as a rider. Yet I had to wear something and the more thickly padded that something was the better for me. I had a vivid picture in my mind of myself, on my fourth day out from base, sitting in my saddle as if it were an electric chair.

So at nine o'clock on the memorable morning I presented myself at Watts the Clothiers, half-way up the main and only street of Builth Wells. This fascinating emporium has made no concessions to false modernity. Its solid mahogany counters are worn smooth by fifty years of selling Welsh tweed to Builth residents at bargain prices. Here hang raincoats built like space-suits to defy the drenching winter rains of the Epynt moorlands. Vast open cupboards along the walls hold hats for all important social occasions, from ministerial funerals at Rhayader and Llandrindod to sheep-trials at Cwmowen and cattle-sales at Craven Arms. If you think, for a moment that Watts are behind the times, Mr Meredith, the man in charge, confounds you by disappearing like a conjurer into the dark, inner fastnesses behind the cupboards and producing the article you require at twice the speed of the languid young men who serve at the giant, chromium-plated London stores.

I entrusted my problem to Mr Meredith. When two Welshmen meet for the first time over business certain formal courtesies must be observed. You discover what denomination you both belong to; then you proceed, by complicated genealogical research, to disentangle the relationship between you. Given time any Welshman can prove that he is the second cousin twice removed of any other Welshman. From this point you are safe to launch into any subject you care to broach.

Mr Meredith at Watts the Clothiers

'Now, hymn writing', said Mr Meredith, 'it used to be what you might call a national sport in these parts. What treasures still remain unsung and unpublished in many a drawer in manse or rectory! We ought to have a research scholarship devoted to the rescue of forgotten hymn tunes.'

'Ah, but times have changed!' I countered. 'The public are more attracted to Mr Acker Bilk than to hymn writers.'

'Changed for the worse,' sighed Mr Meredith, 'like so much

that is going on around Builth Wells. The Forestry has come in. All these English cities are clamouring for reservoirs. Poor old Central Wales—in ten years time they'll have buried all the farms under trees and drowned all the valleys. Still, you'll find a few trails left to ride on at the moment. We'd better get you fitted up before they obliterate them with conifers.'

He then gave me a swift, professional measuring look; I could detect a slight suggestion of alarm in his eyes, but it was quickly concealed by his good manners. 'We've fitted all sorts of people here,' said Mr Meredith, 'I don't think we'll be beaten by you.'

But when I had been whisked into the fitting-room offstage behind the biggest cupboard, I soon realised that I had presented Watts the Clothiers with one of the toughest problems in their history. Certain sports develop special muscles. In the past I have been a keen mountaineer and mountain walker. As a result the calves of my legs are bold and bulging. Since middle age has also brought a certain dignified development to my tummy, my proportions are obviously all wrong for riding. Addiction to the horse, it seems, produces giant thighs and a rather spreading rear—at least that is how the makers of jodhpurs and riding-breeches view their prospective customers. In vain I tried to struggle into numerous garments that Mr Meredith patiently brought to the fitting room-in relays. When they were perfect around the calves they split in the middle; when I felt comfortable around the tummy, I was suffering the tortures of the damned in the legs. It was time to adopt heroic measures.

'Well,' said Mr Meredith, 'there's only one thing for it. We've got some very thick corduroy breeches in stock—they're not very fashionable, I'm afraid, but we keep them for the older shepherds and farmers. You'll be able to get into these all right, for they're only made to one size—the biggest! And we'll have some Welsh socks to cover your legs. One thing I'll guarantee about this outfit: you'll be comfortable in the saddle in the wettest storm you'll get and they're so thick you'll feel that you're riding on rubber.'

The breeches were brought in. They had an eighteenth-century, folk-dancing look about them. They fitted easily about my calves and they were so slack in the middle that I could turn around in them like a tent. I flung fashion to the winds. Who cared what I looked like? I was going to be comfortable. So I left Watts the Clothiers clad in a corduroy suit of armour, finished off with thick Welsh socks.

Several passers-by looked a little hard at me as I now marched with growing confidence towards my rendezvous with the horse. They were summer visitors who obviously thought that old folk customs die hard in the Welsh hills. I paid no attention to them. I made one further stop at Mr Jones the Chemist for a tin of Johnson's Baby Powder. The combination of the contents of that tin with the protection of Mr Meredith's breeches would render me invincible.

I came around the corner on to a scene of furious activity. Immediately my new-found confidence oozed away. Twelve ponies were collected in the open yard at the bottom of the lane or in the small field beyond. In the middle of them stood Biddy Williams, issuing crisp, confident orders to two or three youngsters who seemed to treat the dangerous-looking animals with astonishing familiarity. With them were the trekkers, city girls obviously, yet they, also, had the air of being completely at home with ponies and horses. Everywhere I looked people in jodhpurs or in jeans were slipping bridles over horses' heads, or enjoining their ponies to 'stand still, there, will you,' or giving them a final brush down accompanied by a hissing sound that seemed splendidly professional.

There were restless ponies, head tossing-ponies, ponies that kept backing away and had to be reassured with many an 'Easy, girl', or a long-drawn-out, 'Quiet, quiet now. Stop playing up, Pancho.' The air resounded with slaps on the withers, the scraping of hoofs on the cobbles of the yard, the jingle of harness— which everybody in the know seemed to refer to as 'tack'. Snatches of esoteric conversation floated around:

'Whiskers goes well into bridle, Jill.'

'Wait a minute. Is Pancho favouring a leg?'

'Tighten those girths, old girl, or you'll be in trouble.'

I lingered on the outskirts like a new boy on his first day at school. Biddy spotted me and gave me a hail. 'Come over here. You're riding Tika.'

It was thus that I came face to face with my Horse of Destiny. In the middle of the restless, gyrating mob of ponies stood a grey animal, stock-still and ignoring with mild tolerant eyes all the excitement around. My long study of *The Book of the Horse* enabled me to say to Biddy with an air of authority, 'Ah, you've given me a cob.'

'A Welsh cob,' said Biddy. 'She's as quiet as a lamb.' I'm sure she was about to add, 'Perfect ride for a lady', when she recovered and added, 'She will never put a foot wrong and she'll suit you down to the ground. Get up on her and try. I'll just check up on the others before we move off.'

I looked long at Tika and Tika looked doubtfully back at me. I don't know what was in her mind, but my thoughts were centred on one problem only—how on earth was I to get myself into the saddle. Compared with the wiry Welsh ponies around, Tika looked gigantic. A cob, said my *Book of the Horse*, must be between fourteen and fifteen hands, stout built and docked. I had registered the fact firmly that a hand was somewhere about four inches. So Tika's back was therefore, five feet above the ground. I calculated that it would need an experienced pole-vaulter to swing into Tika's saddle.

But, of course, there was the stirrup. I glanced quickly around. The knowledgeable ones seemed to be grabbing a handful of mane and saddle and heaving themselves up with one easy swing. Now, Tika's mane was close-cropped, so I couldn't get a grip there. I concentrated my attack on the saddle, cranked my left foot up into the stirrup, grasped all the leather in sight and heaved. I collided with some force against Tika's shoulder and was back where I started. Tika did not move an inch.

I took another sly look around. No one was looking my way so I hastily pushed a big brick into position under the stirrup. The extra inches were just what I needed. I wobbled in the stirrup, flung my right leg out like a ballet dancer, grabbed all the bits of leather in sight and suddenly found myself on Tika's back the right way round. Again Tika did not move an inch. I leaned over in what I hoped was the manner of the old hand and patted her neck. 'Good girl,' I said. Tika slowly turned her head around, gave me a resigned look and turned her head away again. 'Ah, well,' she seemed to say, 'here's another of them!'

No matter. I had succeeded in getting on to Tika's back and could now take a good look at my mount. 'Good look' is perhaps an exaggeration, since the View from the Bridge on a horse is strictly limited. All you can see ahead are the neck and the ears; if you swivel around to look astern, you gaze out over a vast expanse of rear. The only evidence for the continued existence of the rest of the animal comes from beneath you in a series of noises of varying degrees of rudeness.

Now a man like myself who has lived long in modern cities has almost forgotten the old elemental world of smells, flies, privies at the bottom of the garden, belches and burps. The food we townsmen eat is wrapped in cellophane, we travel in carefully sprung cars, the slightest suspicion of unpleasantness in the air is exorcised immediately by sprays and chemicals. But once you get on to a horse you go straight back to the Middle Ages.

Your faithful steed has never looked at TV commercials and she is unaware that 'luxurious Camay soothes your skin with an intimate caress'. When she gallops she sweats; in hot weather she throws up a smoke-screen of fumes. She relieves herself anywhere with the noise of Niagara, while her rider has to pretend to gaze with sudden interest at the distant landscape, standing up in the stirrups meanwhile to take off pressure.

All good, earthy stuff! But the air-conditioned modern man takes a little time to get used to it.

Tika, I was happy to note, was not much given to the more embarrassing noises, so I was able to take stock of her calmly. In fact, calmness was the keynote of everything about old Tika— she was the classic embodiment of the great principle in physics of the Conservation of Energy. She never moved unless she had to and then only as far as was necessary. When she did move, unkind spectators in Builth attributed it to the fact that she had heard someone shout 'Milko'.

For Tika had some mysterious episode in her past which occasioned her exile to England, where she served a sentence between the shafts of a milk-cart somewhere near Weybridge. This might account for that gentle resignation she exhibited when asked to stop anywhere. She was obviously waiting orders to move on to the next house. I never hurt her feelings by mentioning this trait—I was glad to know that she had escaped from the plodding round of the suburbs. No longer need she move slowly, day after day, from 'Chez Nous' to 'Torestin' and on to 'Dunromin'. All was forgiven and forgotten and she was back amongst the winds and high bridle-paths of her native hills.

The exact date of this exile was also wrapped in mystery for no one was certain of Tika's age. She must have been well over twelve, for her tail had been docked and the anti-docking law was passed in 1945. Was she fifteen? Well, horses have won the Grand National at that age. Was she over twenty? Maybe, but she still had heart and go, when she wanted to use it. Certain it was that age had taught her philosophy. She had the air of not expecting miracles, but of always hoping for the best. I felt that she would suit me down to the ground.

As for her pedigree—well, that had fallen by the wayside during her English exile. I like to feel that she had some distinguished blood in her, for sometimes she looked like a duchess who had seen better days. Perhaps she could trace her lineage back to one of those legendary horses which always seem to be the starting-point of the breeds of the British Isles. In the case of the Welsh cob we have the splendidly named Trotting Comet, born in the wilds of Cardiganshire around 1836. If a Welsh cob can trace itself back to Trotting Comet she enters the *Debrett* of the cob world.

But the very origin of the Welsh cob is wrapped in designed mystery. Some insist that it springs from an animal vaguely described as 'the old Welsh cart-horse'. No one knows where or when this old Welsh cart-horse flourished: patriots trace it back to the days of the old Welsh princes and would like to assume that it is in direct descent from the war charger of Owain Glyndwr. But even they do not claim that this old Welsh cart-plus-war-horse possessed the splendid trotting gait which is now such a feature of the breed and which brought fame to the stallion so romantically named Alonzo the Brave, foaled in 1866. That gait must have come from English roadsters.

The plain truth is, as my invaluable *Book of the Horse* insists, that there is too close a resemblance between the best of the Welsh cobs, past and present, and the old-world English trotting nags, pictured in the sporting prints of the early nineteenth century. The Welsh drovers, mounted on their sturdy ponies, escorted their huge herds of black cattle into the fairgrounds of London and the big English cities in the days before the railways. These Welsh 'cowboys' were passionate devotees of good trotters. And 'many a good Welsh mare was covered by an English trotting sire and many a good English trotting stallion and colt and many a good mare was taken back to Wales for breeding purposes when the cattle had been handed over and their erstwhile guardians made for home'.

So the Welsh cob, in origin is an Anglo-Celtic promotion. No matter—for the last hundred years Wales has been the chief breeding-ground and the Welsh cob has the speed and action of an English trotter with the toughness and stamina of the Welsh pony. You can use her on the roads, for riding and in the trap. She's the ideal general-purpose horse; and she can jump as well.

All this Biddy told me later. For the moment I was quite happy to be safely mounted on that unassuming descendant of Trotting Comet and Alonzo the Brave—Tika the patient.

My meditations on equine history were interrupted by a shout from Biddy, 'All ready. We'll move off.' Tika, as I expected, didn't stir. She waited until every other pony had moved past and then took up her natural place in the procession—the tail end!

The modern beginner's first few minutes on a horse in motion are extremely disconcerting. Nothing in his motor-car experience has prepared him for the wobbling nature of his mount's progress. The animal does not seem properly sprung and the amount of saddle you can grip with your knees totally inadequate for your safety. You have to balance on top of the horse's heaving backbone and the ground begins to seem an awfully long way below.

Added to which your guide and instructor, no doubt with the best will in the world, begins to bombard you with ancient slogans which must have been the bane of beginners for hundreds of years: 'Head up, hearts up, hands down, heels down.' Fine, no doubt, when you've got used to the motion but whenever I put my head up in those first few minutes, Tika's back gave a lurch and my heart went down to my boots and my hands went up to cling with sudden affection to her neck. As for 'heels down', I was only too pleased that my feet were still in my stirrups to worry about the exact angle made by my heels.

By the time we had reached the end of the lane, however, I had got over the first shock of surprise at the strange nature of a horse's motion. I still felt wobbly, but hoped I didn't look it.

The cavalcade now turned down the main street of Builth and it behoved me to try and look the part of an experienced rider. We passed Mr Webb's the Butcher—'patronised by Edward VIII when Prince of Wales'. I remembered the number of times Edward had been pictured falling off his horse in the hunting field and was not reassured. On past Campbell and Edwards, the auctioneers, with their enticing notices of Hill Farms for Sale— how pleasant it would be to buy a farm named 'Bodnant' or 'Ty'n y Pant' ('sixty acres with grazing rights on the hill') and ride out, with your flocks, like the patriarchs of old, your sheep-dogs at your heels and the larks springing up before you from the close-cropped mountain turf . . . Here Tika's feet skidded slightly on the asphalt and my poetic reverie was cut short as I grabbed at the reins. I had recovered by the time I was opposite Watts the Clothiers, where Mr Meredith waited outside. 'Comfortable?' he inquired. 'Perfect,' I replied after ten minutes' experience of my corduroy armour in the saddle.

So far so good. Now the cavalcade turned up the by-roads and into the lanes that lead on to the mountainside A new hazard presented itself. I had got over my first astonishment at the strange, unmechanical movement of the horse, the sudden lurches and the swift acceleration from scratch; now I had to endure that motion at an angle. The steep lane made certain that this angle was very acute indeed.

I had no idea that a horse, or at least a Welsh cob and pony, could climb up such slopes. I thought these antics were reserved for the horses in *Laramie* or for Cheyenne Brodie, sliding down gullies in the wilds of the Rockies. Tika and her comrades put themselves at the lane with grim determination, as if to get an unpleasant task over quickly. I clung on, swaying backwards in the saddle. These lanes that lead out of the valley at Builth are deep-set in their lower courses. Normally I would have taken great pleasure in our progress. The honeysuckle was out and a rich perfume filled the hollows. The sun was warm and flung a pattern of shadows over us as we passed precariously under the low branches that hung out over the lane. Underfoot the ground was soft—we were away from the hard, unfeeling tarmac that covers most of the highways and by-ways of Britain.

But every time I tried to look at the delights around me I slid gently down Tika's back. I didn't suffer the disgrace of falling off over her tail; a conveniently placed piece of leather at the back of the saddle, which experts call the cantle, seems designed to spare the beginners this embarrassment. But I flopped backwards and jerked forwards and wondered how on earth I would stay on. I tried leaning over Tika's neck and jamming my feet back into the stirrup. This unorthodox trick seemed to work. I was at the tail-end of the procession anyhow and nobody could see what I was up to. So I was still on her back when Tika, plodding steadily upwards, joined the others at the gate which led out on to the open hillside. I had surmounted another crisis in my early riding career.

The track now ran up a spur flung out from the moorlands of the Epynt. Another quarter of an hour's slogging and we were out on the level mountain-top. We drew rein and I thankfully got back to even keel and looked about me.

I was confronting one of those sweeping views which are the glory of the mid-Wales hills, compounded of wave after wave of dark ridges rolling away to the northern fastnesses of Plynlimon. The east was sealed by the bare whaleback of the Radnor Forest. Somewhere beneath us the Wye was struggling through these hills, but cultivation, farmhouses, snug woodlands and the works of modern man were out of sight and out of mind 1,500 feet below. This was a world of space and sun and billowing white clouds drifting slowly across a clear, blue sky. A warm wind rustled the bracken and the sheep formed in single file and wandered through it, heads held high. Lost lambs bleated far away in the sun-drenched hollows of the hills and larks sprang up fluttering and trilling. There was peace here, and all along the southern horizon lay that magic line of high summits that forms the rampart of distant South Wales.

The peaks were dark blue, the air was crystal clear, the track ran away to the lonely little lake on the skyline. This was horseman's country. Biddy gave the order, 'All together. Trot.' Tika pricked up her ears and in a moment my raptures on the scenery died and a new misery began.

No one had warned me about the Trot. I'd pictured it as an amiable kind of motion, with the lulling rhythm of the old Irish ditty, 'Trotting to the Fair'. I'll never sing that phoney folk-song again. Amiable indeed! The Trot is designed to lambast the overconfident beginner, to shake his bones and rattle his teeth and make him regret the day he ever thought he could ride. The Walk is a wobble, but the Trot is a perpetual visit to the Headmaster's Study. You are flung up in the saddle and come down with a bump. 'Rise and fall with the way your horse does,' they tell you. 'Get the rhythm of it.' But every time I rose Tika's back fell and when I fell, it rose—giving me a rousing thump amidships. I tried to sit still in the saddle, but that only made things worse. Bump and thud, bump and thud again! I tried to rein Tika back into the quiet of the walk, but even Tail-end Tika wanted to keep up with the rest over that perfect riding track. Obviously I was not gifted with those legendary horseman's hands which can convey the rider's slightest wish to his steed.

My arms were askew, elbows out. Biddy had advised me at the start, 'Hold your hands as if you had just taken your money out of your pocket.' I would have taken every penny I possessed out of my pocket at that moment if only the misery of the trot would cease.

The only thing to do was to try and get the hang of it. I rose in my stirrups with grim determination, although I felt most precarious as I quitted the comparative safety of the saddle. All miseries come to an end. After a solid mile of bumping and banging we reined up again and gathered on the summit of the ridge. I have complained of my own agony, but I now remembered that poor old Tika was down below. She gave no sign of protest. She was even philosophical when I heaved on the reins to stop her, with the strength of a sailor trying to haul on the mainsail in a gale around Cape Horn. 'Give and take,' your expert shouts at you. 'Pull and then go slack, then pull again.' Most horses, apparently, pull hard against you if you heave against them. Not so old Tika. One hint from me that I wanted to stop and she stopped, too. She was in no hurry to start again either; nor indeed was I after the torture of the trot. I began to perceive that Tika and I would get on excellently together. We came safely down to the lonely Griffin Inn at Cwmowen.

'Into the paddock, unsaddle,' ordered Biddy. Now I had to tackle another problem—how to get off! I thought this would be easy, but I was quickly told that there was a right way and a wrong way to dismount. Like everything else connected with the horse, the correct procedure has been sanctified into a ritual by tradition. In this case I'll admit there's something to it. I kept one foot in the stirrup and swung gaily to ground.

'And what,' inquired Biddy, 'do you think would happen if your horse now grew restless and moved off again?'

I'd have gone hopping around the paddock with my leg up like a ballet dancer, tangled in the stirrup! Good old steadfast

Tika never moved; I blessed her milk-round training and hurriedly unhooked the stirrup from my left foot.

Other ceremonial drills followed. You must slip off the bridle, carefully slide up the stirrup irons to the saddle, loosen the girths and lift off the saddle carefully. And woe betide you if you don't place the saddle the right side up against a selected tree. And even greater woe will befall if you don't tie the halter high enough. Your pony will tangle his legs up in it before you've had time to look round.

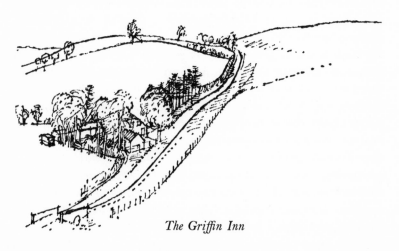

The Griffin Inn

'Your horse isn't a bicycle,' said Biddy, giving me Ancient Saw Number 6. I'll say it isn't. You can prop your bicycle against the wall and slip into The Griffin within two minutes of riding up to the front door. You've got a solid quarter of an hour's fussing ahead of you if you ride up on a horse. If you skimp your saddle drill, for example, you may be laying the foundations for an equine ailment called Sitfast!

What a gloriously old-world Shakespearian flavour the names of horse diseases possess. You can hear them rolling off the tongue of Sir John Falstaff—Bog Spavin, Thrush, Seedy Toe, Windgalls, the Staggers, Thorough-pin!

But one glance at Tika, who wandered gently away to crop

some grass—'she's the only one you can trust without a halter'—
showed me that here was no horse to worry about. She didn't
look as if she was a chronic sufferer from Joint Evil, String Halt
or Capped Hock. She wasn't a Roarer, a Crib-biter or a Wind
Sucker—nasty habits which put a horse beyond the social pale!
She was just a pleasant, friendly Welsh cob of uncertain age,
game to do her best with the minimum of trouble to all concerned. I left her quietly cropping the grass and entered The
Griffin.

Underneath the salted ham, I took stock of my progress.
'You'll be all right,' Biddy assured me. 'On our trip we're not
likely to do much cantering and certainly little galloping. Get
the hang of the trot on the way back and I'll guarantee we'll get
you safely to North Wales.' All through our lunch break I muttered the slogans to myself—'Heads up, hearts up, hands down,
heels down!' 'Give and take.' 'Hold your hands as if you had just
taken money out of your pocket.' The only one I felt made any
real sense was 'Don't treat your horse like a bicycle'. I knew
that Tika would never allow me to do that.

An hour later and we were back in the paddock. 'Saddle up.'
We had to put all the complicated horse furniture back in its
proper place on the animal. The most difficult and dangerous-
looking task for the beginner is the replacing of the bridle and
bit. The expert makes it look easy; he slips the whole contraption into place in one swift movement. But what are you to do
when a horse tosses its head and how on earth do you get it to
open its mouth for the bit? 'Fingers at the back of the mouth,'
they tell you and, greatly daring, you try, and find to your
surprise that the horse doesn't seem to have any teeth in the
corner of his mouth. He can't bite and you can be as bold with
your fingers as the lion-tamer putting his head in the lion's
mouth! Tika, I need hardly say, was a perfect lady. She opened
her mouth as soon as I came near. Saddles were on, girths
tightened, stirrup irons down at the correct length. 'Mount.'

I knew a trick or two about this from experience. I carefully
manoeuvred Tika on to a slope, gained a good six inches to a

foot on my take-off and swung easily into the saddle. I felt that I was making progress. I gathered the reins in the correct style as prescribed by Ancient Saw Number 7, 'Make your hands a lever and not a door-hinge.' Tika took me back to our natural place at the end of the cavalcade and we moved off.

Out once again on to that exhilarating moorland. Again that heart-lifting view of the distant peaks, white cloud billowing over blue sky and miles of lonely pathways through the bracken. Everything conspired to set the blood pacing through the veins of horse and rider. The leading ponies broke into the trot without any urging, then into the canter. Tika and I came up over the horizon to see them pelting ahead, riders with heads down, the ponies with tails streaming out behind. Up went Tika's ears and we started to trot. Rise and fall, bump and bump again! But this time I seemed to get the rhythm. I rose boldly in the saddle as the pace increased and the world began to float faster by. I glanced ahead. We could see the whole mob changing gear and starting to canter, to gallop. Tika had to keep up.

With startling suddenness Tika changed gear, too. Then we went into overdrive—the position was comfortable, but dangerous. There was none of the thumping of the trot; we were floating over the ground with the wind whistling around us. But I had risen automatically from the saddle to balance in my stirrups. I wobbled, but the intoxication of the gallop was upon me. This was speed! I shouted, 'Go on, Tika, go on, lass!' Wind and cloud and the thunder of hoofs on the turf and the far horizon ahead coming nearer and nearer. . . .

All at once I noticed something curious happening to that far horizon. It was starting to tilt: the Brecknock Beacons were slipping sideways, then up-ending themselves. In a flash, in one of those swift moments of insight which are supposed to come to drowning men, the ghastly certainty dawned on me . . . I was falling off.

I hit the ground sideways with a thump that knocked all the breath out of my body. Stars danced before my eyes. For a moment I lay quite still. My first thought was, 'The shame of it.

I've fallen off my horse in front of that crowd!' Indeed, there is something comic and humiliating about falling from a horse. It probably comes from the sudden contrast between your position before and after. One moment you are rising proudly in your saddle, dominating the countryside, the next sees you sprawling with your legs in the air, your cap crushed down over your eyes and your riding-crop flung miles away.

Luckily I landed on a mound of soft turf. I wasn't bruised and slowly got to my knees, fighting for my breath. When the stars stopped dancing before my eyes I could see I was not deserted. Tika had stopped as soon as she felt me go. She was looking around at me and I am sure I detected amused sympathy in her eyes. The humiliation vanished. 'He that is down need fear no fall.' I had simply joined that vast company of notable riders who had fallen off their horses. A rider doesn't know anything about his horse until he has fallen off it once. I realised that I had passed my initiation ceremony and had now joined the tribe.

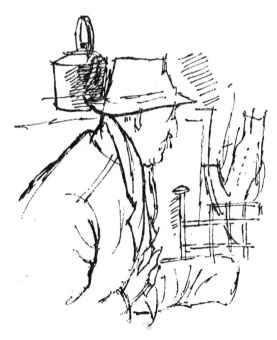

Biddy rode back to find me getting ready to mount again. 'All right?' she inquired. 'Right as rain,' I answered with the confidence of a man who has passed through fire. And carefully I swung back up into the saddle and put Tika into the trot.

'Now let 'em all come,' said I to myself. 'I know the worst that can happen, and I'm sure of one thing—come what may, old Tika will see me through.'

And that was all the riding preparation that I had before I set off to ride the Trails of Wales. With Tika there, it was enough.

3

'SADDLE up!'

At Biddy's command, delivered with all the authority of a TV captain in the U.S. Cavalry, I advanced soon after dawn across a dew-sodden field on the cliff-edge at St David's. I was loaded with 'tack'. The reins seemed to tangle up my feet, and the saddle, bridle and the rest of the paraphernalia you need to get up on the back of a horse made an awkward parcel under my right arm. In my hand I clasped a brush with the bristles worn flat—'You'll give Tika a brisk rub-down before you saddle up,' said Biddy. Fine. But the present problem was how to get near enough to the horses to give them anything at all.

I had assumed that all you had to do to gather in your horse was to shout, 'Whoa, my good fellow', and hold out a lump of sugar. This bunch couldn't have cared less about sugar or any other blandishments. The June sun was coming up warm across the still waters of St Bride's Bay. The gulls were crying around the cliff-edge. The whole world was quiet, undisturbed. And our mounts, with the sun stroking their backs, saw no reason for the thirty-mile trek we were planning for them. They were off, racing around the field—hoofs flashing and with a symphony of snorts and tail-waving.

Biddy had us move up on them like beaters in a pheasant shoot. 'Quiet, boy. Steady, Smatcher. Come here, Shannon.'

There was only one horse out of the bunch who disdained behaving like a juvenile delinquent, old Tika. She stood like a white statue in the midst of this equine riot. Her attitude was that of the Confucian proverb, 'When rape is inevitable, relax and enjoy it.'

While the rest of our party were arm-waving and whoaing like mad, I addressed myself to the task of dressing Tika.

Saddling a horse is just like dressing a restless little boy: you get no active help from your victim. You tug and pull the head-gear over the ears and get the reins at the wrong end of the bridle. You stick your hand at the side of the mouth and whip in the bit when your animal is looking the other way. You do your best to soothe him beforehand by scrubbing him all over with a blunt brush. A portable Hoover for horses sounds a sensible solution to this brushing business and is yet unthinkable. The horse and the machine stand poles apart. It doesn't seem decent to tackle him with electricity.

Getting the saddle on is a battle of wits. The problem is how to get your saddle-girth tight. If it isn't really tight, you will have the delicious experience of suddenly sliding sideways without notice just at the moment when you are trotting through a village and hoping that you look every inch a horseman. I know. It happened twice on this trip.

A cunning horse like Tika deceives the innocent when you saddle her up. She quietly inflates her tummy. You pride yourself on a tight girth. You grasp your saddle to swing up on to her back—and the whole contraption swings around and deposits you smartly on the grass. Old Tika had this tummy inflation trick down to a fine art. She derived a certain enjoyment from it. It was her little morning joke. Even when I knew what she was up to, I felt I had to pretend I was caught out every time.

I acted in the spirit of the two Dublin bookies whom I saw

losing money to an old man who was doing the three-card trick at Cahirsiveen Races in the wilds of County Kerry. 'But you surely can't be taken in by this old stuff,' I protested. 'Quiet, now,' said the biggest bookie with a wink, 'sure it's a charity to be deceived by the poor fellah!'

Tika was now safely saddled and then came problem number two. What do you do with your personal luggage? Where's that convenient boot of a car into which you throw things gaily at the last moment? The horse hasn't got one.

What about a commodious rucksack? Ah, there's a terrible catch in a rucksack in a literal sense. Against all advice I insisted on wearing one during my trial trots in Builth Wells. I soon found that I received a continual back-thumping at any speed. But worse was to come. Our cavalcade plunged under a thick-set hedgerow on the mountainside. We swayed down in our saddles to avoid the low-hanging boughs. Suddenly I felt a violent jerk on my back. A giant hand seemed to be hauling me out of the saddle. Tika went on. I didn't.

To my infinite shame and confusion I remained suspended in mid-air, legs dangling, arms waving. The rest of the cavalcade stopped, turned to look and roared with laughter.

It was like a scene out of an old Buster Keaton silent comedy. A stout branch had gone under one of the straps of my rucksack and neatly skewered me, six feet above the ground. Now I know what a fish feels like when it's suddenly yanked out of the water! One minute you are happily swimming along with the crowd; the next sees you ludicrously sprawling on the bank. You have no hope of recovery.

No rucksack on horseback ever again for me! The thing to do is to strap your property around the saddle. Let it bounce up and down on its own. And carry the minimum in a heavy mac in front and some pyjamas and toilet utensils rolled up in a waterproof bag behind you. Keep your sandwiches in your pocket. A four-hour ride with sandwiches fastened to the saddle will turn them into papiermâché. And a final tip: be careful about waving maps around once you have mounted.

By this time my more experienced comrades were up in the saddle and ready to go. I pulled the map out of my pocket and opened it up to check the route. In a moment, all was chaos. Horses backed, shied, and bumped into one another. I had a glimpse of Rowland hanging on wildly to the neck of his powerful bay, Shannon, and Biddy holding in a rearing Smatcher and shouting, 'Put that map down.'

Of course, anything large and white suddenly flapped before their eyes is bound to startle horses. But I have a theory that they are particularly allergic to maps. Maps belong to hikers and motorists. The old horse is designed to wander anyhow across country. The proper thing for a horseman to do when he wants to find the way is to lean down from his saddle and inquire of a passing yokel. You can see the correct attitude in the hunting-field jokes in any number of *Punch* before 1939.

But as I had now pulled out the map and was still safely on Tika's back—naturally she was the only one who had not moved a yard in this panic—I felt I might as well check our day's route carefully. We'd planned a complicated zigzag along the coast of northern Pembrokeshire for this first section of our ride through the heart of Wild Wales, from its Land's End in the south-west at St David's to its John o' Groats in the north-east at Point of Air.

We would, first of all, trot to the door of St David's Cathedral, where the Dean had promised to give us a short blessing. Then out through St David's itself and along the road that runs a few miles inland northwards to Trevine. Next down to the coast and in and out of the bays. A circuit to dodge Fishguard and a glorious final ride over 1,000-foot Carn Ingli to our night's rest at Llwyngwair Manor just beyond the little town of Newport (Pembs). In all about thirty miles of highly varied riding—ambling along lonely roads, through bramble-lined lanes, across sands swept by the tide, up over wild moorlands. It would be the longest time I had ever spent on the back of a horse and there would be seven more days exactly like it to follow. I had a secret anxiety about my power to sit through it all. I felt in need of that blessing by the Dean.

We walked our horses slowly out of the field and along the narrow lane that leads to the Cathedral. Somehow it seemed exactly right that we should approach the grey shrine of St David through a gorse-lined lane. This is the most secret, tucked away and unexpected of the great religious buildings of Britain. It is hidden in a wild, stony valley. You don't march towards it over miles of level land as you do to most of our cathedrals. You suddenly fall into it, over the ledge of rock that marks the rim of the valley. It is the only cathedral I know that has a trout stream running in front of the Great West Door. Outside it is grey, Norman, stern; as firmly planted on the rock as a prehistoric cromlech. Inside it has a strange splendour of Tudor roofwork. Either way it's an astonishing experience.

The Dean and a few friends stood in a little group before the dark tower. The bells sounded far off in the warm air. Everything was very still on that perfect early summer's morning as he wished us 'God-speed'. Tika blinked and almost bowed her head. That experienced old horse had a sense of occasion. We moved off slowly, almost like pilgrims setting out on a journey fraught with fabulous perils and delights. And still at 7 a.m. we had the whole world to ourselves.

St David's Cathedral

Now we clip-clopped through the village—or rather the city, the smallest in Britain. Past the old market cross and through the one narrow street. Immediately I discovered another advantage of travelling on horseback. You are perched high above any other forms of traffic, higher than the highest lorry-driver. You have a splendid view straight into the front bedrooms of the two-storied houses that line the village streets. Not that we saw anything out of order in the eminently respectable upper bedrooms of St David's City.

Only two sleepy-eyed little boys in pyjamas, standing on the bed and peeping through the curtains at the cavalcade going by.

'Ooh! Look at the white horse,' eight years old whispered.

'She's not a horse. She's a pony,' said knowledgeable ten years old. 'Can't you see she's last?'

Of course she was. Tika had taken the place which she retained as by natural right to the end of our journey.

I welcomed being on Tail-end Tika in those clear morning hours of our first day out. We were riding through a country that has held a special charm for me since I first came to it over thirty years ago, fresh from my first term at Oxford. Landscapes that excite you before you are twenty-one never lose their grip on your mind. This is a gnarled, sea-surrounded, rock-outcrop of a land, spoke-shaved by the winter wind. The coast is a jagged procession of cliffs and pinnacles, speckled with secret coves and even now not altogether caravan-covered. The old pilgrims who came to St David's in the Middle Ages must have felt they had come to the end of the known world. Beyond was the savage Atlantic, and in the winter the wind and the waves came in non-stop from Newfoundland.

This strange peninsula is speckled with rock-outcrops like the tors on Dartmoor. They shoot up above the pattern of rock-walls like miniature mountain peaks. St David's Head and Pen Beri are under 600 feet, but in this treeless landscape they can look like the Matterhorn—if there's winter mist about.

On this warm June morning they seemed friendly, near. And as we dawdled our horses gently along the deserted road we looked beyond the out-crops to the real Land's End of Wales—Ramsey Island and the welter of dark rocks, called the Bishops and the Clerks, that ends in the South Bishop lighthouse. Old George Owen, the Tudor historian of Pembrokeshire, had a wonderful phrase for them. 'These Bishops and their Clerks preach deadly doctrine to the souls of poor mariners in the nights of winter amidst the wastes of the waters.'

Ramsey is a marvellous whaleback of an island, the finest off the coast. It is cut off from the mainland by a tide race that was a challenge to me in my early youth. Today it looked as smooth as silk, just a quiet ripple off the line of rocks known as the Bitches that run out into the middle of the sound from Ramsey. But I remember shooting it with the tide in a half-decked sailing-boat—holding my breath as the helmsman struggled to keep her straight amid the roaring waters, with our eyes blinded by the spray from the overfalls. The races around the Pembrokeshire islands on bad days have an evil, inhuman savagery about them. We came in under in the lee of the Bitches, half drowned and bailing for our lives. We stayed on the security of Ramsey for a month!

The race died down and the skies became clear; it would have been easy to retreat to the mainland. But Ramsey in those far-off untroubled days of 1929 seemed an enchanted place to me. You are either a natural island-dweller or you hate them like Hell. I am a completely island-crazed man. Steamy-hot or glacier-covered, inhabited or uninhabited, flat or mountainous—I can take them all. Of course, it's escapism at it's worst and most anti-social, but the waters that you cross to get to islands seem to cleanse you of crowded suburbs, piped music, the whine of jet-engines, the bird-cages of power lines. I have never had to live all my life on an island, so perhaps I might change my tune. We are not realists in our dreams. All of us keep at the back of our minds some picture of a place where we can slip out of the mundane world and live the perfect life, where the Earthly Paradise would be made visible and viable.

On its western side Ramsey tumbled into the sea in high, grey cliffs. The waters around were littered with the rock fangs of the Bishops and the Clerks. The seals came in to breed in the clefts of the rocks. You could never look down from the cliff-tops of Ramsey without seeing a friendly, dog-like grey head popping out of the creaming breakers.

Overhead floated the Golden Eagle. Back in 1914 a Mr Neale, perhaps with romantic dreams of restoring this noble bird to

Wales released a pair of them on Skomer Island. You could do a thing like that in 1914 and no questions asked. What a howl would go up from the farmers if you tried it today. But these Pembrokeshire isles, before the advent of myxomatosis, swarmed with rabbits and at first the pair had a field day. Then one of them was shot on the mainland by a 'sportsman' and the survivor soared across to Ramsey and lived there in lonely state for eighteen years. We expect long life from an eagle in Wales—the old romance of Kilhwch and Olwen named the Eagle of Gwern Abwy as the second oldest thing in the whole world. And this fierce, disainful bird ruled the air of Ramsey until 1932.

When I first camped on Ramsey the eagle was still there. You would sometimes come upon her with her talons fastened into a rabbit—lazily she would spread her wings, that always looked enormous, and insolently float away with effortless ease far out over Ramsey Sound. The eagle was the pride of Ramsey, but the island's most remarkable inhabitant was the man who then farmed it, if you could call farming his taking a rather half-hearted interest in a singularly independent flock of sheep. Mr Edwards came to the island after the First World War. It suited him to claim that he had come to cultivate Ramsey, but what he really wanted to cultivate was bird-watching, seal-friendship and the art of telling stories.

What farming that went on seemed to be conducted by Mr Edwards's Welsh assistant, old William. To us young men, William seemed fabulously old. His splendidly aquiline profile was set off with flowing white hair. He looked like an Old Testament prophet who was partial to a nice drop of beer in between his sessions of sin-denouncing. Mr Edwards at his side was neat, country-bred, English-looking in the plus-fours of the epoch. Conventional—until he started to talk! He was the first gifted story-teller I ever met, genuine artist in the spoken word, for he would have nothing to do with writing.

'Why don't you write your memoirs?' we used to urge him.

'Write things down!' he snorted in disgust. 'Printer's ink is one of the great killers of our time.'

He had something there. The story-teller with a pen or type-writer is a different and duller bird from the vocal artist. The vocal story-teller needs a background and he needs time. He's no good on television. The pace is too fast. He ends up in anecdote and wisecracks. In 1929 Mr Edwards had all the time in the world to deploy his effects and we had all the time in the world to listen.

The setting was unfailingly right—the wide kitchen of the old farmhouse on a wet evening, with the cold-nosed farm dogs nuzzling our hands and the firelight playing on William's face as he underlined Mr Edwards's narration with 'Very, very true, Mr Edwards, bach. Very, very true'—like a deacon in chapel counterpointing the preacher. All Mr Edwards's stories needed William's reassuring murmurs. Even at eighteen we were a bit worried about the absolute historicity of some of them.

For example there was the story of how Mr Edwards had saved the whole of the British Army in the great retreat of 1918 and thus saved the free world.

'Ah, boys, you will never know—and pray heaven you will never know—the horror of War.' (In 1929 we had no idea of what 1939 would bring.) 'I was just an ordinary Tommy—No, I'd no desire for the trappings of command, although naturally they kept pressing me to take a commision. I knew I was of more value keeping up the morale of the men in the trenches. Then in March 1918 the blow fell. Gough's disaster! The Germans smashed our front. My unit was scattered like confetti. Day and night we retreated. Dog-tired, turning to fire, then falling back until I alone was left. I trudged back in the falling rain. I didn't know where the front was or if I was behind it or before it.'

'Suddenly a staff car came past, splashing me with mud. It pulled up and a glittering figure with highly polished boots got out. I trudged up to it and managed a weary salute. You know the old army proverb, "If it moves, salute it; if it doesn't move paint it."

'The figure condescended to speak.

' "Tell me, my man, you are a typical British Tommy. What

would you say to the troops that would rally them and make them turn and fight?"

'I said quite simply, "Tell them this. There is no other course open to us but to fight it out! Every position must be held to the last man: there must be no retirement. With our backs to the wall, and believing in the justice of our cause, each one of us must fight on to the end!"

'The glittering figure said nothing, saluted, got back into the car, which squelched off through the rain and gave me a final spattering of mud as it went!

'At dawn next morning I staggered into a ruined French village. There on the wall was a notice. It was Haig's famous Backs to the Wall Dispatch, word for word as I'd said it. You all know the result of that great rallying-cry. The men took fresh heart. They stopped retreating. They stood like a rock before the final German assault. Europe was saved.'

'Very, very true, boys,' said William, 'every word of it.'

'You got your reward, Mr Edwards?' we asked.

'Indeed I did, in a way that you, starting on the voyage of life, should take to heart. The year is now 1919. We are in Germany. I am part of the guard of honour on the bridge of Cologne. The Field-Marshal, in even more glittering medals and boots, comes slowly down the line. He has a word for each man. He notices each ribbon, he congratulates each veteran. At last he stands opposite me, looks at me . . . and passes without a word. Ah, boys, put not your trust in princes or in field-marshals.'

'True, true, Mr Edwards. Very, very true,' echoed William, 'true every word.'

'But,' said Mr Edwards, with the resignation of an unpublished philosopher, 'what do I want with the empty trappings of public recognition. Enough for me to know, in my heart, that I had saved Europe. Like a Welsh Cincinnatus I have retired to my farm, happy to live out of the world, happy to speak to the birds and to the seals. I mean that literally, of course.'

'You mean,' we inquired in astonishment, 'that you can actually understand what the seals are barking about.'

'Certainly, once you live close to them on an island like this, you soon get to understand their language. More important still, they understand me. As a matter of fact, I've established a bit of ascendancy over a group of seals that usually lie out on that little beach under Ynys Cantwr. I drill them—usual army drill. Be there tomorrow morning and I'll put them through their paces for you.'

We were there next morning, for this time we felt in our bones that Mr Edwards had gone too far.

The south end of Ramsey breaks down into a huddle of small islets and the nearest one, Ynys Cantwr, 'the Singing Isle', protects a little beach under the cliffs of the main island. We crawled cautiously to the edge and looked down. Three seals were lying up on the seaweed and shingle. They had flopped in through a narrow passage in the rocks. Mr Edwards whispered, 'that's my squad. Just look down and watch me give them their drill.'

He slipped off and worked his way down the cliff out of sight. There were the three seals basking on the warm rocks, fat, comatose and unmovable. Nothing, not even a cat in front of a fire, looks so totally at peace with the world as a seal asleep on a summer's beach.

Suddenly Mr Edwards appeared from behind a rock. He stood in a splendid military posture and shouted his order, 'Att . . . en . . . tion.' The seals' heads came up. 'Eyes right!' Every head swivelled towards him. 'Single file!' The seals scrambled into line. 'Quick march!' Smartly the seal line set off towards the sea. 'Right wheel!' The flopping file swung right and plunged into the breakers.

We nearly fell over the cliff in our astonishment. Mr Edwards rejoined us. 'Well, what do you think of them? Smart, eh? I'll have to ask Frances Pitt, the naturalist, across to see this. Highly important, I think, for the future. We've got to communicate with our wild friends. When I really get to understand them, just think what we can do together!'

We drifted back through the heather, with the dogs chasing the rabbits as they came out of the farm to greet us. We had a vision of Mr Edwards and his trained seals revolutionising the fishing around St David's, running an underwater messenger service. Anything seemed possible.

'We don't know the boundaries of knowledge, boys,' said Mr Edwards. 'I'm trying to extend them in my humble way.'

'Quite right,' chorused William. 'This time it's even truer than the truth.'

It wasn't until we were back for some days in the semi-sober atmosphere of St David's on the mainland that we realised what Mr Edwards had done. How stupid we'd been. The solution was obvious.

It wouldn't have mattered what noise Mr Edwards had made when he stepped out from behind his rock. The seals would have looked up towards the source of danger, and then made for the sea. They would have to go single file, since they were forced to pass a narrow rock passage and then turn right to get to the safety of the breakers. All Mr Edwards did was to give the appropriate order a split second before the seals did what came naturally. It was a masterpiece of timing, that was all.

I have always regretted the loss of illusions. It would have been pleasant to go through life believing that somewhere, somehow, on some lonely island around our coast there is a man who can communicate with the Grey Seal.

I had been absorbed in memories of island delights and had almost forgotten that we were travelling firmly on the mainland. We had come well clear of St David's City and had already come four miles past cottages with names of old ships like 'Morning Star' and the first of the five hundred chapels we would pass on our journey.

I looked towards the fading peak of Carn Llundain, the highest summit of Ramsey. Even at Tika's slow plod, it was falling behind. We were moving, I calculated, at a splendid five miles an hour. All around us the countryside was still undisturbed in the warm, new-minted morning. Not even the distant revving of a car. Just the pleasant clip-clop of Tika's hoofs as we went steadily on between the stone walls bordering the road. The rest of our cavalcade was about fifty yards ahead. Tika refused to be hurried. There is no more drowsy, soothing sound in nature than the slow sound of horses' hoofs on a warm morning.

I could sit on Tika's back and dream of the past and Ramsey Island or gaze abstractly around at the pleasant, unspoilt landscape. This was an enormous pleasure for me. The others could have all the fiery-spirited mounts they wanted—all eager to go, starting into the trot before you gave them the slightest indication. Before Tika condescended to trot I had to give her two minutes' solid exhortation: 'Come on, old girl. Get up there, Tika. Get up, I say.' And I went on saying it until Tika, in her own time, changed gear. This morning she'd decided to keep walking. So slowly we ambled northwards from St David's.

My private chats with Tika became a habit with me. All the horse experts advise you to talk to your horse and explain what you want her to do. The famous Victorian horse-tamers like Sullivan and Rarey, who won world fame by their ability to get savage 'killer' horses to eat out of their hands, set enormous store on whispering into the horse's ear. Tika was no killer, and needed no exhortation from me to 'take it easy'. But I felt sure she liked to hear a friendly noise coming from somewhere on her back. Even if it did nothing for Tika, it did a lot to reassure me. And we had now come to something completely beyond her experience. Our road turned westward and came out on to the actual edge of the sea.

Of course, the feeling of the sea had been with us for some time, for we had seen Ramsey in the distance, but the country here has a curious saucerlike quality, rising to the rim along the sea's edge. You come up over the rim and suddenly the sea is immediately below.

Now, Tika was a completely land-bred horse. She had never smelt the salt tang of the waves or seen the shifting green carpet of the ocean—so much more dangerous than the wildest of mountainsides. She wrinkled her nostrils a little uneasily. Clearly her attitude was that of the old Yoruba chief who was invited to Lagos for the first time and taken to look at the sea. He gazed with astonishment at the waves crashing on to the beach and then said to the interpreter, 'Tell me,' he said, 'how long has this been going on?'

'This,' I said firmly to Tika, 'is the sea. Now, my girl, the sea is . . . ' But there I stopped, for how can you explain the sea? I had always claimed to be a seafarer. I have sailed boats around the Welsh coast with enthusiasm, I once even started to work for a mate's ticket; I take to blue water whenever I get a chance.

'Tika,' I continued, 'what you see before you is the sea as understood by the ordinary folk, sailors and such-like. But you don't see the half—no, not one-eighth of what it really means. Now look down below.'

I have no idea if the eye of the horse allows her to see into the ocean deeps, but I didn't care. For on this day the water off the Welsh coast was of Mediterranean clarity. The bright sun may have had something to do with it, but you could see twenty feet down, and my mind immediately went back to the coast near Marseilles where I had only recently been shown that there is another, more exciting, more dangerous and yet far more fascinating sea than the old, familiar wrinkled water-plain we are used to. I had been introduced to the fourth dimension of living—under-water exploration. My initiator was none other than Captain Cousteau himself.

I remember talking about the underwater world with him on board his yacht, the *Calypso*, as we prepared for the first sub-aqua TV broadcast from a sunken Greek galley. The white cliffs of the Calanque coast plunged down before us into water so clear that I could imagine that I could see the outline of the wrecked galley a hundred feet below.

Cousteau was lithe, brown from the sun; you felt that his body had become almost as streamlined and swift as that of a fish from long immersion in salt water. He was obviously a man born to command—what he said in his quiet voice went without dispute. His smile was given to his team as a medal of achievement: it did not appear often, but when it did it made everything worth while. Around us the *techniciens* of French television were busy slinging cameras down into the water or heaving masses of equipment up on to the rock face of the island. Everything they did defied the practice of the BBC and even the basic laws of electrical engineering, but somehow it would work!

Cousteau looked around a little sadly.

'All this television publicity—I wonder how far I should go— if I have already gone too far. I hear everybody saying, "*Cousteau est un peu cinema.*" I may have overstepped the permissible limits, but I struggle very hard not too. Money must come for my work but how to avoid being caught in its web?'

We looked overboard at a shoal of bright fish moving under the stern of the *Calypso*. Cousteau said, 'When we first went down in the 1930s with the beginning of the aqua-lung we went into a marvellous new world: all was innocence. The fish were our friends, now they are learning to hate us. We do not see them making love any more . . . *Ils sont pudiques, ils se cachent.*'

Cousteau's little dog gambolled up to us. 'Taillez tried to make him a suit, but so far he has not succeeded. We have made everyone free of the sea, anyone can dive. My father went down at the age of seventy-five, all my family live in the water. But how long can we keep this under-water paradise? Already the great merou, that slow majestic guardian of the wrecks, is getting rare. The coral is broken. We have no under-water police force. It is like the moment when Captain Cook first came to Tahiti. When he first landed the country was happy, lazy and enchanting. Fifty years later half the islanders were dead and the rest were dressed in cast-off Western clothes and were singing hymns. Will it be the same in the sea? . . . '

We were riding now along a coastline cut by a series of small creeks—none of them big enough to hold the sort of fishing village you find in Cornwall, only a few houses or two and a pub at the most. In the past the small ketches out of Fishguard used to bring up all the supplies that this remote area needed. Hence the presence of hidden, tucked-away inns which always cultivated a flexible attitude to the great problem of the Welsh countryside, Sunday Closing.

We turned down into Aber Eiddy, where, in the 1880s, there was a small slate quarry. Pembrokeshire slate at its best has a deep, olive-green sheen, and when the big industrial towns of England were expanding in a housing explosion Aber Eiddy must have seemed a gold-mine. But the boom faded, the quarries shut, leaving behind them some deep holes on the cliff-face and a fascinating fact, firmly recorded in local memory, that only sixty odd years ago some quarrymen looked over the cliffs hereabout and saw a mermaid. Apparently she was an educated mermaid who—very conveniently—spoke excellent Welsh. She uttered a cryptic statement before plunging back into the sea, '*Medi yn Sir Penfro a chwynnu yn Sir Gar*'—'Reaping in Pembrokeshire and weeding in Carmarthenshire!' You can make what you like of this mystic utterance.

The only comparable statement that I collected from this coastline as we rode along was a bit of gossip I overheard as we dismounted in the next village along the coast, Trevine. Said one lady to the other.

'You ought to have seen the picture last night.'

'A or X?'

'X, of course. It was lovely and terrible, all about Vampires. I thought about that Vampire all night. It had a face like Mr Rees, Frongoch.'

Trevine lies along the hill that leads out of a small cove. It consists of one wide street, large enough to hold the annual November St Martin's Fair which was the pride of the place until the end of the nineteenth century. I got the recipe for the famous mutton pasties which used to bring the farmers on pilgrimage, just to taste them. 'But,' said my seventy-year-old informant, 'don't forget, you've got to flatten the pastry by hand. None of that old rolling-pin business.' The old lady remembered a far-off, happy Trevine—correctly Trêfin, in Welsh. Half the men went to sea in the days of the windjammers. 'Yes, and the wives went to sea with the captains everywhere, round Cape Horn, Valparaiso, India. You couldn't find a house here without a curio from the far ends of the earth. We were right on the very edge of Wales and England, but we knew more about the wide world than any of those London or Birmingham people, poor souls. Imagine living all your life among those buses and trams and no sea!'

'Has the old place changed?' I asked her.

'No, it's not places that change,' she said, 'it's us. You know, if I only had my middle age again I'd be as airy as a lark.'

But Trevine has changed in one important respect—the mill has gone. The old water-wheel has rusted and the little stream that once turned it tumbles unheedingly over the cliff, choked by rushes. The walls are yellow with moss . . . and from here on every Welsh-speaking child can continue this description in verse.

For the ruined mill at Trevine is the theme of one of the most popular poems in modern Welsh, written by the Rev. Crwys Williams, who is approaching his ninetieth year, but is still as upright and lively as ever he was. He made one of the most distinguished of Archdruids; a man of splendid presence who looked, in the midst of his white-robed fellow bards at the National Eisteddfod, as if he were one of those impressive head Druids who lined the shores of the Menai Straits long ago and struck terror and reluctant admiration into the hesitant Roman legions about to defile the sacred groves of Anglesey.

Crwys's poem is simple yet unforgettable, but how on earth do you convey its effects in English? I pondered over this business of translation as I rescued Tika from her admirers and followed the procession out of Trevine. Tika, by the way, had begun to collect her fans, for we had published details of our route in the *Radio Times* and a little crowd was waiting at Trevine to offer the riders morning coffee. Tika was our only grey horse and this gave her an unfair edge when it came to attention. She also arrived five minutes after the others, so she was guaranteed her publicity build-up. She soon realised the advantage of this. She would loiter gently to get exactly the right distance, then prick up her ears and trot briskly up to the Welcoming Committee. She scooped all the sugar and monopolised the fuss of delighted children. I had difficulty in rescuing her from the friendly pattings of the juvenile population of Trevine.

But away we went in fine style, with Tika pretending to trot up the hill until we were out of sight over the brow. Then, immediately, she abandoned her temporary impersonation of the trot. We were back to five miles an hour at the tail end.

As we went slowly past the gorse-lined hedges—and all North Pembrokeshire is full of the yellow glory of the gorse in flower at Whitsuntide—I returned to my meditation on the appalling difficulty of translation, of using another language completely naturally. For example, I am supposed to be completely bi-lingual, but I am still uncertain about the correct use of 'shall' and 'will'. I am consoled to read in the great Fowler, whose 1906 book on the King's English is still my grammatical gospel, 'It is unfortunate that the idiomatic use [of these words] . . . while it comes by nature to Southern Englishmen, is so complicated that those who are not to the manner born can hardly acquire it.'

So I have deep sympathy for anyone who has to write English and is yet 'not to the manner born'. The results can be charm-ingly unexpected. In Nigeria, during the Korean war, I was en-chanted to see the banner headline, 'Macarthur Flies Back to Front'.

The greatest piece of joyous mistranslation I have ever come across was handed to me at the Liberation of Naples in 1943.

The ingenious Dr Alfano realised that the first need of the keen liberator was a phrase-book telling him what to liberate. The Doctor hurriedly ransacked all available dictionaries and produced the *Modern Polyglot Conversational Italian*. It became an immediate best seller-with the troops. The soldiery were instructed in the correct conversation to use in every difficult situation. No doubt the Italian was impeccable, but the wild glory of the *Modern Polyglot* lay in its English sentences. Here is the conversation you were supposed to hold with your barber from the section, 'Al Barbiere.' The customer speaks first:

Customer: Be quick and put on my wrapper and a white napkin and strap your razors when you have lathered me . . . Ah! you have put the brush into my mouth.

Barber: It was because you spoke when I did not expect it. The young bride's hair was black, thick, coarse, her forehead broad and square. An ordinary hair-dresser would not have been able to hide the sternness of her features, but I have given her head a gentle and languishing expression.

Customer: Truly, I am struck with admiration. But, Mister Artist, for all your talent, you have cut me. I am bleeding. You have been shaving against the grain.

Barber: No, sir, I have only taken off a little pimple. With a bit of court plaster, it will not be seen.

Customer: Doesn't my hair need to be freshened up a little?

Barber: I will cut a little off behind, but I will not touch the tuft on the forehead or about the ears.

Customer: Why ever not?

Barber: Because, sir, you would then appear to have too low a forehead and ears too long. Do you wish me to give you a touch of the curling irons?

Customer: It is unnecessary. My hair curls naturally.

Barber: Shall I put on a little oil or pomatum?

Customer: Put on a little scented oil.

Barber: Look in the glass.

And when the customer does look in the glass he is invited to burst out with a '*Va benissimo*. It will do very well. I see you are an artist worthy to shave and trim your contemporaries.' I only wish I could hold such a conversation with my own barber. I would like to see his reaction to the 'touch of the curling irons'.

The memory of Dr Alfano and his *Modern Polyglot* put out of my mind any thought of trying to translate Crwys's poem on the old mill at Trevine. In any case we were now over the brow of the hill with the temptation of a notice, No Through Road, before us. A horse goes happily where a car gets into trouble. We turned off the tarmac. The lane changed from rough stone into grass and we savoured the pleasure of moving over grateful ground, the sort of yielding, springy turf that horses love.

Away went Shannon, Smatcher and Seamus. Even old Tika stepped out into a gentle trot. The sun was warm, the scent of broom in the air and we came to the cliff-edge to a glorious view of rock and sea. The sea was a dark blue, creased like shot silk. The coast stretched away in lonely coves to the grey bulk of Strumble Head, where the French landed in 1797 for the last invasion of these islands. It was an inept affair, the worst-managed combined operation in history. The French troops were the sweepings of the jails and the galleys and their commander, Tate, was an American adventurer. The whole foray was simply meant to distract attention from a serious plan to invade Ireland.

The troops came ashore in February on a cliff that would have puzzled modern commandos. There was looting, a little skirmish with the locals—one gallant heroine, Jemima Nicholas, rounded up twelve of the invaders with her pitchfork. Within a day or two the French laid down their arms on Goodwick sands.

When we looked at that succession of cliffs and jagged rocks stretching to the climax of Strumble, we wondered who, on the French side, had ever thought that this was an ideal place to start a beach-head.

I managed things better in the last invasion in which I was involved: the Allied landing in the South of France in 1944. Sober military historians call it 'Operation Anvil'. To me, it will always be the 'Champagne Campaign'.

I can see myself now—as dawn broke on that warm August day in 1944—crouching against the steel sides of a packed LCT, with recording gear festooned all over my ill-fitting battledress. We were racing for the shore in the approved style for well-conducted amphibious assaults. The shells from the fleet whistled overhead and burst with a roar on the enemy defences. Or we hoped they did. The GIs around me swore like Norman Mailer heroes and looked as if they were already signed up for Darrell Zanuck's *Longest Day*. Our objective, of all places, was the sands of St Raphael in the South of France.

A thick smoke-screen drifted across the beach ahead. Our LCT grounded in luke-warm water, down came the ramp and we splashed through the smoke to the shore. The GIs prepared to sell their lives dearly and I prepared to record them doing it. A whistle shrilled somewhere in the murk and we ran forward. At any moment the machine-guns would be opening up. The light was increasing in spite of the smoke-screen. Suddenly we were out of the smoke and blinking in the first sunshine of the day. Ahead of us, no German strongpoint but a Riviera villa which had escaped all our shells. The door opened, and an immaculately dressed Frenchman appeared. He carried a tray on which were ten glasses and a bottle of Veuve Clicquot '34. We stopped the war immediately and crowded around. Carefully he poured out the wine and handed glasses to the sweating and astonished GIs.

'*Messieurs les Americans.*' he said, '*soyez les bienvenus*', and then added, gently, even' if you are a little late'.

He set the keynote for the stern days that followed. The experts still argue learnedly and acidly about this point of the Champagne Campaign. Perhaps after this long interval one needs reminding that it took place two months after D-Day in Normandy. The Americans under General Patch and the French under General de Lattre de Tassigny landed on the Riviera and swept up the Rhône valley to link forces with General Eisenhower's troops advancing across northern France. 'Vital to the task of smashing the Germans before they reach the Rhine,' insisted Eisenhower. 'Fatal to our hopes of forestalling the Russians in the Balkans,' lamented Churchill.

But time softens controversy, and the history of distant wars grows mellow like '49 burgundy. At last we can see Anvil in its true perspective. It wasn't fought for military motives at all. One glance at the map and the route taken by the invading armies makes the *raison d'être* of the Champagne Campaign crystal clear.

Ahead of the advancing troops was grouped such a collection of noble names that the mouth waters as the hand types them: Châteauneuf du Pape, Tavel, Tain-l'Hermitage, Chateau Grillet, the Côte Rotie. And, beyond, the greatest objective of them all—Burgundy and the Côte d'Or!

Was it possible—when the German front had started to crumble elsewhere—that these oenological strongpoints should be left at the mercy of the Nazis, especially with the vintage only a few months ahead? General Eisenhower and Sir Winston Churchill may not quite have appreciated the urgency of the situation, but there was one man who did. General de Montsabert was one of the most trusted generals of the new French army. He was a soldier of energy and resource, but, more important for the future of France and for our own cellars, he was a lover of wine. He was in the centre of the planning of Anvil. I need say no more.

I admit that I have no documentary evidence that the gastronomic General played the decisive role in swinging the invasion towards the threatened vineyards, but historians cling too readily to official documents. I prefer to trust the subtle hints that the General himself gave me when the Champagne Campaign was safely over and we were enjoying the grateful hospitality of the wine-growers of Nuits St Georges.

We were pouring out bottles of such quality that the General's usual sense of security became slightly less strict than usual. We fought all over again the campaigns we had covered together, and I broached the vital question, 'Why did we have to land in France? Would it not have been better to continue up Italy with full strength and with the Germans on the run?'

'My friend,' said the General, 'you do not sufficiently consider one great difficulty. In Italy we were fighting our way through an art gallery and a museum. It was no longer the Art of War but the War of Art. How could we deploy our full strength? The fifteenth century? I could not attack, but had to make an outflanking movement. The sixteenth? Then I permitted myself a little machine-gun fire. The seventeenth? Ah! Now we could have artillery support. The eighteenth meant tanks and for the nineteenth, monsieur, I had no hesitation in calling in the air. If only Italy had all been built in the twentieth century we should be on the Alps by now!'

'And Anvil?'

'Let us rechristen it "Winepress". I admit it commanded my immediate support. In Italy all we could do was smash things and the outside world doesn't like to hear of works of art being smashed, even in the best of causes. But in this campaign we came as saviours of the greatest works of art in the world.'

'Works of art, mon General?'

'But certainly—the vineyards of Burgundy.'

So it was that the Champagne Campaign combined glory with pleasure in a way never before or since achieved in modern war. In the actual plan of the advance I detected the subtle thinking behind the scenes of a Man of Wine. Take, for instance, the lines of attack assigned to the different commands. The American army swung north from the Riviera through the rough country of the Basses Alpes, with the task of cutting into the German army retreating up the actual valley of the Rhône. Their job was vital and took them through superb country, but the vinously minded historian will note that it did not take them near a single vineyard of quality, with the possible exception of a slight reconnaissance towards Clairette de Dié. Frankly, I cannot see Clairette de Dié inscribed on the flags of General Patch's army as one of its notable battle honours.

Now follow the advance of the French army. The soldiers of de Lattre de Tassigny and of Montsabert took the valley and the left bank of the Rhône. Swiftly they possessed themselves of Tavel, and after making sure that all was well with one of the finest *vins rosés* in France, struck fiercely for Châteauneuf du Pape. Northward they raced for St Peray and Hermitage. The Côte Rotie fell to a well-planned flanking attack. It was then only a matter of days before the French were masters of the Mâconnais in every sense of the word.

On the surface all was going well, with the Germans on the run and the Americans racing through the Jura towards Besançon. But when I dropped into American HQ for a briefing on the general situation I detected a slight anxiety in the air. As a war correspondent I had become a connoisseur of briefings and had been fascinated by the differences in each Allied army's approach to this esoteric branch of the military art. Instinctively the British officer tends to avoid the vivid word, wisely feeling that he can minimise the horror of war if he can describe it in everyday terms drawn from the vocabulary of sport. If he is a senior officer that sport will be fox-hunting. When Field-Marshal Montgomery told a group of Americans that his men had their tails 'well up', a puzzled colonel asked a British officer in the group, 'Excuse me—up what?'

I remember at Anzio listening to a British officer putting the Americans in the picture about a tank clash up the Albano road. He stood in front of a map on which every position was meticulously marked. 'Well, gentlemen,' he proceeded, 'our tins were hacking along the road with their swedes out of the lid when they got a bloody nose. The question is, shall we thicken up the party or do an Oscar? In any case we'll have to tie the whole thing up on the old-boy net.' Said one American anxiously to me, 'Thomas, are we advancing or are we retreating?'

The French method was in complete contrast. It naturally derived from the Napoleonic communiqué. Every statement had to be '*court, énergétiquet décisif*'. General de Lattre, standing before the flag of France but with no map, explained how he pierced the Gap of Belfort. 'First it was the optimism of the morning. Then came the pessimism of the evening. And then, Messieurs de la Presse, we consulted the final reports and, *pouf, c'etait la Victoire!*'

The Americans also believe in the swift punch-line. When I discussed the problems facing Anvil with General Patch I asked him how he proposed to solve them. 'Sir,' he replied, 'we don't solve our problems; we overwhelm them.' The American briefers certainly overwhelmed me. I always came out from a session with them slightly dizzy but boundlessly confident. Men who could make wisecracks with such effortless ease were obviously men of resource. As the briefer told us before the Anzio break-out, 'General Mark Clark has got fifty-seven different plans and he's going to use every one of them!'

But on this occasion I detected a slight lack of the usual

buoyancy in the air. General Patch might well have had fifty-seven different plans up his sleeve, but clearly he was now a little uncertain about which one to use.

After the briefing, a colonel on the staff—an old comrade-in-arms of Anzio days—took me aside.

'You're going across to see the Frogs this afternoon, I hear?' I had, indeed, intended to go scouting through the vague no-man's-land of fifty miles which now separated the two armies.

'Well,' said the colonel thoughtfully, 'I wonder if you'd give me your private opinion, while you're there, on a little problem that's got us kinda worried. I've got a feeling that the Frogs are doing a little bit of a "go slow" on us. I've got no proof. On paper, all's well. But in this game I've found that it's sometimes wise to back a hunch, and right now I've a hunch that our friends are staying a little too long at this place Chalon something or other. Not like them, either. Those babies can move all right when they want to.'

Chalon something or other! Obviously this was Chalon-sur-Saône. I felt that I already had a shrewd idea why the 'Frogs were dragging their feet'.

That evening I presented myself at the field HQ of Monstsabert and received the usual warm welcome. The Intelligence Officer took me to the map tent and we reviewed the situation. There was no doubt that the enemy was retreating, but the point was—how fast was he moving? Was he prepared to fight a strong rearguard action before Dijon? 'I need hardly tell you,' said my friend, 'the terrible consequences of such a decision. It would mean war, mechanised war, among the Grands Crus! Would France forgive us if we allowed such a thing to happen? We must not forget 1870.'

I confess that I had long ago forgotten what happened in Burgundy in 1870. But the Colonel swiftly reminded me that one of the last battles of the Franco-Prussian War took place around Nuits St Georges: 'Shells fell on Les Cras, the German reserves swept forward over La Tache, Romanée-Conti and Richebourg. This must never be allowed to happen again.'

We both looked thoughtfully at the Colonel's private map of the German positions. They were—quite properly—marked with care on the relevant sheet of Larmat's *Atlas Vinicole de la France*. There had been reports of a Tiger tank at Meursault and of demolitions prepared at Chassagne-Montrachet. There might even be a strong German rearguard assembled behind Beaune. A picture immediately leapt into my mind of air attacks on Chambolle-Musigny, of tanks rolling forward over the carefully tended vines of Vosne-Romanée, of smoke rising from the burnt-out château of Clos de Vougeot.

Then occurred one of those dramatic strokes that are the speciality of the French at war. A young *sous-lieutenant* entered, hurriedly saluted and, with a smile illuminating his face, declared, 'Great news, mon Colonel, we have found the weak point in the German defences. Every one is on a vineyard of inferior quality.'

We both recognised that we had reached a turning-point in the battle. Said the Colonel, 'General de Montsabert must know at once, but he will give only one order, *"J'attaque"*'.

Attack he did, and to such effect that in a matter of twenty-four hours the Germans were bundled out of Burgundy and the schedule of the French advance jumped boldly ahead of the Americans. None of us can forget the glorious days that followed. Les Trois Glorieuses are celebrated every year at Dijon and in the Côte d'Or as a feast of wine and gastronomy. It has been my pleasure and privilege to attend the sale of wine at the Hospices, the feast of the Confrérie du Tasterin at the château of Clos de Vougeot and the fabulous three days of the Liberation of Burgundy. For a brief moment the cellar doors of the Côte d'Or opened almost of their own accord. . . .

No wonder General de Montsabert's eyes sparkled as we raced up Route National 74 in his jeep, close on the heels of his forward tanks. A blown bridge here, a demolished house there—what could these matter beside the great, overriding fact of the undamaged vineyards stretching mile after mile before us?

To our left rose the long line of the hills of the Côte; it was as if the Cotswold escarpment had been planted with vines and bathed in mellow sunshine. 'Decidedly,' said the General, 'in the matter of wine you must count me a man of the Left.'

I must admit that, at this point, I lost touch with the advanced elements of the French army. A sound military maxim teaches the enlightened warrior that his first duty after victory is to make sure of his base. Accordingly I disappeared into the cellars of Beaune and Nuits St Georges to make sure that our objective had remained undamaged.

I have drunk great wines in many parts of France, but never have I tasted such nectar as was offered to me during the early days of the Liberation of Burgundy. That whole enchanted period of my life is a symphony of popping corks, through which the voices of the Cadets de Bourgogne reach me, accompanied by the endearingly uncertain hunting horns of the Cor de Chasse de St Hubert singing the theme song of Burgundian Liberation:

'Toujours buveurs, jamais ivrognes!'

But on the third day, as we tackled our twentieth cellar, my friend the Colonel of Intelligence suddenly recalled that the outer world still existed. *'Les braves Américains,'* he declared, *'anciens camarades de la France. Il faut les envoyer quelque chose!'* Quickly my jeep was filled with some of the rarer treasures of the Côte. Outside one of the noblest cellars a little ceremony of historic importance was performed. The guard of honour saluted the great bottles destined for American consumption.

I drove my precious jeep-load of noble bottles back over the bumpy roads of La Bresse to American HQ, now safely established in Besancon. Hurriedly I sought out my American contact and consigned the treasures to his care. All of them? Let me be honest: some of them, by an unaccountable chance of wartime transport, found their way into my cellar in the year after the war. Still, the bottles I handed over to the Americans were enough to make the fortune of any London restaurant in these overpriced years of the 1960s.

'These are the greatest wines of France,' I said with a flamboyant flourish. 'Guard them with care; rest them; and make certain that they are *chambré* before you serve them.'

'Don't worry,' the gallant U.S. soldier reassured me, 'the Doc knows all about this Frog liquor. And while we're about it we'll invite them over to drink it.'

So it was in a certain eighteenth-century palace at Besançon that the ancient splendours of the *Belle Époque* were gloriously revived. The French guests advanced up flights of stairs lined on one side with Spahis and on the other with American military police, the Snowdrops. The Americans awaited them in a salon worthy of the receptions of Pompadour, trumpets sounded, and a column of waiters marched in bearing bottles on silver trays. My heart gave a warning thump—the bottles were from Burgundy, the noblest gifts of the Côte, and, horror of horrors, they were bubbling gently.

'We're in luck,' my American colonel whispered to me, 'the Doc's hotted this stuff up with medical alcohol.'

A look of incredulous horror flickered over the faces of the French. All eyes were turned to de Montsabert. He had led them through the campaigns of North Africa and across the snow-clad mountains of Italy. Faced with the greatest crisis so far in Franco-American relations—how would he behave?

He fixed his staff with a stern glare of command. 'Gentlemen, take up your glasses.' Reluctantly the French reached out their hands. 'To our comrades-in-arms, *les braves Américains*,' he ordered, in a ringing voice. He drained his glass with panache— every drop! Then, in a quieter voice that only the nearest Frenchman could hear, he murmured: 'Liberation, Liberation, what crimes have been committed in thy name!'

How long ago all that seemed to me as I rode along the Pembrokeshire coastline'. I wondered what Montsabert would have said to the commander of the Fishguard Invasion! We left traces of our passage through Burgundy in a trail of noble but empty bottles. All that remains of the Fishguard affair is a memorial stone set up long after the event, some bullet-holes still proudly preserved in the rafters of the old farms on the headland and the table on which the surrender was signed preserved in a pub at Fishguard. Today the profound peace of the countryside made any thought of invasion impossibly remote.

Immediately below us lay the curve of Aber Mawr—the Big Bay, a sweep of pebbles under low earth banks, with a gleaming beach before them and a pattern of green fields and crags behind. And no one there in the warm, sleepy sun!

Aber Mawr

We came carefully down the steep path and slid down the earth slope on to the beach. The little waves came caressing the sands at our feet. Biddy said, 'See how the horses will take it.'

For, as we had discovered at Trevine, they were all inland bred; not one of them had ever put foot in salt water or even been within sight of the sea before that day. And what a fuss they made of it! They were like a lot of children taken paddling by stern nursemaids. No horse likes having movement he doesn't understand going on under his feet.

'Put them at it,' ordered Biddy; 'they've got to obey.'

Then followed a wonderful display of sideways reluctance. Felicity got Seamus in and he made a fiery splashing with his hoofs. The waves caught Shannon before he could retreat. Biddy now made Smatcher go in right up to his knees and the rest took courage and went in after him—all except Tika! She went tip-toeing backwards every time a little wave came near her.

'Come on, Tika, don't be a baby!' I urged.

But it was no good; she found the whole affair of dabbling in this mysterious element completely upsetting and unladylike. She backed away on to the pebbles and plainly indicated that as far as she was concerned the sea was a dead loss. She was clearly determined to leave this new sensation to giddy youngsters. Tika retired to the earth bank and gazed reflectively towards Strumble Head and carefully avoided any view which included water of any sort.

Yet I know that horses do enjoy galloping amongst small waves when they get used to them, for I saw them at it down in the Camargue, that vast, marshy, level loneliness at the mouth of the Rhône in the South of France. There the owners of the *mas* or farms breed troops of horses, and let them wander at will over the marshlands and the miles of shallow water in the lagoons. This is a country which looks like the fenlands drenched in the sun. Great roseate flights of flamingos move lazily over the marshes, the gleaming water-channels are fringed with the feathery embroidery of waving reed-beds and, away in the distance, the blue line of the Alpine foothills. Nothing could be less like the landscape immediately before us—the rugged end-of-the-western-world country of Aber Mawr and Strumble. But watching Seamus and Shannon now facing the waves with growing confidence took me back to the time immediately after the war when I first saw the horses of the Camargue.

I didn't dare get on to their backs: those were the days when I admired horses from a distance. But while watching one of the troops of the most famous of the *masardiers*, Denys Colomb, coming dashing through the shallows, the spray rising in flashing fountains from their hoofs and the mares and foals lifting their heads in a wild, tossing rhythm to get them out of the spray, I got carried away by my enthusiasm: 'This is poetry,' I shouted, 'poetry you can see!'

We drove along the wide grass track that led around the verge of the lagoon, where the flamingos were standing on one leg out in the shallows. The middle-aged lady guest from

Rouen, who was with us, started the inevitable inquiry that no Frenchman or Frenchwoman can resist: 'But your stallions run with the herd, how can you tell who creates the offspring?'

'But easily,' said Denys. 'There can be only one stallion—the strongest, who fights like a fiend for his love rights. My Crain Blanc is magnificent. The other day he scented the nostrils wrinkle of a pair of young stallions at a quarter of a mile distance: he tore after them in a flash. The fights between stallions are terrific, but you cannot appreciate the splendour of a stallion until you see him at the moment of love. Then his eyes flash fire, every line of his muscles stands out, he is the furious embodiment of the Life Force. I am filming this and matching it, as in a ballet, to noble music.'

The French lady sighed, 'How well I understand the inspiration behind that work of art.'

But after the war the Camargue started to change. Will this last paradise of the horse disappear as the marshes are controlled by the vast Mondragon Power Scheme and rice farms displace the flamingos?

'Will they leave us nothing, these damned engineers?' Denys fulminated as his cowboys came riding up from the herd to escort our car, like Bengal lancers around the old Viceroy of India. 'Rice culture, indeed! The man who plants rice is the most inelegant of peasants; his life is spent bottom-up grubbing in the mud. Contrast that row of slowly advancing posteriors with the free carriage and upright glance of my horsemen of the Camargue. We are being engineered into insignificance. We do not want to become the slaves of co-operatives: we must reject these tempters. We will be the last place left in this France of the cheap car, the power-line and the mass tourist where you can come and say, "Here I will still see man in his natural state, religious, drunk, talkative, believing in honour and fearing pain and death." '

I remember how impressed I was with those words. It is a Welsh weakness. We are a nation brought up to believe that eloquence is important: if a man cannot speak easily, we distrust him. 'Doesn't say much,' we note; 'must be hiding something.' When I began my career as a commentator I was rather flattered than otherwise to discover that I was becoming known as Thomas the Talk: and the oratory of the Camargue is as flamboyant as that of Wales.

Alas, my last news of the last-ditchers of the Camargue was of the great estates being turned into dude ranches, '10,000 francs a week and all found, including a bull fight and Crain Blanc in action.' My informant added sadly, 'Down here we live a picture-postcard life.' I remembered my interview with a splendidly bearded ancient, known as Clan-Clan, who was once a waiter in the cafe painted by Van Gogh.

'You must have known him and seen him often,' I said; 'tell me what he was like.'

Clan-Clan sighed through his white beard. 'But there were so many artists, monsieur. We just fed them. And it wasn't like today: we did not think of tourism.'

Clan-Clan might have made a happy living in his old age as the man who remembered Van Gogh if he had only thought of tourism. Tourism! The universal solution for all our problems. Pembrokeshire has leapt at it. The caravan-farmer is busy in the land and the visitors pour in their millions towards the sea. But miraculously you can still find your way on horseback into countryside that savours of the pre-car age—a Pembrokeshire of grass lanes, hill tracks, beaches to which you must walk or trot rather than queue up for a car park. And I cannot conceive of the farmers of Aber Mawr and Strumble turning their farms into dude ranches or living 'the life of the picture-postcard'.

But the sun at least had the warmth of the Camargue as, at last, the rest of the party came out of the sea and Tika fell in behind. We scrambled with difficulty up the earth bank and into a lane that led inland. The open country of Pembrokeshire, where the strong wind can sweep straight in from the Atlantic, is clean and bare, but once you duck down into the little valleys deep cut into the ancient rock, you find trees and trout streams clattering down under tangled boughs. We came up a leafy track where the flies happily fastened on us like long-lost friends.

The horses shivered their flanks and swished their tails. I've often wondered why a rider shouldn't carry a Flit gun and spray the flanks of his irritated mount as he goes along: but again, this is one of those things that a beginner dare not suggest. I suppose we would look a little strange, moving along in an artificial mist, but it would get rid of one of the slight drawbacks of summer riding—the occasional horse-fly that prefers you to the horse.

Luckily the lane didn't last long. We came out on to a little green set amongst the trees, with a low white-walled building on one side and a farmhouse opposite. There was a cool sound of water tumbling from a stone channel on to a vast water-wheel. We had arrived at the Tre Gwynt Woollen Mill. Proprietors H. Griffiths and Son, 'Tweeds of tasteful design available for Town and Country Wear, in attendance at The Mill daily, Fishguard Market on every Thursday.' And lunch.

Out side the mill door we took off the saddles and tethered the horses. All except Tika. She was a self-tetherer. You had to tie up the others or else they would have meandered off down the lane and you'd have been in for half an hour's hunt for them. Worse still they would have rolled on their backs. I had no idea high-spirited horses could be so stupid. But apparently certain horses simply wait for your back to be turned before rolling with infinite relish on their own. Thus a ten-second frolic can cost you plenty of hard cash. One happy roll will wreck saddles, stirrups, girths and the rest of the expensive 'tack'. No wonder the experts keep on reminding you, 'Your horse is not a bicycle.' No bicycle would be quite so perverse.

While our horses browsed, we sat down to a midday guzzle cooked by Mrs Griffiths. All the old Welsh favourites were provided, including *bara brith* (a sort of currant bread) and Welsh cakes, made from dough placed on a cast-iron griddle.

I never cease to marvel at the contrast between public and private cooking in Wales. There are now some delightful exceptions to the general rule that public cooking in Wales is a form of self-inflicted gastronomic penance. The *Good Food Guide* lists them in lyric prose and the tourists flock to them. But they have no connection with any form of Welsh cuisine. And far too often you find yourself in establishments where the food served to the visitor represents the Welsh revenge for the defeat of Owain Glyndwr.

I once entertained a French gastronome at a Pembrokeshire hotel (not even a back-rolling horse would drag the name of the hotel out of me). My French friend ordered roast beef and Yorkshire pudding. When it arrived he saw the strange raft of yellow cardboard floating in a muddy sea of gravy. He prodded it nervously with his fork, cut off a corner and lifted it with misgiving to his mouth. He tasted it and hurriedly returned it to his plate. *'Mon Dieu, c'est du plastique.'*

But Welsh farmhouse cooking has flavour, as long as it sticks to Welsh farmhouse ingredients. I was brought up on non-tinned materials, prepared in the old-fashioned way. I can remember the complicated ritual, which embraced the whole family, for creating jugged hare, and the splendid, mouthwatering sizzle from the frying-pan as Mother served us the traditional Gower dish of laverbread and bacon.

Laverbread! Now, that's a unique Welsh delicacy, a breakfast food made from seaweed. You must gather the laver-weed from a limestone coastline; Gower and South Pembrokeshire are the fountainhead. You must wash it and then boil it in a cast-iron pot for twelve hours over one of those everlasting fires of culm (powdered anthracite mixed with clay) or good Glamorgan steam coal. Then sprinkle it with oatmeal. You eat laverbread for breakfast, fried in bacon fat. The enthusiasts call it Welsh caviare! I've never tasted it anywhere else, and certain English visitors when they saw the appearance of laverbread on their breakfast plates might have exclaimed, 'And no wonder.' For truth to tell laverbread looks like a pat of oozy tar speckled with bits of plaster. One indignant eater even went as far as to call it an 'edible cow-pat'. This could be a title of honour. One of the finest cheeses of the Loire Valley proudly calls itself 'Croton (cow-pat) de Sauvignon'. And who has seriously maintained that the appearance of food has anything to do with its taste? Mrs Griffiths prepared her Welsh cakes according to the correct recipe: you want lard, baking-powder, flour, sugar, currants, a teaspoonful of mixed spice, an egg and milk. Mix into a stiff paste. You roll out the paste, cut into rounds and bake on a girdle. I can still see the old, black, cast-iron girdle that used to hang in my mother's kitchen, and smell the aroma of cooking that filled the air when she made Welsh cakes!

We were happy with Welsh cake and the horses with the lush grass they pulled from the hedges. Up the lane from Tre Gwynt we trotted with new gusto. Out again on to the plateau, but away to the eastward there was a new splendour on the skyline. We had come to the edge of the Preselly Hills. This range of lonely moorlands covers most of northern Pembrokeshire. The highest summit is Frenni Fawr, 1700 feet. But again it's not height that matters. Preselly Top is pointed and graceful and acts as the weather gauge of the county. We were all taught at school the old rhyme:

> When Presselly weareth his hat
> All Pembrokeshire shall wet from that.

Today the whole range was crystal-clear, and promised well for tomorrow, when we had planned to ride the whole length of it. For the moment our route took us through tangled lanes out on to the slopes of an outlier of the main range. This was Carn Ingli, just on 1,000 feet, but a most romantic summit, set high above the sea and littered with stone circles, cromlechs and strange outcrops of rock which give it a feeling of immeasurable age. We had planned our ride over Carn Ingli to be the climax of the day.

I approached it with a slight misgiving. Once out on wide-open moorland, our horses would certainly canter, even gallop. Tika, herself, might be infected by the craze for speed. I knew I could survive the trot, I might even hang on for the canter, but if Tika galloped I faced disaster. I had vivid memories of my fall during my training period on just such a moorland as Carn Ingli. Somehow we always assume that falling off a horse is comic and that the horseman always lands safely on a soft tuft of grass. I've fallen off far too often and I must admit that I have, until now, always found a providential soft cushion spread for me by a kindly and amused guardian angel. But I can't be certain that I will always find my falling body neatly fielded. Sooner or later the odds will shorten and I will pick out a large rock concealed in the heather for my alighting place. Or perhaps there is a simpler solution, as Rowland Lucas pointed out: 'Why not learn to ride better?'

But these, after all, were my early days on horseback, and I had not gained any confidence in my ability to stay in the saddle, let alone control my horse at a gallop. I needed moral support and encouragement from someone who knew all the local pitfalls. I was relieved, therefore, to find an old friend waiting for me as we came down through tangled lanes to the little hamlet of Llanychaer, in the bottom of the Gwuan Valley. Mounted on a sturdy Welsh pony and accompanied by a fellow farmer, J. V. Wynne Jones greeted me on the old stone bridge across the sparkling river. Now I normally associate 'Jeevers' with a microphone and rugby grounds. Yet here he was in his hunting tweeds, riding-breeches and brown bowler and looking every inch the squire as pictured in the photographs that used to grace the old *Tatler*; with his partner at his side on an equally fiery pony which was pawing the ground and impatient to be off. Jeevers, at that time, owned a flourishing county club at Dinas Cross between Carn Ingli and the sea.

But all South Wales knows him as one of the Voices of Rugby and this gives him a special aura which is peculiar to South Wales, where rugby is a religion, an article of faith, a furious assertion of nationality.

There are many differences between North and South Wales, but one of the most profound is the shape of the ball with which they play football. I remember the irony in the voice of our geography master at school when we talked of North Wales. 'Oh, all they produce up there is slate, sausages-and-mash for tourists—and soccer.' Nobody who played soccer, we felt, could be really trusted. Up in the mining valleys of my early youth there were two men who shed social glory around them as they walked the streets—the conductor of the local choir and the local International. There was an awed drop in the voice as the rugby champion was introduced: 'You know Dai Rees, of course—played for Wales.'

When the local team took the field, especially against a visiting English side, they went out to do battle like the Spartans of old: 'Conquer or come off the field in the ambulance.' I was present at one epic encounter up the Valleys on a ground hewn from an old coal-tip and laid out by the local surveyor, with a cunning slope to the west known only to the home team. 'Good for one try at least before the others tumble to it,' said the locals. But on this occasion disaster struck. The English, by some unexplained freak of luck, were the first to score. The game was resumed in numbed silence until a voice behind me rallied the Welsh ranks with the heart-warming shout: 'Rub their faces in the dirt, boys bach—in a sporting fashion, of course.'

Where did this mixture of friendly ferocity and savage sportsmanship originate? Why did Welsh rugby, from its birth, vigorously reject the well-played-old-man, Twickers tradition of England. The solution of the mystery was about to be revealed, for beyond Llanyrchain and the Gwuan Valley we were going to ride towards the country where the Welsh first introduced ferocity into football. The story is told by that most attractive of Tudor historians, George Owen of Henllys in northern Pembrokeshire—or to give him full due, Lord Marcher of Cemaes, Vice-Admiral of Pembrokeshire, author of *The Description of Pembrokeshire*, and father of ten children by his first wife and seven by his second. A lusty, strong-sinewed and learned man!

He gives an elaborate account of the great game of Knappan, which was played every Shrove Tuesday between the men of

Newport and the men of Nevern. Other great tussles took place between the men of the Hundred of Cemaes and the Hundred of Emlyn in Cardiganshire and in certain other places along the border between Cardiganshire, Carmarthenshire and Pembrokeshire. All that was required was a feast-day and a challenge and the battle was on. For battle it undoubtedly was. The teams might be a thousand a side, surely the mightiest scrum history records, and this figure leaves out the horseman on the wings. The field was the whole country, between the homes of the rival teams, and the spectators in vast hordes gathered out of harm's way on some near-by hillside, regaling themselves with food and drinks as the heroes below prepared themselves for the fray.

The footmen stripped to the waist while the horsemen armed themselves with clubs three and a half feet long. The referees, who soon disappeared, were supposed to check that these weapons were not too thick to pass through a regulation ring. The ball was of wood and was thrown from player to player as in the passing action of modern rugby, but it was also boiled in tallow to make it slippery, which may account for the inherited skill of the Welsh three-quarters on a wet day.

Then with a blood-curdling howl from the players the ball was thrown in and probably disappeared for the rest of the afternoon. I have a feeling that the direct descendant of that howl is the singing of the crowd at Cardiff Arms Park when Wales are about to score a try. Didn't a well-known New Zealand player tell me once, 'You never beat us, you sung us out of the game!'

The footmen hurled themselves at each other, for Knappan was played on the celebrated principle of 'Never mind the ball, let's get on with the game'. The horsemen cudgelled each other black and blue, and the game continued until one of the teams succeeded in removing the ball from the field altogether—there was no nonsense about goals.

The heroic traditions of Knappan were carried, I am sure, into the industrial valleys and emerged again to give the players of one small area of South Wales power to pulverise the national rugby might of England, Scotland and Ireland—on occasions, anyhow!

I didn't elaborate this theory to Jeevers. In any case I was too busy getting Tika to follow the cavalcade at a reasonable pace. For we were now climbing up through the steep lanes that would take us out on to the upper moorlands of Carn Ingli. Jeevers's little Welsh pony was fresh; so was that of his fellow farmer. They went up that lane with ballet dancer's steps. They had Arab blood in them, they tossed their heads with spirit, they seemed always on the edge of cantering even at the walk. Tika had no intention of doing anything as reckless as cantering uphill. She climbed the slope with the slow determination and steady puffing of the engine on the Snowdon rack railway. She had every excuse, for we had already come a good twenty miles that day.

At the end of the procession, as usual, I took the chance, when Tika indulged in one of her calculated pauses, to turn in the saddle and look back over the way we had come. The sea far below lay drowsy in the late afternoon sun. The air was so still that I imagined I could almost hear the ripple of the Gwuan running down to the snug little harbour of Lower Fishguard. I could see the woodlands near the mouth of the Gwuan that marked the grounds of the old mansion of Glynymel. I felt I should lift my cap to Glyn-y-Mel—'The Vale of Honey'. Here lived my predecessor on this business of riding through Wales, Richard Fenton.

Fenton was one of those people who seem extraordinarily attractive even across the long gap of time. If we had been riding over Carn Ingli 150 years ago, I'm sure he would have welcomed us in to the elegant new house he had built to his own design in one of the pleasantest little 'hide-outs' in Pembroke-shire. He was a scholar and also spoke Welsh. He married a French woman and cut a dash in London in the days of his youth as a friend of Johnson, Burke, Goldsmith and the rest of the big literary names of the time.

Then he settled down again in his native country. He was a

lawyer, and a man of restless curiosity, always riding through Wales, making a list of the local rarities, 'cracking cromlechs' and 'bursting open tumuli' in company with his distinguished friend and fellow archaeologist, Sir Richard Colt Hoare. Their methods of excavation would make Professor Glyn Daniel's hair stand on end, but they were pioneers, and Fenton, at least, left records of what he found.

How pleasant to have sat with Fenton in the elegant drawing-room of his house with the woodlands rising beyond the river meadows, and our horses wandering in the lush pastures. The room is still there and so is the charming curved flight of steps leading up to the front door, while a later owner has left the garden full of unexpected inscriptions to pet dogs and horses.

> Of all the dogs a sportsman e'er possessed,
> Lucy, my noble setter, was the best,
> Fain would I weep, and on thy memory dwell,
> But all, like thee, must die—so fare thee well.

He also set up a tall stone carved with what I took to be an ancient post-Roman inscription: FORAS SESTOR RUBON. The old squire used to chuckle as learned visiting professors struggled to decipher the Celto-Roman language, when all it signified was the English sentence, 'For asses to rub on.' They had a simple sense of humour in those days.

We would have discussed Fenton's ambitious plans for his *History of Wales*, which he never carried beyond the stage of voluminous notes—how many vast volumes did I sketch out in my youth when time seemed limitless and I felt that it wasn't beyond the capacity of one man to learn Arabic and Russian and Old Norse and any other scholarly and splendid piece of antique obscurity! Above all, I would have enjoyed actually riding through Wales with him; a Wales without a motor-car on any road, without a pylon on the skyline, without the noise of an aeroplane in the loneliest part of the hills. And how easy it was then to ride a horse anywhere in the Principality. You went straight down the middle of the main roads—no working your way through lanes or lost bridle-paths, no anxieties about where to put your horses for the night in a world where all the inn stables have been turned into garages. You flung the reins to a waiting ostler, who led your steed to a well-appointed stable while you settled down before a brisk fire and made an entry in your leather-bound diary, recording the splendid, restorative spread already prepared for you by the beaming landlord. Fenton's diaries abound with entries that bring back the pleasant sizzling of bacon across the centuries—'had a damper of eggs and bacon at the New Inn with a draught of good ale'. And the inn parlour was full of rich characters like Squire Corbett, whom Fenton met at Barmouth carrying a hunting-pole and dressed in a gold 'Bobbin' waistcoat with a gold-lined front and with three or four terriers at his heels. The Squire was a great 'smoking man' and boasted of the days when he used to smoke in the Druid Society at the sign of the Old Bull, and the room was filled with 'as much Smoke as when the Groves of Mona were fired by the Romans in the time of the old Druids; when the old King of Spain and he, though their Pipes touched, could not see each other for half and hour. . . . He remembered a young Barrister entering this smoking room once, with whom he talked, knowing him by his voice, through a cloud for half and hour. Conversation very mellow through such a medium; but I suddenly lost him, for he had slunk away by force of the cloud of smoke to the Ladies.'

The formidable smoking Squire had nothing but contempt for such a pusillanimous non-smoker—'a mere milksop, not fit for the company of such enlightened beings as we were in the clouds; a fellow full of small talk and poetry, famous at handing round a plate of light cakes, and could write an ode on the head of a pin'.

My sympathy was all with that milksop of a young man. My one fury—the only thing on which I become totally irrational—is public pipe-smoking. Why should I have to absorb the reek of something that smells to me like rags in an incinerator every time I travel in a tube?

Cigars? No, they are another matter, bringers of illusions of wealth and well-being after a first-class dinner! Fenton bravely tackled his first cigar at Llandovery when he was past sixty, for the highest possible motives.

'To my great joy heard from my excellent friend Sir Richard Hoare, and to my no small confusion of head, smoked a Segar in company with my oldest friend, Doctor Symmons. I know not if it be worth while serving so disagreeable an Apprenticeship to learn the Art; but if I could once get over the little sickness it occasions, I have reason to think that it might contribute to help and concentrate thought, which I much stand in need of.'

A splendid excuse for acquiring a pleasant new vice in your old age. I have a fellow-feeling for Fenton, for I, too, have never learnt to 'concentrate thought'. I am always ready to turn aside into a tempting by-way—which is just what I've done now.

I came hurriedly back to the insistent present when I looked away from the south and realised that slowly Tika had brought me up out of the lane and that now the open moorland lay ahead. On the skyline the little group of horsemen was waiting for me. Tika ambled up to join them.

Ahead of us a path meandered through low heather. Three miles away lay the actual cairn of Carn Ingli, a huge clutter of giant, dark rocks. There was warm air flowing over the wide hills. The sea glittered to the west. There were larks singing and the scent of crushed heather-bells hung around us. The horses picked up their ears. This was the moment for the gallop—and my heart sank.

The farmer led the way. His wiry little pony had lived all her life on this moorland. She knew every stone and bump that lay ahead. The sheep that were cropping the grass in the hidden hollows suddenly came to life and scattered for safety. Away went the rest of our party, in a cavalry charge that took them half-way to Carn Ingli in minutes.

Jeevers stayed just ahead of me on his pony to tempt Tika onwards. The old girl decided she would have her last skittish fling of the day, she actually began to trot. I concentrated grimly on rising and falling correctly in the saddle. Not too badly, so far; then Jeevers put on speed, and Tika changed gear—she began to canter. 'That's the stuff,' Jeevers shouted back at me. 'Let her go.'

Tika now seemed to me to be travelling at high speed, although she was clearly not going to do anything as reckless as changing up into the gallop. It was fast enough for me. I made no attempt to control her; I hung on. And miraculously, as we came quickly out on to the road that crosses the very centre of Carn Ingli, I was still in the saddle. Could it be that at long last, I was getting the hang of it?

The others gave me an ironic cheer as I joined them. Together we moved slowly down the long mountain road that leads off Carn Ingli into the little town of Newport (Pembs). I was happy in the saddle. I hadn't fallen off. I had hopes of getting to North Wales in safety provided that Tika didn't gallop, and, above all, didn't jump. I felt I could rely on her to save me those two unnecessary ordeals.

Only one further anxiety remained. It was now five o'clock. We had been travelling for ten hours: leisurely hours, it is true, with plenty of pauses for refreshment and contemplation, but still the longest hours I had ever spent in the saddle. The great question rose in my mind of the Act of Dismounting. Would my weary limbs be equal to an elegant slide off Tika's back or were they so set in the mould of fatigue that I would have to be lifted off by a crane like the knights of old? I moved my legs cautiously as we got to the first houses of Newport. Not bad—a slight creak in my left knee and a hint of stiffness in the leg muscles, but nothing serious. I addressed myself to the task of looking every inch a horseman as we clattered through the centre of the town. Away through dreaming Newport with the inhabitants coming out at the doors to give us a wave; along the high road in the early evening with only a mile to go and the landscape still mellow in the warm sun. No haste. I could let Tika drift steadily home.

So we came past the early nineteenth-century lodge of the drive leading to Llwyngwair, our journey's end on our first eventful day. The old house lies back from the road. It is a quiet mansion, friendly and unpretentiously graceful. Cemaes and indeed the whole of Welsh West Wales never went in for the Great House and the Castle of the sort you find littered over the English countryside. True there are some splendid landed estates in South Pembrokeshire, but that's in the English-speaking part of the county. For the rest you will find no Badminton, Cliveden or Arundel in the length and breadth of Carmarthenshire, Pembrokeshire or Cardigan. Glamorgan and North Wales are the places in Wales where you could see

> The rich man in his Castle
> The poor man at his gate.

The mansions of West Wales are more modest, and give a broad hint that there was never a great deal of money knocking about in this part of the world.

Still, old Sir John Bowen built as gracefully as he could at Llwyngwair, and in later years John Wesley rode up the very drive we were now following. Llwyngwair is now a guesthouse and Mr and Mrs Marchington, the present proprietors, came out with what I suppose would be a very un-Wesleyan 'stirrup cup'. Although in all fairness the old original Nonconformists were not so anti-alcholohic as their nineteenth-century successors. I still have in my possession two elegant wine decanters from which Peter Williams used to refresh himself when writing his celebrated commentary on the Welsh Bible.

Tika, of course, brought me in last to make certain of her sugar and applause. Then came the critical moment. I had to dismount. I disentangled my feet from the stirrups, swung my right leg in a ballet dancer's circle over Tika's backside and slid suddenly to the ground. To my astonishment I was able to stand up. True my knees bent a little, rather like those of the American astronauts stepping out of their capsule after their fortnight of orbiting the earth; and I felt as if I had travelled twice as far as they had done. But I was able to walk with dignity to the door. Johnson's Baby Powder and Mr Meredith's Welsh shepherd's breeches had seen me safely through my Longest Day.

Ah, I'd forgotten one important factor—old Tika. I don't care what her real motives were, but she had firmly set a pace designed for middle-age comfort. I watched her go slowly, unhurriedly after the others, out to the near-by field. I felt a deep sympathy growing between me and that horse. She, too, had made up her mind that, over the next few days, we would extract the maximum pleasure from the minimum effort.

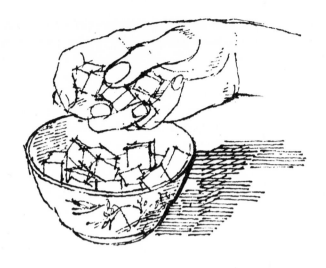

4

I f you are attached to a horse you are committed to the practice
of at least one virtue—you become a confirmed early riser.
None of that easy business of just strolling out to the car,
throwing your luggage in the boot, pressing the starter and
away. The horse demands an hour's ritual before every 'take-
off'. You've got to round him up, soothe him down and turn
him out looking like an Alfred Munnings painting; at any rate
for the beginning of the ride. All horsemen set enormous store
on looking good when they start off, no matter how they look
on their return. Notice how you always see photographs of the
meet of a hunt, never of the finale. The Master is splendidly
garbed, the hunt servants are in pinker than pink and the
hounds are all washed in Omo.

Snap them ten hours later and they look like a collection of
Irish farmers who have been celebrating St Patrick's Day all
night in the back parlour of the Widow Clancy's drapery and
porter shop in Ballynahinch.

It was exactly the same with our little party. Biddy insisted that we gave our mounts a complete valet service every morning. We rubbed them down, checked over every part of their anatomy, inspected the 'tack' and finally laid in a supply of lump sugar. This last business was very important. All progress on horseback depends on a constant supply of lump sugar. The horses expect it as a sort of equine trade union tea-break! Horse-lovers go to extraordinary lengths to meet the demand.

I soon learnt one thing fast, no horse-lover ever buys sugar for his animal when he travels. It's a point of honour to beg, borrow or steal the stuff. You can always tell a horsy man by the fact that his pockets are full of other people's lump sugar. After breakfast the sugar-bowl is always ruthlessly emptied. I've even blushed to hear Biddy ordering up another full bowl when it was obvious, even to the most innocent waitress, that we were already saturated with the stuff.

All this demands time in the morning, so the alarm was set for the pitiless hour of 5.30 a.m. Normally I am a confirmed early riser. I like to be stirring at six, when the world is uninhabited and your mind is as crisp and clear as the early-morning air. But this particular morning had a legacy from the previous day's ride in my aching muscles and I was tempted to snuggle back amongst the bedclothes in the spirit of the famous Hebridean verse:

> Ah, wad the peats would cut themselves,
> The fish leap to the shore,
> So thou and I might lie abed
> And love for evermore!

Just over the hill from Llwyngwair I could have found another verse encouraging morning laziness. Two miles away is the ancient church of St Brynach at Nevern, my favourite amongst all the small churches of West Wales. The old church with its squat tower lies on the slope of a wooded hill overlooking the little Nyfer river tumbling down from the Presellies. More legends have gathered around this spot than any other in Pembrokeshire. St Brynach himself is a bit of a mystery. The pious monks who commemorated him a good six hundred years after his death were not troubled about verisimilitude. They relate how the good man retired to this lonely spot to escape the torments of the flesh as personified by a most desirable young widow, how he floated easily up to the top of Carn Ingli for a week-end chat with the angels, how he had a special power over animals which allowed him to call two stags out of the woods to pull his furniture around whenever he wanted to move house and how the cuckoo became his specially favoured bird.

So much so that the cuckoo always came first to Nevern on 7 April, St Brynach's Day. And the parish priest, in later years, never began Mass until the cuckoo arrived to perch on the marvellously carved St Brynach's Cross in the churchyard and sing its twin notes.

But one day, so our old friend George Owen reported, the bird did not appear. Anxiously the priest and his congregation waited. Surely the cuckoo would not let them down. Then at last the bird fluttered on to the stone. Storms had delayed him in his long flight from the south. He had battled on against the headwinds for hundreds of miles. But for generations his family had been given the honour of starting mass on St Brynach's day at St Brynach's own church. He gave every ounce of strength he possessed, and bedraggled and exhausted though he was, he kept faith. He sang his first two notes—and then dropped dead.

Only a few yards away lies the tombstone of someone who set a totally different example. The inscription is in Welsh, but I will risk a rough translation:

> Here in this grave is Lazy Dai,
> As snug in earth as he can lie,
> If he loves his grave as he loved his bed,
> He'll be last when they awaken the dead.

As I also lay snug in my bed at Llwyngwair I wondered which example I should follow—Dai or the cuckoo? After a struggle the cuckoo won. I felt like dropping dead myself, but

I managed to shave, anoint myself liberally with Johnson's Baby Powder and struggle into my riding armour.

By the time I had creaked my way downstairs Biddy and the horses were at the door. Again the early-morning sun was generous with its warmth. All the sounds dear to a horseman were around me—the snort of the horses as they cleared their throats, the gentle swish of their tails, the tinkle of the irons as we flung the saddles over their backs—little sounds of no importance, but they stay in the unconscious library of the memory. When I hear them anywhere I am back in my mind to those blissful early starts, and see the sun on the slopes of the Presellies, and St Brynach's cuckoo calling in the woodlands, and Rowland bravely finishing Mr Marchington's stirrup-cup concocted as a parting depth-charge out of whisky, sherry, vodka and cloves, and our little procession on its way out of the drive into the lane that led upwards towards the wild stone tors on the northern hillside of Carn Ingli. Ahead of us a long, long journey over lonely country with all the time in the world at our command.

We had planned our route, as usual, to give us a ride away from cars, crowds and congestion. We would ride eastward along the whole length of the Preselly range, then on through the unfrequented lanes and odd patches of moorland along the borders of Carmarthenshire, Pembrokeshire and Cardiganshire. No tourists penetrate here. This is a piece of country that most Welshmen pass by unnoticed. At 5.30 p.m., after ten hours in the saddle, we proposed to come safely down into the Teifi valley at the little town of Llandyssul. I felt it was just as well that I couldn't ask Tika's opinion of the day's journey. She would have to walk and trot nearly forty miles.

She followed the others up the lane on to the western slopes of the hill as if she had a shrewd suspicion that there was a long day ahead.

Now the view broadened out; the vast checker-pattern of the fields of Cardiganshire to the north with the Teifi twisting its way through woodlands and gorges to the sea. Behind us the first outliers of the strange rock outcrops that cover the Presellies.

The whole of this world seems immeasurably old, haunted and remote in time. King Arthur passed this way, so legend says, which is hardly surprising, since there isn't a foot of Welsh soil which the great race-hero didn't tread at one time or another.

But Arthur and his knights were newcomers compared with the earliest settlers in these parts, the Beaker folk, who came from the sun of the south and the Mediterranean and slowly crept up along the wild Atlantic coast from headland to headland to come at last to this lost, western end of Wales. It must have happened over two thousand years before the birth of Christ, long before Arthur or St Brynach and St David and the Welsh themselves arrived in these parts. Their memorials are the grey stones of the cromlechs, the standing stones and circles that litter the hillsides of the Barony of Cemaes. The greatest and most famous of these cromlechs is Pentre Evan.

The authorities have now tidied up the approach to it. You walk along a neat pathway between railings to the huge, dark stones. They seem part of the mountainside and the whole place still has mystery in spite of the official park railings. Somehow, I wish we didn't have to tidy up our ancient monuments. I know that the flood of tourists now pouring over the land forces the Ministry to take protective measures, but I like my ruins to look like ruins. I am glad I saw Pentre Evan before the railings arrived—although the cromlech nearly brought my riding career to a sudden and very unpleasant end!

Biddy had dismounted and had lifted back the broken gate that then led into the field, which was surrounded by a high bank of earth and stones, surmounted by a ragged fence of barbed wire. The farmer had placed a log along the foot of the gate to prevent his sheep squeezing out, for all Welsh mountain sheep are professional acrobats and can escape from anywhere. I conceived the mad thought that I might actually make Tika jump over the log. Hop would be the better word, for the whole thing was only a foot high. My success in staying in the saddle without falling for the whole of the previous day had clearly made me bold. Why shouldn't I try a little gentle hop over this minute barrier.

Pentre Evan

I gave Tika a prod and she started to trot towards the gap in the hedge, ahead of the others for once. 'Here goes,' I said to myself, and settled firmly in the saddle. Then suddenly Biddy gave a shout, 'Wire!'

Tika seemed to skid and slither: I felt something sharp brush across my head as I was flung forwards with a grinding shock on to Tika's neck. She recovered and then, very carefully, put her feet across the log to stand inside the field.

I straightened myself up and looked behind. High up across the gap that led into the field was a strand of barbed wire; it had been strung so clear of any dismounted man that we hadn't noticed it. It was perfectly placed to have wrapped itself around my throat or across my eyes.

I slid out of the saddle and stood very still as Biddy, Rowland and Felicity came up. I dare say incidents like this are commonplace to all experienced cross-country riders, since barbed wire is everywhere in rural Britain. It made a powerful impression on me. I got used to accidents of this sort in wartime, but it seemed a sinister thing to have happened within sight of those grey, prehistoric stones on a warm summer's morning. Was there an atmosphere about Pentre Evan that was hostile to riders?

One thing was quite clear to me, old Tika somehow or other had seen the danger and had saved me by her slithering.

'Are you certain she wasn't just lazy and simply didn't want to jump?' said Rowland with practical common sense.

Of course I was certain; I knew that I had now cemented a firm alliance with old Tika. I felt in my pocket and gave her a full ration of sugar. I hoped she would realise that it was the only way I had of saying 'thank you'.

Three miles farther on we came out on to the saddle on the upper slopes of Freni Fawr. The road dropped away steeply to the southward. In that direction lay English Pembrokeshire and the winding shores of Milford Haven. To the eastward lay miles of open moorland with sheep tracks winding between the rocky outcrops and no sign of any human handiwork.

'Trot,' ordered Biddy and away our little cavalcade went over the springing turf with the larks whistling overhead and the world at our feet. You can see everything on a clear day from this high tent-ridge of the Presellies—the sweep of Cardigan Bay, with Bardsey Island and Lleyn to the north, Plynlimon, the Carmarthenshire Vans and Gower to the east, even the Wicklow Hills in Ireland when the western sky has been washed by rain.

The view and the steady rhythm of the trot set a tune running in my head; it could only be the famous old Welsh tune of the 'Mochyn Du', 'The Black Pig'. Far below us lay the farm of Felin Wrdan, where lived John Owen, a young farm servant who wrote the words of this ballad which swept Wales in the 1830s and related in mock-heroic style the burial of a favourite pig belonging to Deio Thomas, Penymaes—we could also pick out this farm from our lofty viewpoint. The pig played an important part in the economy of Pembrokeshire in those days, and the funeral took on the splendours of an Irish wake. But as the ballad swept the country until it became, as it were, the undisputed Top of the Pops—especially when it was sung by the famous ballad singer, Levi Gibbon—the unhappy author struggled to get the thing out of his life. He had become converted and was entering the Methodist Ministry. The rollicking Black Pig was no companion for a highly respectable minister, especially as his song was undoubtedly more popular than his preaching. The poor man even bought up the complete bundle of a ballad-singer, who was doing a roaring business with the Mochyn Du on Carmarthen bridge, on the very day the Rev. John Owen was attending the general meeting of his denomination.

The tune goes marching on. They used to sing it in South Wales with words describing the exploits of Crawshay Bailey, the great Merthyr iron-master, and rugby club reunions still rock to improvised male voice choirs of hefty forwards:

> Crawshay Bailey had an engine,
> It was puffing and was blowing.
> It could go right round the Gower
> At twenty miles an hour.

Chorus. Was you ever see, was you ever see,
Was you ever see such a funny thing before.

> When Crawshay Bailey died
> All the people cried
> And they raised two hundred pound
> Just to put him underground!

And do I not detect traces of its rhythm in the immortal marching song of the old Indian Army that was still going strong when I was out in the Punjab. Perhaps I was slightly misled by the fact that all Punjabis sing with an accent that makes them sound as if they had been converted by Welsh missionaries, but surely the old 'Mochyn Du'—in spite of celebrating an animal which is not exactly a favourite among Muslims and Hindus— is present as the Punjabis step out to the tune, fitted by some long defunct Kiplinesque subaltern with words of irrepressible but totally misplaced optimism:

> Cooch parwani. Good time coming!
> Queen Victoria very fine man.
> Get up in the morning, look-it up early,
> See Britannia rule-it wave.

> Lying in Calcutta gutter, leading very happy life.
> Lying in Calcutta gutter, Britons never shall be slave.

> Cooch parwani, etc.
> Ten long years you court my daughter,
> Now you leave for Blighty, sah'b,
> May the ship that carries you over,
> Sink to the bottom of the pani, sahab.

By the time we had trotted a mile along the lonely ridge of the Presellies I seemed to have got both tunes running in my head and had discovered one more thing about the horse—you can't sing on horseback. It's even more dangerous to whistle, worse than whistling on board ship. The horse, as far as I can discover, is tone deaf. Music means nothing to him. It's just a piercing noise that can startle and dismay.

The mounted bands of the Household Cavalry and the Garde Républicaine retain their seats only because their animals have been laboriously trained not to notice the rumpus crashing around them, just as police horses are disciplined to ignore fireworks thrown under their feet. I had cherished fond hopes that old Tika might be an exception and possess a musical ear. It would have been pleasant to have gone trotting along to the rhythm of some old song, preferably one of the folk-songs with a swing to them that I picked up in my early days—before the folk-song world became a racket and was annexed by bearded young men with guitars and check shirts or dark angular ladies with corpse-faces peering out at you from a tangle of dank hair.

I was lucky enough, at the BBC's expense, to spend a month with Seamus Ennis in Ireland just after the war, drifting happily around Kerry, watching him collect folk-songs. In those days the tourists were non-existent, petrol could only be obtained by having a quiet chat 'over a jar' with someone who knew someone else who had a licence to run a peat lorry. 'Ah, peat's the trouble now,' they would tell me; 'they're burning poor old Ireland sod by sod.' And every pub we went to west of Bantry seemed to be full of what the barman described as 'easy singing gentlemen'.

It was the time of Puck Fair at Killorglin and the countryside was on the move under horse-power—tinkers, 'bonedry travellers' and the good singing men. In the back bar of Regan's combined grocery, drapery, butcher's shop and pub the boys were gathered and the songs were flowing with the porter. Offstage, discreetly hidden by the overalls and print dresses that hung in clouds from the rafters, a somewhat sad-faced lady was disconsolately looking at an empty glass.

'Well, to tell yer the truth, 'tis a poor lady that comes down from Dublin every Puck Fair to practise her art on the young fellahs, if you understand me,' said Mr Regan with a nudge and a wink. 'She's downhearted, because she hasn't had any luck at all, and you know'—Mr Regan dropped his voice—'Ireland is not a country where you can talk about this sort of thing. We're very strict country indeed, a most moral country, and no one has much of a word for the likes of her.'

'Ah well,' said Seamus, 'give her a drop on us, and no harm meant.'

Meanwhile the singing men were in full swing, ready to keep it up all night. 'What about the licensing laws,' I asked Mr Regan. 'Ah, don't worry about such things,' he replied. 'We shut, but we don't close.'

From under the hanging hams and the fly-papers a voice floated, giving full value to a ballad with the mournful last line:

> But 'twas the dealer men, from Armagh Glen,
> Put the whisky in me tay.

In Wales a chorus would have immediately joined in with fruity harmony. Everybody in Wales is born either a prospective tenor or a baritone and as long as you tap on the bar and start a hymn going you'll have every one singing away in four parts. But Ireland is a soloist's paradise. And the older folk-song singers make certain that you don't escape, by always singing standing up and grasping you firmly by the hand. They've then got their audience safe for the next forty-three verses.

Inevitably the ballads became political; soon we were singing of the '98, and the Rising and the Troubles and back to Cromwell and Brian Boru for good measure, including a ballad which concluded:

> So Lloyd George, when he dies
> Will go up to the skies,
> Borne in a flaming- chariot,
> Seated in state
> On a red-hot plate
> Next door to Judas Iscariot.
>
> And Judas will say
> When he comes up that way,
> My claim to prec-ee-dence now fails.
> Come a bit nigher,
> Come away from the fire
> To make room for that b'hastard from Wales, me bhoys,
> To make room for that b'hastard from Wales!

'Ah,' said Seamus, 'a grand song, but Mr Thomas here—he's from Wales, too.' Immediate consternation, and all the Irish countryman's natural politeness poured over me in apologetic bucketfuls. ' 'Twas only a song'. Sure we're always singing about the murdering British and standing them pints at the same time! Have another jar and another song. . . .'

It was exactly like the way Brendan Behan used to behave twenty years later. I'd gone down to record him in a top flat at a house in the middle of Blackheath, which we entered by the fire-escape. Brendan was in full blast on the telephone. From the right-hand side he looked like a reincarnation of Michael Collins, from the left like Nero after a thick night out at the

Coliseum. If you lay on the carpet and looked upwards over his ample tummy, you saw a Falstaff who had learned Gaelic. He was bellowing expletives down the receiver to his correspondent at the far end. He held the phone with disgust at arm's length, while a disembodied voice floated through the room, 'But may I say, Mr Behan, in the matter of royalties, we will most willingly meet you in all possible . . .'

'Ah, b—— you,' bellowed Mr Behan, still holding the receiver as if it were a cat about to misbehave itself in a drawing-room. 'What will you have, boys? Powers?' He poured out two stiff tots with his free hand and downed one of them in a gulp.

'Oh, God. I'm —— well destroyed. Bloody awful. . . . No not you, you bastard'—this to the far-distant gentleman on the telephone who kept on murmuring to himself as the receiver lay on the table, 'I am sure you will find us, Mr Behan, may I say, not ungenerous in the matter of payment, providing we might discuss the right format . . .' 'Ah, hell,' said Brendan and banged down the phone, 'I'm destroyed, I tell you. Let's go out for a drink.'

'You must do your interview first on the state of the drama.'

'It's the state of the dramatist you've got to bother with now.'

'What do you think of Mr. John Osborne?'

'Him, an angry young man! He's about as angry as Mrs Ruddy Dale. You haven't got a real theatre; a nation of fifty million and you can't support Joan Littlewood. And we in Ireland can support a national theatre and send the actors to the sea for their holidays.'

'You don't like the English?'

'Switch that bloody thing off. Sure I like the English, but you know bloody what? It wouldn't be commercially profitable for me to admit it.'

And he burst into song: 'Twas the night the holy picture fell . . . '

Poor Brendan! I can never understand why people of creative

power are driven to destroy themselves. I don't have any such demon inside me, and besides I enjoy myself too easily. One day like that day on Preselly, all sunshine and lark-song and the scurrying of the sheep over the lonely hillside—and I'm ready to believe that 'All is for the best in this best of all possible worlds'.

We were now well along the summit ridge, riding amongst the great tors of dark rock from which, in the remote mists of prehistory, the bluestones were dragged down to the waters of Milford Haven and then floated around the coast to be set up in Stonehenge.

As we came quietly downwind around the rock a vixen started up with two cubs and slipped away amongst the tangle of scree. I couldn't help feeling that I was watching one of the oldest inhabitants of Wales, for foxes must have been breeding here since the ice disappeared as the glaciers retreated. They rule the roost on these hills. There was a time when somebody attempted to thin them out and lay down grouse. The boys at Llwyngwair chuckled, 'Nobody wanted that sort of shooting around here, spoiling everything. But it didn't matter. You know, once the east wind gets behind a grouse it can't stop. The whole lot got blown out to sea.' The foxes remain. Was the vixen the direct descendant of the foxes who were slinking around here over three thousand years ago, watching the Beaker folk quarrying these stone blocks of four tons weight and hauling and tugging them down the long slopes to the water's edge to start their 140-mile journey to Salisbury Plain? I cannot see why not. In spite of hunting and shooting, the foxes have hung on through the centuries and were here long before the Welsh arrived.

At this time I felt I ought to put a fire-cracker under old Tika to get her to move a little. The others were almost out of sight by the time I had come around the last of the great tors. I decided to trot down the long grassy trackway that led off the main ridge of the hills to the little village of Crymmych Arms.

I made the orthodox clucking noises, 'Come on, old girl', and as a gesture to me more than from a sense of obligation, Tika began to trot. I rose and fell in the saddle and, to my pleasure, covered the last mile at speed. True it was downhill which accounted for Tika's willingness, but trotting downhill isn't easy for a beginner. You find yourself continually bouncing forward in your stirrups, losing balance and rhythm, struggling to right yourself before the next bump arrives.

But I did manage to trot up to the door of the Crymmych Arms and join the others in the friendly bar. There were farmers come in to sell sheep, notices of farm sales on the walls, and a young lady, a student at Swansea University, who was sipping a daring gin-and-tonic.

'This is a quiet spot?' I asked.

'Not a bit of it. Crymmych is the hot spot of this countryside. There's something on every night; dances, classes—oh! plenty of things to do.'

'Well,' said the quiet, middle-aged man in the corner, 'I had no idea little Crymmych was so lively. It depends on your age group.'

Said the landlord, 'I thought the last real excitement they had in Crymmych, now that they've closed the railway station, was the Rebecca Riots.'

As soon as he mentioned the words Rebecca Riots I had a feeling of going back fifty years. I was once again a small boy, sitting with Mother in her work parlour, listening spellbound as she knitted and related the great family saga, of how my grandfather narrowly escaped being transported for his part in destroying the toll gates in 1844 and how as a result I, and the rest of the family also, escaped being born Australians.

When I started to learn history seriously at school I was amazed to discover that hardly anyone had heard of these epoch-making events and that the most they rated in the school books of that time was an obscure footnote. To me at the age of six they were as great a turning-point in world history as the French Revolution. Mother made it seem so, for she had such pride in Grandfather's one act of social defiance that she made me almost feel I was back a hundred years ago in the Welsh countryside, where the farmers were smouldering with fury at the spread of the toll gates over the main roads, and Grandfather was getting ready to lead his posse to smash the hated gates at midnight.

The whole thing started not very far from Crymmych Arms in 1839, when this out-of-the-way part of the country had a particularly bad turnpike trust; the farmers paid excessive tolls and no one was surprised when the gate at Efailwen was smashed at night. This was Wales and therefore the rioters immediately turned up their Bibles and found a good text out of Genesis 25:60. 'And they blessed Rebekah, and said unto her, Thou art our sister, be thou the mother of thousands of millions, and let thy seed possess the gate of those which hate them.' They naturally didn't look at the next verse in Genesis, where it said that 'they rode on camels'. They elected their leader as Rebecca, dressed themselves in women's clothes and chopped up all the toll gates in sight.

By 1842 the movement had spread across to Glamorgan to the village of Pontardulais, which was where my grandfather came in.

'He was a natural leader,' mother used to say; 'he knew the law and so the farmers came to him and made him Rebecca. They used to blacken their faces and dress in women's clothes so that no one should recognise them. Your grandmother was forbidden by her parents to have anything to do with this reckless young man, but she had heard that he was going to call the Daughters of Rebecca together to smash the hated gate on the Swansea road. So she got a friend to smuggle her into the attic of the Fountain Inn, that gave a splendid view over the whole proceedings. Then as darkness fell, in the deep quiet that then held the countryside in the days before the motor-car was thought of, they heard a voice calling in Welsh from the steel hillside, "Come along, my little daughters, come along, there's work to do."

'Then, led by your grandfather on a white horse, down came the Daughters of Rebecca—they were all riding ponies, all with mob-caps and their wives' and sweethearts' dresses on. The old soldier who kept the gate was quickly persuaded to retire to the nearest inn and within three minutes there wasn't a stick left. And the yeomanry from Swansea had been neatly sent off on a false scent and were guarding a gate miles away.

'Ah, but there was a traitor in Pontardulais. He gave a tip to the magistrates that Daniel Lewis, your grandfather, was Rebecca. The police arrived and his poor mother begged your grandfather to walk down the steep lane to the carriage, but he knew the law; he made the police bring it to the door. So he and Jones Dantwyn were lodged in jail and all the farmers kept bringing them chickens and eggs and the choicest lamb—oh! Grandfather used to say he had never eaten so well as in his Swansea cell.

'And, of course, when the trial came on and they called for witnesses, not a man, woman or child came forward. Everybody knew, but no one spoke. And there was the judge threatening to pack him off with penal servitude to Botany Bay and your grandfather calmly asking him to produce proof—which they couldn't do.'

'Why not?' I asked Mother.

'They'd kidnapped the traitor and held him in the mountains
And everyone swore that Daniel Lewis had been at home quietly
writing a poem while the gate was being broken up.'

'Wasn't that perjury?'

'Of course, but it was for a good cause and on a heroic scale.
So out he came from court a free man and that's why'—and
here Mother would give a little chuckle—'you are not an
Australian.'

'What about Grandmother,' I asked, 'did they let her marry
him?'

'Well, Wynford, they had to, for the traitor in the camp was
the very man her family had in mind as her husband. The whole
countryside sent him to Coventry and he fled the village—
perhaps it was he who went to Australia in the long run. But
her family got one revenge on her. They didn't give her the best
timber from the farm to make her wedding dresser and her
chairs, which it was their duty to do for daughters in those
days—and that, as you remember, led to the great disaster.'

The great family disaster was the terrible morning—I was
very small at the time—when Mother tugged at the drawer
of the dresser and brought the whole thing crashing down on to
the stone-flagged floor of the kitchen. Into a thousand pieces
went the Swansea and Nantgarw china and my chance of
inheriting a fortune was swept into the dustbin. What would
it fetch at a sale today? I daren't read of the prices at Sotheby's
and Christie's without feeling ill.

But the dresser is still there and the oak chairs are set around
my table, polished until they have a mirror surface. I can't look
at them without seeing all the work put into them by women's
hands. How the housewives slaved in those days, even with all
their maidservants around them; and with it all, my grandmother found time to bring up ten children and almost run
Grandfather's woollen factory. As for Grandfather, he remained
a rebel all his life, although a somewhat tamed one, and staged
a death-bed piece of repartee which has puzzled our family
ever since.

The minister reassured him, 'Mr Lewis, if ever a man is going to see his Maker face to face, you are that man.'

My grandfather smiled gently and his last recorded words were, 'Well, in that case, there are one or two pertinent questions I'll want to put to him!'

His gravestone carries his name and his virtues inscribed in a Bardic Alphabet known as Coelbren y Beirdd, which no one reads nowadays and in any case was probably a seventeenth-century fake. It was my grandfather's final joke and last attempt at social revolution.

My grandfather on his white horse leading his rioters to smash the Pontardulais gate and now, 120 years later, myself on my white horse, old Tika, trotting through the countryside with the utmost respectability! These are the moments in time and place when history seems to get foreshortened and telescoped. I almost imagined I was trotting back towards 1840 as we went on from Crymmych over the last waves of the Presellies, and up and down into the deep-cut valleys. For this is country that cannot have changed much since those days; upland, with scattered, lonely farms and not a sign of modernity beyond the tarmac that has now crept outwards from the main roads of Wales to give its soulless, hard surface to every soft byway.

Tarmac is just another sign of the modern hostility to the horse. Twenty years ago we'd have gone cantering through these lanes at speed. Today we had to ration ourselves to a strict time-table of cantering and trotting. Once you put your horse into the trot on tarmac down come its feet with twice the impact, and with twice the jarring thud on its leg-bones and muscles. Some horses are tough and can stand it. Old Tika had the advantage here; she is a cob, whose ancestors were specially bred for tough legs in the days when they went bowling along with traps and 'gambos'.

But Biddy and Rowland were on hunters and their mounts were designed for cross-country, soft going. We kept a wary eye on them, with a pause every five miles for a check-up—rather as a motorist keeps checking a leaking radiator.

That simile crept in by mistake. I hadn't been long enough in the saddle to get used to the proper horsy language, although I was learning fast. After two or three checks on the feet, I discovered where the pasterns were, and that fetlocks could be too hairy and should be trimmed with scissors and that you used the leg as a sort of horse thermometer. When you put your hand on his lower leg you may find it slightly warm; beware, your horse may be going lame!

But what I'd have done about it if old Tika had gone lame I still hadn't the slightest idea. I had shed my early dream that all you had to do with a horse was to get on its back and ride it. I realised that I was now astride one of the most complicated and pernickety bags of tricks in the natural world—I'd got to soothe it, agree with its irrational tantrums, cook for it, stroke its brow if it was off colour, cut its hair and take it out to dinner as a treat, just as I would a wife. There was only one advantage: Tika couldn't answer me back!

So we trotted away over this high, bleak plateau country, when, ahead, in a field on the side of the road, we spotted a strange, yellow-panelled object. We kept on trying to guess what on earth it might be and we had an unexpected surprise as we came nearer. It was a glider, the last thing one would expect to find out on this lonely hillslope. And its owner was even more unexpected. He turned out to be a German who had fled from East Germany after the war and had taken over a Welsh hill farm. Here he bred cattle and sent his son, little Hans, to the village school, where this six-year-old uprooted German learned to speak Welsh. We reined up and gossiped with father Hans over the hedge.

'Why did you settle here, of all places?'

'I looked at the map of Europe and said to myself that I must go as far away from the Communists as my money would allow. And I couldn't get farther west without falling into the sea or going to America. And I don't think they would like me much in America! And I wouldn't like them either. So I see this place marked Wales on the map and here I come.'

'Can you make a living out of this land?'

'Not very good. I'm a worker, I can work hard, but they taught me to fly in the war and to glide. So I saw this glider advertised and I thought that I could make some money when the tourists come. And I've got an old car in the field to run it off—my wife comes out and drives it. So all costs nothing.'

'You're a bit out of the way for tourists here!'

'They will come, I am sure. And for me, no matter if I do not make much money—nobody ever asks me what I think or orders me to do this or that. This is why I am here.'

He looked out over the bleak uplands, which were warm today in the sun, but which are so chill and rain-drenched in the winter. He could take all the chill and winter rain simply because there was an easy freedom in the Welsh air. But I wondered what his wife felt. She just smiled and said, 'Ja, Hans,' to every word he said.

'Come up,' he invited me and I would have done so if Biddy hadn't looked warningly at her watch; for I enjoy the silent bird-flight of a glider close to the ground far more than any of the endless commercial flights I am now compelled to take. Once they've got you capsulated with 120 other standardised citizens in some pressurised super-airliner, they take the magic out of flight. You are now compelled to race around the world in pieces of flying suburbia.

For flight to be real, worth while, you have to feel in touch with the air. It's the same with the sea. One rough passage across the channel between West Wales and Ireland taught me more about the sea than any amount of crossing the Atlantic on the *Queen Mary*. The small craft for me every time. The space explorers must feel it. When they are up there on their own, floating through that strange silent world on the edge of space, they must have a sense of rare adventure which will be totally lost once the big space craft arrive. It so happened that, not long before setting out on horseback through Wales, I had made the nearest approach to space I am ever likely to get. I was shot off the flight deck of one of our aircraft carriers off

100

the coast of Norway and in a matter of minutes found myself at 50,000 feet. Of course, there is a vast difference between a mere hop for half an hour up to nine miles above the Earth and a week spent at two hundred. But I did discover one secret about space travel and weightlessness that all the space explorers seem tactfully to conceal.

I was the guest of the aircraft carrier *Ark Royal* during NATO manoeuvres off northern Norway and naturally they all insisted, 'You've got to fly. We'll catapult you off tomorrow at 4 p.m. You'd better wrap up, for you'll be going up beyond 45,000 feet and it can be mighty cold up there if the heaters give out. Better be boiled than frozen.' I was an extremely portly figure by the time I reported to the dressing-room and was jammed into rubber armour to the accompaniment of a pleasantly sardonic commentary by the petty officer in charge.

'Now, first, your immersion suit—you'll be jolly glad of that when you fall into the drink. You're all sealed up and you'll float for ten minutes before the cold gets you. And, boy, can it be cold. Your Mae West and a whistle for you to blow when you are floating around in the dark, and here's a new one, pull this and it will release a dye and you'll be in the middle of a nice yellow spot in the sea and they'll be bound to spot you— although we've got some clots in this ship that would miss anything. A little radio set around your tummy and you're ready for hoisting on board.'

I was lifted up into the rear seat of the Venom like a French knight being hoisted on to his horse in the Agincourt film. A final word of advice before they clamped down the Perspex hood: 'Your floating dinghy will blow up with compressed air as soon as you hit the sea. Mind you, it can come adrift in the cockpit and then Heaven help you, it will inflate and squeeze you against the roof or out of the plane. Stick it with a knife: you've lost your boat, but you've saved yourself from becoming strawberry jam!'

Then we were joggled into position on the launching-gear. My pilot lifted his thumb—and we received a smart kick in the

101

pants, my body went forward and my stomach caught up with it a few seconds later to find that we were airborne. The pilot pulled her nose up, and the Venom seemed to stand on its tail as it shot, arrowlike, through a thin canopy of cloud. Then up it went, at a prodigious rate for one used to travel in sedate airliners. At first the clouds looked like towering Himalayas, then swiftly they diminished into a fleecy, woolly blanket; then, away beyond the blanket's edge came the coast of Norway with the mountains flattened to a brown map flecked with specks of white.

Forty-five thousand feet, and we ourselves were specks in a steel-blue sky. Never had I felt such loneliness. There was one human being in front of me, but he was so encased with rubber, plastics, Perspex, that he seemed part of the plane. The air all around was crystal clear: you could look up and almost feel yourself going steadily away towards outer space, with the sky getting a deeper, harder blue—until you felt you were dropping away altogether from the earth and its gravitational field and all its small, petty, inexplicable affairs. Far, far away below two aircraft left trails of silver across the blanket of cloud. The sun shone with a dazzling intensity. We hung in the midst of a crystal ball of pure, unsullied light. I knew that our aircraft had a ceiling of only 50,000 feet, but I still couldn't get over the sense of being lost in outer space.

Then, suddenly, voices crackled in my ear, reaching up to us from the lost Earth far below; voices chanting the mystic jargon of military technology. Again and again, as I listen to the comments of the gallant astronauts circling the earth two hundred miles up, I weep for their banality. Couldn't we shoot a poet or a man with the gift of tongues into space, who could thrill us with his descriptions of what it really looks and feels like. All we get is 'All systems go, everything is just swell', or else 'Fervent greetings to the Commissars of Astrakhan, the pioneers of the Red Toffee Factory and our glorious leaders'.

What I got in my ear on the edge of outer space was even more extraordinary. Another aircraft, American, was somewhere in this crystal ball of the sky. The two pilots sang this duet together.

'I'm Nabob Papoose. I'm friendly. Are you?'

'Affirmative.'

'I have a cruiser below me. Is she on your side?'

'Wait . . . Nabob Papoose, I have two destroyers down below. Are *they* friendly?'

'Anyface three, Anyface three, this is Nabob Papoose, two days ago they were friendly, but, Jeeze, I don't know what they are now.'

'Papoose, Papoose. Anyface three authenticate Alpha Echo Pa-pa.'

'Roger, wait.'

'Papoose Papa, if you don't authenticate Alpha Echo Pa-pa shortly I'm going to shoot you down.'

'Oh, Jeeze, I didn't get that; try Whisky Hotel.'

'That's affirmative, Papoose. O.K. Welcome friend!'

Such is the new language of outer space. But I didn't have any fuller chance to study it, for as we hung in splendid isolation in that clear loneliness above the Earth I became aware of a certain 'puzzlement amongst my natural winds', as the celebrated Mrs McCaferty described it. No one had hinted to me before I left the surface of the Earth that, as you went higher, the pressure on your body eased and the gases in your stomach expanded.

The puzzlement became more intense: soon I was battling for my personal honour 45,000 feet above the Earth. Did this ever happen to Major Gagarin and Colonel Glen and the rest of the astronauts? They have obviously kept very quiet about this great hazard to man's conquest of outer space. Here is the most difficult barrier of all to penetrate—the Embarrassment Layer. Scientists have given us a very clear picture of the various layers in the earth's atmosphere—from the troposhpere up through the stratosphere, past the hydroxyl zone and the E layer, on through the ionosphere to the rarest of them all, the exosphere. They have tactfully omitted the Embarrassment

Layer from their plan. Have too many explorers already come to grief in it? I was about to be the next martyr to science, when a voice came roaring in on my headphones.

'Solid Clancy, Solid Clancy, strangle your bell-hop.'

It was the modern military way of saying to us, 'Thank you, your services are no longer required. Please come home.'

My pilot put our plane over and we plummeted down; in a minute my problem was solved. We shot through the Constipation Layer. I can chart it accurately at 36,000 feet. I must have it officially inserted in all plans of the upper air. It is essential knowledge for all future space-men. I am proud indeed—and profoundly relieved—to have discovered it.

We shot in over the round-down. A jerk and we were hooked on to the arrester wire. We were back in the everyday world as our aircraft taxied to one side of the deck, folding its wings as it went.

Of one thing I could be sure; Hans's glider would never take me up to the Embarrassment Layer. In fact, from horseback the whole of the flying world seemed incredibly remote. The horse and the aeroplane do not mix. Outer space, after all, is reserved for very few and most of us must be content to look at it through other eyes. No wonder that supreme realist, Sir Winston Churchill, remarked as we were proudly displaying to him the model of the Universe in the Space Hall of the Festival of Britain: 'Show me the Earth; that's all I'm interested in.'

Biddy pulled me back hurriedly from outer space by reminding us that we still had ten miles to go and that it was half-past three. 'Now we'll really have to trot. Come up, Tika.'

We went off like a posse in search of an outlaw, all together thundering through the lanes. Biddy shouted, 'Keep Tika at it, tickle her up if she drops behind.' Tickle her up, actually hit her! Impossible! I know horsemen all carry whips and switches, but I'd always thought that kindness was the great secret of getting on with your horse. It never entered my head that you used switches seriously. Yet apparently the theory of 'spare the rod, spoil the child' is still applied to the horse. Not violently, of course, since a vast change has come over the handling of the horse in the last hundred years. He's ceased to be a workman and become, in fact, a pet. When everybody had to use or handle horses to get the world's work done the poor animal got some pretty rough treatment. Today you don't keep a horse unless you have some affection for him. And when you have to use the switch, it's for his own good.

Biddy had cut me a small switch from the hedge, and I waved it about for form's sake. But I never put any force into it; I had a feeling that Tika wouldn't have noticed it any more than a fly. I've got no venom in me, no urge to dominate anyone or anything. Tika co-operated by putting in a burst of speed now and then to keep up appearances and smartly dropping back as soon as she felt Biddy wasn't looking.

So, at the end of the procession as usual, we trotted down into the narrow tree-filled valley of Glyn Cych. Occasionally little rivers cut their way down through this upland region on their way to the Teifi. Their valleys are unfrequented, full of the murmur of fast-running water under woodlands, and Glyn Cych is the cream of them. No Welshman, who was educated in Wales as I was, can trot down into Glyn Cych without immediately recalling the opening sentences of that wonderful collection of mediaeval Welsh stories, *The Mabinogion*, when 'in the youth of the day', Pwyll, the Prince of Dyfed, came to Glyn Cych and 'let slip his hounds in the woodland, sounded his horn and starting the quarry, followed his hounds and lost his companions'. But in a clearing in the woodland, as his hounds pulled down the deer, he met a mysterious fellow hunter, who turned out to be none other than the King of the Underworld. The whole of the story of Pwyll is filled with the remote magic of a pre-Christian Britain and a countryside still wild and almost uninhabited. I remember reading it first in my father's study in Swansea, curled up in a deep chair with the warm sun streaming in and the sound of the piano playing Debussy in the distance. I must have been about ten at the time and I had no idea where Glyn Cych was. I pictured it as a sort of vast Sherwood Forest, full of giant oaks and always full of sunlight filtering down through the canopy of green boughs— a place where there was no school, or algebra, or any of the things I was no good at, only freedom and bird-song all through the long, lost summer days.

Now, nearly half a century later, I was riding down into Glyn Cych for the first time in my life. Of course, it was not a bit as I had dreamt about it. There was a country road along the riverside, farms here and there; peaceful, charming, yes, but magical, alas, no: until from the distance came the unmistakable sound of a hound giving tongue. Immediately *The Mabinogion* came rushing back into my mind. Pwyll could still be hunting here after all.

Then, around the corner, filling the whole roadway with a moving flood of waving tails and padding feet, came the pack of the Teifiside Hunt being walked by huntsman Jack Scarrett. In a moment we were engulfed by the hounds, handlicking, sniffing, yelping in a deluge of overeager canine friendliness. Jack called them off—and we found that all the hounds had English names. The Welsh seemed to have stopped naming hounds once the country was absorbed legally into England. The anglicised squires who created the modern packs firmly stuck to names such as Wellington, Challenger, Bellman—the sort of names John Peel would have shouted in mid-career. But, as Jack explained, the Master of a hunt who didn't speak Welsh would have found it extremely difficult, as the fox burst from a covert, if he had to rally the pack with enthusiastic shouts of 'Come on, Cadwaladr, Maredudd, Cadwgan, Mae-lienydd, Rhydderch and Cynwrig ap Rhiwallon'. The fox would have been in the next county by the time he had got all his hounds moving.

In fact, the huntsman was up against the old problem which has haunted Wales ever since the Act of Union with England— how are we to christen ourselves? In the old days all was well. Wales was a small, princely society, and when people met it was important that your ancestry was correctly traced back for generations before you shook hands. Introductions must have been a form of choral music: when two gentlemen met they almost sang a duet of names. Each ancestor came into the song prefaced by 'ap', meaning 'the son of'.

'Who are you?' they might inquire as you pulled up at the castle gate. Proudly you would answer, 'I am Iorewerth ap Iolo ap Owain ap Tudor ap Llewelyn ap Ieuan ap Pryderi ap Rhys ap Iolo Goch'—by which time the waiting Englishman had run out of patience and his lawyer had run out of parchment.

'Make this business simple,' commanded the conquerors. My theory—and I don't care if serious historians make mincemeat of it—is that the Welsh obliged by choosing the simplest names to hand which could be understood by the English. Within two hundred years of the advent of the Tudors, the whole landscape was alive with Thomases, Williamses and Evanses, and Wales became the one country at least where there was no difficulty in keeping up with the Joneses. The difficulty was to get away from them.

The only method of distinguishing one Jones or Thomas from another was by the bestowal of an extra name on Jones to indicate what he did. Hence the spate of Evans the Milk and Williams the Bank and Jones Petrol and the rest of them which cover the pages of Welsh novels and erupt into TV programmes. Some of these appendices have charm. One gentleman in my youth, a pillar of the extra-mural classes in philosophy, was therefore known to all and sundry as Rees Elevated Thought. Or the lady from Pontardulais to whom Mother continually referred as Mary Cottage by the Sea, because at all local concerts it was impossible to stop her obliging with the moving ballad, 'I love my sweet cottage beside the wild sea'. She was the only one who did.

Williams the Death was my favourite undertaker. I cherish his description of a funeral operation which involved him driving his only hearse from a lonely part of West Wales to fetch a coffin at Southampton.

'A challenge to me, Mr Thomas, for until that moment I had never buried farther east than Newport in my life.'

However, he bravely drove to Southampton Docks and collected an outsize in caskets. 'An overdone job,' Williams the Death described it, since the poor man had died in New York and had received the 'Loved One' treatment. The widow and the best friend drove on ahead to pilot Williams back to Wales, and stopped from time to time to assuage their grief at a succession of welcoming inns. Suddenly at Chepstow they came out of their ninth hostelry and saw with a shock that Williams and his hearse had disappeared.

The police obliged with an alert all over the West and finally headed off the puzzled Williams making as fast as possible towards Exeter and Land's End. After all, he had driven westwards in the direction in which Wales was always supposed to be, but, as he lamented to me, 'How was I to know that this ruddy country forked!'

How indeed! For there is always a problem in adjusting yourself to the customs of one country when you are brought up from birth in another. The Welsh made a mess of their attempt to give themselves names intelligible to the English. Just as my good friends in Ghana went somewhat astray when they decided to celebrate the advent of Freedom with the first beauty competition ever held in West Africa.

My sympathies were completely with them. A beauty competition is a fantastic Western ritual whose rules are very difficult to explain to the average Westerner, let alone to the inhabitants of Accra. So it was not surprising that there were some unusual moments when the entrants arrived at the Community Centre in a bus marked 'Mass Education'. There had been six hundred applicants and now here were the finalists, competing for a free trip to London and the battle for the title of Miss World. Other countries in Africa had their eyes on the title, however. The local Press that very morning had warned Ghana of the dangers of competition: 'Six Dakar Cuties Couched by French Experts for World Honour'.

When we arrived the Community Centre was besieged by amorous wolves who kept up a running fire of comment as the ladies be-bussed.

'Ah, man, man, that's a Jaguar girl.'

'What you think this girl?'

'At all.'

'She drink kellie-wellie?'

'Oh, master, I beg of you.'

My friendly Ghanaian guide explained, as we were ushered into the reserved seats, 'Now, do not expect to see what you see in Europe or U.K. These ladies will be well clothed. Miss Northern Territory and Miss Trans-Volta will not be very lively; it is only Miss Western Territory who will do that. She has danced much High Life—this dance is very suggestive without meaning anything. But she has lived a carefree life. Maybe the judges do not like this.'

The privileged guests—black, white, Indian and Lebanese— were no sooner seated than there was a roar like a dam bursting: the wolves were storming the hall. A fierce struggle broke out at the back, chairs cracked and fists flashed. 'Ah,' said my friend, 'it is only the power of love.'

Then the contestants came on to the stage and once again the hall fairly rocked with a roar from the audience. Each young girl came shyly up to the microphone, against a backdrop inscribed 'Mass Education' and made a little speech to the assembled public. Miss N.T. was clad in a splendidly voluminous gown which was at the opposite pole from a Western beauty queen's traditional bikini. Her actual figure remained a mystery Said my guide, 'How difficult it will be to decide on what we are to judge. Are we to cheer for our traditional type of beauty when we are demanding a nice lady with much comfortable fat, or for your new Western type where everything is displayed, but is very thin. I am thinking it will be the African beauty we will be preferring here, but maybe we should send you Miss Accra, who is a real Jaguar girl and has no fat.'

Miss N.T. was extremely traditional. She murmured softly

into the mike, 'My name is Monica, I am seventeen years old and I am still at school. When I grow older I will be an infant teacher, for I love little children. I have four brothers and a sister at home just like me.'

How I wish I could hear a speech like that from a Butlin's Camp beauty! Then came the sensation, Miss Trans-Volta Togoland. She had everything that the Ghanaiean wolves demanded—a deliciously coffee-coloured skin, ample areas of satiny flesh and a smile like a row of pearls dropped into a cup of chocolate. She started, 'My name is . . .'

But it didn't really matter what her name was; for the moment she had scooped the kitty.

Miss Eastern Region, with the attractive first name of Comfort, tried to recapture interest with a quick potted biography: 'I am a seamstress and I live with my mother, for my father has died. I have been taught by the Scottish missionaries.' In vain. No one could believe that the worthy missionaries could have taught Miss Comfort what girls learn easily in Togoland.

Miss Accra had plastered her hair into snake coils and shot Medusa-like glances at her rival. Miss Western Region did her best, while coo-ing softly, 'I live alone with my father', to fulfil expectations as a 'carefree girl'. Her supporters, for a moment, seemed to win the noise competition and chaos filled the hall. A neutral Lebanese tried to suggest a compromise between African and Western standards of beauty: 'Why not judge on the proportions of the Venus de Milo?'

There was a storm of protest. 'That lady is not in the competition.' Miss Upper Volta Togoland rolled her generously proportioned figure and swept everything before her. The prize was awarded to Ghana's own *Boule de Suif*. And quite right, too!

How on earth have I got to Ghana from Glyn Cych? Blame it on the magic of *The Mabinogion* and Pwyll, Prince of Dyfed, which must still be active in these parts. Or on the pleasure of riding on horseback on a warm summer day, where every mile presents an irresistible temptation to meander and turn aside. But our time-table was going astray. We were due in Llandyssul by 5.30 p.m. and we had an hour to make it.

It is now that the horse comes into his own. I've always been a keen walker over rough country and when I'm on form think nothing of thirty miles a day over mountains. I confess that secretly I had listened to a lot of horseman's talk with a quiet sense of superiority. They made such a fuss about a hard day in the saddle, when they've only covered about twenty miles and, after all is said and done, it's the old horse who does all the work. And then all those learned discussions about resting your horse and nursing him carefully over soft ground! I'd begun to feel that, in the course of a long day, I would at least walk the same distance in more time but with less fuss. Until the end of this afternoon eastwards from Glyn Cych.

The horse produced reserves of power I would not have suspected. Away we went in a sort of horse 'Boy Scout's Pace'; trot a mile, walk a mile, trot again. Now that I was getting the rhythm of the trot I began to enjoy this up-and-down bouncing in the saddle in the glow of the afternoon sun, until, at last, we came down off the high ground into the green trough of the Teifi vale. Over the bridge and into Llandyssul.

Now Llandyssul is one of those fortunate places which have stayed out of sight for the last two hundred years. No doubt it's had a history of a sort. There must have been a visit by St Tyssilio back in the Dark Ages, a battle or two between the Normans and the Welsh and a sprinkling of eminent preachers born in or around the place later on. For the rest, Llandyssul has slept peacefully beside the Teifi. It has a main street with an outer ring of villas, a collection of chemists' shops and drapery stores, the regulation issue of assorted chapels, an ancient church and—with its back to the graveyard—our journey's end, the old-fashioned, wholly delightful Porth Inn.

The Porth Inn

5

THERE'S a pleasure in awakening with the dawn in the country, to feel yourself stirring at the exact moment when the first birds are singing, the fox is slinking home after his prowl around the hen roosts, the Teifi is singing under your window and there isn't a sound of a lorry changing gear within twenty miles. From my window I had a choice view of the churchyard, a rickety footbridge across the river and the church tower festooned with ivy. Biddy had already got the horses corralled in the yard below. In my bedroom was a genuine feather bed, a text on the wall, a wash-hand basin with vast china bowls decorated with floral designs—all the delights of 1898 miraculously preserved into the 1960s. Perhaps they have disappeared since and the Porth has been given the usual brewery face-lift. I devoutly hope not. I would like to preserve the Porth and a few other of the old Welsh country inns as a sort of alcoholic annex to the Welsh Folk Museum.

The hunting prints were still on the walls. The breakfast room had a vast mahogany sideboard with silver chafing-dishes, the meal was served on that single central table, with elaborately carved legs, which used to be the essential feature of all respectable Welsh country hotels. None of that modern nonsense about separate tables and vast menus constructed around refrigerated food. Here you took the bacon and eggs brought in all together on a plate as large as a 1910 cartwheel hat at Ascot. As we tucked into a monumental breakfast I thought of all the characters who must have sat down to do justice to the food around this very table over the last seventy years—the election agents discreetly rallying their voters during the stormy Lloyd George elections; the squire entertaining his lawyer before raising the rent of half his farms; the visiting school inspector meditating on his report back to Whitehall on the teaching of Welsh in the local schools; even my grandfather on one of his tours around this area as an auctioneer in the '80s, ready to sell off the furniture of the Big House after the family had ruined themselves by investing in those newfangled coal-mines in the Rhondda.

The whole cavalcade of these departed frequenters of the dining-room of the Porth Inn became real and present when the waitress brought us the Visitors' Book to sign. This was a solid volume, bound in black leather and dating back to 1898. The entries evoked the lost, leisurely world of wealthy fishermen, Victorian light verse and endlessly rainy week-ends. Where is Bertie Cherlock who scribbled so industriously in 1908:

> Our hosts, the Smiths, so genial and bright
> Looked to our comfort by day and night.
> May they flourish and with them all go right
> As the burning of their brilliant acetylene light.

And who was Robert Blake who arrived in 1899 and gave his address as Patagonia and the Falkland Islands, and who made the enigmatic entry: 'Fished successfully—and caught what I wanted.' What, indeed? But the most indiscreet entry of all was written in May 1901: 'John Jones, with Miss Erlys Evans of Cardiff.' To which a wit has added 'and very nice, too!'

These old volumes, scattered here and there around Wales, give me pleasure wherever I find them. Visitors' Books, minutes of long-disbanded societies, diaries of forgotten organisations—they seem to be more valuable in bringing back the real feel of the past than all the solemn official documents historians dig up so industriously. Thus, if I want to relive the great crises of the last war as they affected the Welsh country-side, I turn to the War Diary of the Bow Street Home Guard.

Bow Street is a straggling village just north of Aberystwyth and the Home Guard was embodied on 11 November 1940, when the village at last felt itself threatened by a possible German invasion in Cardigan Bay. The gallant volunteers formed up outside the Memorial Hall and marched out to war as the women and children ran beside them shouting, 'Come back safe!' They swung smartly down the road and turned sharp left into the strongpoint they were to hold with grim determination through the rest of the war, the ladies' waiting-room at Bow Street station.

That evening they made their first important entry in their War Diary (which, I am glad to say, has been carefully pre-served by the railway authorities). The state of the defences was carefully noted: 'Equipment checked 8.30 p.m., 1 teapot, 1 kettle, 1 dartboard, 3 darts, 2 mugs, 1 shotgun, 5 rounds, pack of cards missing. All quiet.'

Conditions got tough during the grim winter of 1940. In December came the disconcerting report, 'Hole burnt in blanket', But the defences remained at full strength: 'January 29th, 1941. Equipment checked 8.0 p.m., 1 teapot (spout broken), 1 kettle, 1 dartboard, 3 darts, 2 mugs, 2 shotguns, pack of cards (joker missing), All quiet.'

Then as Hitler's panzer division crashed through Russia, the Bow Street Home Guard also faced their stern test. 'July 2nd, 1941. When I came on duty this morning the guard had been throwing lumps of bread on the floor. Soon this place will be alive with rats.'

The war strain deepened. By August conditions had become

desperate: 'Aug. 12th, 1941. Password Chips and Beans. Can't sleep; Evans is pushing me out of bed.' But action and danger were at hand. 'Dec. 10th, 1942. Alerted the guard. Police reported suspicious character on road to Aberystwyth. Person examined, who appeared to be on a mission of an amorous nature. Allowed to proceed. Patrol continued up road and found freshly painted inscription, "To Hell with Churchill, Freedom for Wales".' At last the enemy had attacked!

But steadily through 1942 the ladies' waiting-room on the down platform was strengthened, the guns available went up to three, and two teapots and a new pack of cards were added to the defences. So, bravely checking their darts, clinging to their burnt blankets and shouting 'Chips and Beans' to each other through the lonely watches of the night, the Home Guard of Bow Street saw out the war. Or did they? From the Diary, it seems uncertain that they've yet realised that the war has ended, for the last entry simply reads, with commendable caution, 'All Clear—presumably!'

This caution was natural. Bow Street is in Cardiganshire and everyone in the rest of Wales knows—or thinks he knows—all about the character of the Cardiganshire man, or the 'Cardi' as they call him. He is a Welsh Aberdonian, careful of his money and with his eye on the main chance. He is the only Welshman, they say, who will come to a pair of swing doors behind you and emerge in front of you. Well, here we were setting out to ride through the country, into the very heart of it. We would keep our eyes skinned and our minds open as we bearded the Cardi in his den. Like all such reputations, this one might turn out to be totally unjustified.

Once again we had the delights of an early start on a perfect summer's morning; all the countryside to ourselves and fresh horses beneath us. We had received local advice the night before and took a route through lanes and across fields that gave us a whole morning away from main roads. Cardiganshire is a land of small farms, chapels at cross-roads and slightly out-of-date black Austin cars—'handy for market or for a funeral'. The

Teifi is its pride and the Aeron Valley its secret. We were now riding across the high ridge between these two rivers.

Biddy and Rowland took to galloping at every field we crossed. Even Tika cantered. We had now cemented our alliance, she and I. I never asked her to do anything she didn't feel like doing; she in her turn did just enough to keep me in the picture. Cardiganshire, as we rode through it, seemed unexpectedly full of horses. Every farm seemed to have a pony or two; and I found that there must be some strange telepathy amongst horses. Even if we were miles away, far across the valleys horses would start running around their fields as if they sensed our presence. We stirred up the whole of the horse population. Perhaps they were just lonely, but we never passed a field containing a horse without that animal snorting, tossing up its heels and racing parallel with us on the other side of the hedge. In a relay of welcome from the horse population, we came down into the hamlet of Llwyn Rhydowen—'The Grove at Owen's ford'.

At first I thought I was in a typical Cardiganshire village: a few houses with names like 'Catref' (Home) or 'Llys Teg' (Fair Dwelling), newly plastered and with lace curtains in the windows; a shop 'pob peth'—which sells everything from boot-laces to herbal remedies; two elderly inhabitants leaning over a bridge looking at the trout and discussing the evil ways of the Milk Marketing Board—and a chapel, Zoar or Sion or Hebron, with the inevitable notice, built 1839, rebuilt 1859, enlarged 1872, reconstructed 1898, and still as four-square to the winds of Heavens as when it started.

The chapel at Rhydowen had the patina of age on it and no trace of reconstruction. 'Early Baptist Perpendicular,' I said to myself, for I am a connoisseur of chapel architecture, 'and with stables attached'. It looked so peaceful on the slope of a green hill; nothing ever happened here except a dispute over the next venue of the Sunday-school treat. But one of the bridge-leaners passed and saw me looking at the old chapel.

'That's a nice thing to see a man riding a horse around here again,' he said. 'When I was a boy the chapel stable was full. The ministers rode over from Llandyssul. And after all it was a bit of an honour to preach in Gwilym Marles's old chapel!'

As soon as he mentioned Gwilym Marles I had a feeling of instant recognition. I was back in Swansea talking to my school fellow, Dylan Thomas, and I remember him saying to me that his poetic gift was something that had always been in the family. 'My middle name is Marlais, after all,' he said. Marlais is just another form of Marles and the fiery radical minister of

The chapel at Rhydowen

Rhyd Owen was Dylan's great-uncle. Just as I cherish my grandfather leading the Rebecca rioters, so Dylan's family had their great protest hero in Gwilym Marles. He was indeed a remarkable man. He took his degree at Glasgow University in 1860, when degrees were not so common in poor Welsh families. He became a prominent Unitarian minister and flung himself whole-heartedly into the radical politics that were rocking the Cardigan countryside in the 1870s. The landlords had his name on the black list and got their revenge by evicting him and his congregation from the old chapel. Defiantly he built a new chapel, and although he died soon after, he made a powerful impact on this lonely part of Wales. But I wonder what he'd have made of Dylan.

I think Dylan's father told him a great deal of the family saga. Dylan didn't speak Welsh and didn't acknowledge any Welsh influence on his poetry, but he couldn't escape the soft persuasive charm of the South Wales landscape. Cardiganshire isn't the scene of *Under Milk Wood*, but it's got the feel of the Milk Wood country all over it.

Dylan's father was our English master at the local Grammar School and a rather terrifying figure to us boys. He had a taste for biting sarcasm and perhaps a feeling that he had not fulfilled himself, that he had missed the big prize in life of the gift of creative power. I can see him now glowering down on me like a black bat in his M.A. gown, and rapping my fingers with a pencil as I misquoted a line of Chaucer. But he knew what the standards were, and when young Dylan showed a power of using English which was denied to D.J., Dylan's father felt a recompense for his own personal failure. He knew early on that he had a genius growing up in his house. 'There was young Dylan,' as his mother said, 'always scribbling. When it was wet, all I had to do to entertain him was to give him a pencil and up he'd go to his bedroom and write about anything. His sister used to get fed up with him asking, "What shall I write about now?" and once said to him, "Bother it, write about the kitchen sink." And, do you know, he produced a poem about that. And a very good poem too!'

As far back as I remember Dylan, he had blandly announced that he was going to be a poet, and nothing else. 'All right, boy,' said our most tolerant of headmasters, 'only I'll never forgive you if you're a bad one.'

He was the despair and the pride of the Swansea Grammar School; and the most daring cub reporter on the local paper. I always prefered this Dylan to the figure I call Public Dylan—the ranting, hard-drinking, Roaring Boy from Wales whom the Americans built into a legend. When we met him in Swansea after his forays into London and across the U.S.A., he was always half apologetic about Public Dylan. 'They've got me tied, boy,' he'd grin and groan. 'There's another professor

119

writing a book about me in the Middle West and I've got to live up to his Chapter Six.'

But my Private Dylan, in his early youth, had an immense charm, a gift of making commonplace, ill-planned Swansea glow with excitement when you met him. I remember in his early reporter days how he said to me, 'Care to meet an actress tonight?' and he spoke the words with studied unconcern. 'I've got the entrée backstage.'

Dylan made it sound as if he was making me free of the whole romantic world of grease-paint, dazzling young stars, stage-door johnnies, and champagne suppers. We arrived, breathless, at the dressing-room. A voice as cracked as the paint on the door called out, 'Come in, dearie', and we found ourselves in the presence of none other than dear old Nellie Wallace! Dylan rose to the occasion. 'Miss Wallace, we bring you the homage of the artists of the future to the artists of the past.'

'Variety or legit?' inquired Miss Wallace.

'Legit,' we replied. We didn't know what it meant, but it sounded better.

'In that case, boys, you've got a hell of a road to travel. Have some gin.' Miss Wallace produced a bottle from behind a pile of cosmetics and poured out the first and strongest gin I've ever tasted in my life. It exploded in Dylan and myself with devastating effect.

'Take it easy, boys, take it easy,' Miss Wallace chuckled. 'Here's one thing at any rate in which the artists of the past can wipe the floor with the artists of the future.' And she dealt with the rest of the gin with a quick gulp.

'This,' said the youthful Dylan afterwards with solemn emphasis, 'will be an incident for our memoirs.'

Dylan never wrote memoirs, but no man depended more completely for his inspiration on his home town, his early memories and upon the green, unsullied landscape of Carmarthen and Cardigan. He used to return to them like a homing pigeon every time he had work to do. Come to think of it, I never saw him actually write a poem in London. He needed the seclusion of the little summer house annexe to the boat house at Laugharne where he sat polishing and repolishing every phrase and word, and covering the floor with rejected drafts. He didn't care what became of them. All his friends have endless versions of his poems and the definitive edition of Dylan Thomas texts will keep American editors busy for the next twenty years and reduce most of them to tears. Still, these continually altered drafts with their long lists of alternative words, show what a hard-working craftsman Dylan was when it came to poetry. The Roaring Boy disappeared and the dedicated artist took his place.

His drinking died down, too. Whatever he may have done in his extrovert act around America, Swansea in his early days saw him as a melodious, companionable drinker, with a marvellous gift of almost spontaneous humorous verse. I only wish that I had noted down half the songs, lampoons and the rest of them he scattered around with a lavish hand—including a marvellous comic poem on the secret life of New Quay, Pembrokeshire, which was side-splitting and scandalous.

But I do remember a singing party in which I became involved with Dylan and Vernon Watkins in a secluded pub in Gower before the war. The closing hours of this Welsh pub were as elastic as those of the Kerry inn. By eleven o'clock the song was in full blast. Dylan was improvising a verse threatening the local council with the visitation of a Welsh vampire:

> Councillors' jugulars suck I with glee.
> Oh ho, for the taste of a scrumptious J.P.
> Tremble, ye aldermen! Town Clerk beware!
> As I hoover the veins of your succulent Mayor!

'Who's that singing?' the landlord inquired with awe.
'The greatest poet in Wales,' I announced.
'I don't know about the greatest,' said the landlord, 'but I'm sure of one thing though, he's by far the loudest.'
That is how I'll remember him, being natural with people

he knew and liked and not acting the Great Bohemian. I talked about Dylan to Dame Edith Sitwell; it was in the year she died and although she was ill and lay in her bed to talk, she looked like a splendid medieval queen still receiving her courtiers in her chamber of state, clad in black gloves and extended upon a coverlet of red velvet. Dylan rated his meeting with her, when he first came to London, as the beginning of his real career as a poet. 'I've seen her,' he told me in triumph. 'A marvellous talking missal from the middle ages, and she positively gloats over my poems.'

'How did he behave when he first met you?' I asked Dame Edith.

'Beautifully.' And then she gave a slow smile. 'Beautifully, but I've never seen him behave anything but beautifully with me. He always behaved with me like a son with his mother.'

'Did he never overstep the mark?'

'Well, one day he came to lunch with me—that was the only time when I have seen him a little—perhaps a little over, do you see? And he said, "I'm sorry to smell so awful, Edith, it's Margate." "Ah," I said, "yes, of course my dear boy, naturally it's Margate. I quite understand *that*!"'

Dylan, frankly, was a little afraid of Edith Sitwell. He was delighted to have her approval, but frightened of the disaster of misbehaving in her presence. He need not have worried. She had the perfect manners of the nineteenth century. She would have soothed over his wildest social disasters with splendid tact. Others were not so kind or understanding.

And now the Dylan we knew has been swallowed by the legend. I have to keep reminding myself that Public Dylan wasn't the real Dylan. I turn up letters he wrote, usually asking for money—and no one wrote more splendidly persuasive and unusual begging letters than he did.

'This is, I think, the first time I've written to you—treasure the paper, boy!—and, oh, for what a reason. I'm whimpering in bed, with mumps and gout, the music-hall duo, and cannot work and am, quite suddenly, utterly without money and horribly in debt. My face is a sad bladder and my big toes full of teeth. And tradesmen bludgeon the door all day and summonses fall like grouse. There's no one here to borrow a mite from . . . and I'm writing to ask you if you could temporarily (oh cringing word!) help me with a little money however little. If you can, I will send you a cheque post-dated eight weeks hence when I begin again to write film-scripts in London where, God, I must live for the winter. Snarl and throw this over the Devonshire Castle if you must, but try your best, and do not think too hardly of your mumpish and gehenna-toed, Dylan.'

I never cashed that post-dated cheque or any of the others that followed. Why should I? It is not everybody's luck to have gone to school with a great poet and been privileged to help him occasionally out of his permanent temporary difficulties; and, in addition, to receive payment in words you are compelled to remember, that came singing back to me as we rode on past the dark chapel where Dylan's great-uncle preached his powerful, defiant sermons,

> Into the bright sun, in the first, spinning place,
> The spellbound horses walking warm
> Out of the whinnying green stable
> On to the fields of praise.

And in this pleasant haze of drifting through the countryside, 'a springful of larks in a rolling cloud and the roadside bushes brimming with whistling blackbirds', we came over the watershed and down into the Vale of Aeron.

This is fat, milkman's country. A great deal of Cardiganshire is high, sparse land and farmers have to struggle to make a reasonable living out of it. The Cardi got his character out of the struggle; he could afford to give nothing away. But the Aeron on that warm day in early summer was a gentle successful river, running through green pastures and woodlands. Tika pricked up her ears and sensed the midday rest ahead. I must give that horse credit, she knew exactly when and where we were going to. As the final mile approached she showed a surprising turn of speed and trotted gaily up to join the leaders.

So we formed a pleasingly compact little troop as we rode down the drive into Llan Llyr, the house in the river meadows where Captain Hext-Lewis, then Lord Lieutenant of Cardiganshire, had a lush pasture awaiting us. We unsaddled and let the horses loose in a vast field. Seamus, Smatcher and Shannon kicked up their heels and raced off like schoolboys let loose on the playground. Tika strolled quietly to the most shady part of the pasture and settled down—a clubman looking forward to a glass of port after lunch. We went into the cool of the old house.

Llan Llyr is early nineteenth century, pleasant and orderly. The site goes back a long way in Welsh history, but the house and the estate have had their ups and downs. The mansion remains one of the few Welsh manor houses inhabited by the descendants of the original family. We talked over lunch of the Captain's work in rebuilding the fortunes of Llan Llyr, of making the land work for its living, of finding old pictures in the attics, of re-creating a house that had been in danger of disintegrating.

As we talked I admit that a certain feeling of mild envy came over me. I earn my living by throwing words about in front of a microphone. Occasionally they are filed away on disc and tape, but most of them disappear—deservedly—into thin air. And I wondered if any words of mine had ever created something as solid as this pleasant old house of Llan Llyr.

Well, perhaps there was one moment in my commentating career when talk did actually lead to worthwhile action; and it naturally took place in the far-off days of World War II.

I'd been the BBC correspondent on the Anzio beach-head and felt as if I'd been to jail for four and a half months. In the heady atmosphere of freedom that followed the breakout and the fall of Rome, I seemed to be set free to meander joyously over the whole front. Ahead of us now lay the next great artistic prize, Florence, and along with Eric Linklater and Sy Korman of the *Chicago Tribune* I drove in my jeep through the July heat towards the front to see how the battle was going.

We made a very strange jeep-load. Eric Linklater is short, slightly bald, wears glasses, and is the last man in the world whom you would immediately recognise for what he is—a brilliant novelist, a distinguished military historian and a soldier with a heroic record in the First World War. Sy Korman was tall, gaunt, raw-boned, and his uniform looked as if it had been issued to him by a relief organisation during a famine. He was brave, untiring in pursuit of a story and the employee of the *Chicago Tribune*, which was then still under the powerful control of Colonel McCormack. The Colonel felt the British, and especially the BBC, were not Allies but potential enemies of the U.S.A., determined to reverse the result of Yorktown as soon as this war ended. Yet Sy and I had struck up a close alliance, behind the backs of our bosses. As for myself, I was a red-faced roly-poly sort of soldier, a fugitive from Falstaff's army.

We came to the high ridges that guard Florence, and reported to the HQ of the hospitable 8th Indian Division. Captain Uni Nayar, their Press Officer, did us proud. He produced a curry of epic proportions and we tucked in; so heartily that when the time came to move poor Sy Korman had tummy trouble on a big scale.

'Stay where you are,' I reassured him. 'I'll tell you if there's anything happening.' Nayer, Linklater and Quereshi, the Reuter correspondent with the 8th Indians, now joined me in my jeep and we drove north through a landscape of cypress trees, white-walled Renaissance villas and vine-clad hillsides. The war had erupted itself over a painting by Fra Lippo Lippi.

The silence of fear held the countryside. The guns thudded here and there and a stray shell whistled overhead on a pointless mission across a powdery-blue sky. On the brow of the ridge before us stood a medieval castle, complete with towers, turrets, battlements and a view towards the distant domes of Florence. We raced up through the dust to avoid giving an easy target to snipers and machine-gunners—for the front was all around us and no old soldier takes any risks he can conveniently dodge.

We shot into the safety of a small courtyard. Indian soldiers were everywhere, some squatting in the corners clapping their hands over the circular *chapattis* that seemed so strange in Renaissance Italy. We had come to the HQ company of the Mahratta Light Infantry. The Colonel was upstairs asleep after being up all night dealing with a Tiger Tank at the bottom of the garden.

We went into the castle itself. Two great golden crucifixes leant against the walls of the entrance, alongside them a Virgin and Child on a dark, wooden panel. 'They are very good,' said Linklater. 'Too good,' said I. 'They must be copies.'

We went into the drawing-room. Cases were stacked against the wall, and a few British soldiers from the signals company attached to the Mahrattas, were rummaging amongst the shelves. A pile of invitation cards were still on a table near the door. I picked one up and read that Lady Ida Sitwell would be at home at Montegufoni and that there would be dancing.

Montegufoni! Of course, it was Sir George Sitwell's castle we were in. Sitwell on gardens littered the shelves. Everywhere were books, photographs and *objets d'art* which bore the hallmark of the marvellous and terrifying eccentric who was the father of Osbert, Edith and Sacheverell. Linklater, as a friend of the family, felt he ought gently to expostulate with the sergeant. 'We were only looking for something like an Agatha Christie, sir,' he explained, 'but there's damn all here.'

How wrong he was! At that moment I felt myself being tugged on the arm. I was surrounded by a group of Italian refugees, papa, mamma and all the garlic-perfumed bambinos. They shouted, *'Capolavori degli Uffizi. E vero, e vero'*, and propelled me towards the main hall. As they opened the doors I could see stacks of dark frames inside in the gloom. Then papa shouted, *'Moment', aspett'*. He raced around the hall, opening the huge shutters. As he opened each shutter a shaft of sunlight shot down, like the spots in a theatre, and lit up the frames. Down shot the first shaft—and I gave a gasp of delight and astonishment. There before me was one of the world's greatest paintings, Botticelli's 'Primavera'. Down came the second shaft: Again a glorious revelation—Uccello's 'Battle of San Romano'. On through the hall, with shaft after shaft of the sun lighting up picture after picture, Giottos, Cimabues, Andrea del Sartos, Lippo Lippis—the greatest concentration of superb painting I had ever seen. And all at my mercy! For a moment I was overcome with a wild temptation. Not even the Great Train Robbers had been given such an opportunity. I could have put an assorted pair of masterpieces in my jeep, whipped them back via the BBC and spent the rest of my life enjoying Bootlegged Botticelli in the bathroom.

But at that moment a triumphant cry of '*Il Professore*' echoed around the hall and my 'moment of truth' ended. Il Professore entered at the run, one of the librarians of the Uffizi. These were indeed the masterpieces of the gallery. The Allies had bombed the marshalling yards and in panic the Fascists had ordered the paintings to be scattered around Florence. The war rolled north, the Germans had no transport to spare and there was the anguished Professore bicycling from castle to castle appealing to unheeding soldiers, on both sides, who had a battle on their hands, to stop shooting in the cause of the Renaissance! He didn't get far.

Now, at last, he had hopes. He turned to Linklater. 'You are a Colonel. Quick, you must stop the war.'

We did our best. We roused the C.O. from sleep. He'd noticed some paintings about, but he had a Tiger Tank to deal with and painting wasn't exactly his line, though the wife did a certain amount of water-colours. But once we'd explained the position, he acted promptly. He cleared out the refugees eating their salami and drinking their Chianti amongst the Fra Angelicos. Dark Mahratta soldiers stood on guard over the Uccellos. As for the Botticelli—Eric Linklater adjusted his glasses to make sure he'd got the right woman and, on our behalf, imprinted a kiss on the lips of Primavera.

Later, led by the Professore, we ducked and dodged our way along the skyline to the two neighbouring castles of Montagnana and Poppino. The Professore made light of the odd bullets that whistled over. 'I, Cesare Fasola, was an ancient Alpini'; and away he bounded with his green pork-pie hat decorated with a small feather.

More pictures, some damaged, some hidden in wine vats for safety and which to the end of time will exude a slight perfume of Chianti into the exclusive air of art galleries on warm days.

'Now, you have seen with your own eyes, you must stop the war!'

We decided that Linklater as senior man had more chance of stopping the war than I had. He would stay at divisional HQ; I would race back and send a discreetly worded dispatch to the BBC. We pondered carefully how we would describe Montegufoni so that there would be no danger of bringing down German gunfire on it. 'An old Italian farmhouse' was our best effort. Alas, when they heard it in England, the Sitwells were naturally indignant at hearing the lordly castle on which their family had lavished so much care demoted to a decrepit old farmhouse. But later Edith Sitwell forgave me in the same way as she forgave Dylan for Margate.

Yet perhaps I ought still to feel guilty, for as I picked up Sy Korman and sped back to the Press Camp to send my dispatch, a new temptation overwhelmed me. For the first and only time in my life I had a world scoop on my hands. What should an honest man do? Tell Sy? I just couldn't. When Sy asked me, 'Did you bump into anything interesting up there?' I heard myself replying as from a great distance, 'Not a thing, everything as quiet as the grave.' Sy has long since forgiven me, but if ever a reporter committed journalist mayhem, I was that man.

But my words took effect. They were heard and the Allied Art Commission raced up its experts. Linklater, on his side, has eloquently pleaded the cause of art with the generals, who sealed off this small but precious section of the front. Between us I think we helped to save the Primavera and her sisters. May it be accounted to me as my one good deed of the war.

When I returned to the Uffizi after the war Cesare Fasola welcomed me. We walked through the newly hung galleries. Everything was guarded, untouchable, reverenced. We passed the pictures which I had last seen propped against corridors and surrounded by peasant families. Now they seemed to have become impossibly remote once again. At last we stood before the 'Primavera'. I remembered how I had touched the painted panel and my surprise at discovering that it was full of little worm holes.

Two American ladies stood beside us as we looked at the marvellously patterned colours, the delicate, heart-moving fragile beauty of spring. One turned to the other and said, 'I think she doesn't look very healthy, do you?' The other replied, 'I wonder why they make such a fuss about her'.

Il Professore and I made no comment. We knew what the fuss was about. We felt that from now on we had a secret understanding with Primavera. I was glad to find she came safely through the floods of 1966 that did more damage to Florence in twenty-four hours than the Allies did in four years of war!

By the time I had finished telling the story over lunch—and I'll admit I'm a difficult man to stop when I've got well into a story, especially if my wife isn't there to give me a quiet tap under the table—we were running behind our time-table. The moment had come to collect our horses once again, and the heat outside was now worthy of an Italian summer.

Tika was easy to catch and saddle, as usual, but the others were troublesome. The vast green water-meadow gave them plenty of room to manoeuvre. No wonder the cowboys had to hobble their horses on the prairies. There's nothing more irritating than an animal that has taken it into its head to stay free. It waits until you are almost there and then calmly trots past you, out of the corner where you've fondly hoped you've got him corralled, and you're in for another five minutes' careful stalking. The correct solution was an elaborate combined operation with much chorusing of calming sounds and offering of sugar until at last the troop was saddled up, and out we rode onwards up the Aeron valley.

The country was drowsy in the summer heat. We went across fields and forded the river, Wild West style. It's curious how horses which make a tremendous fuss about wetting their feet in the sea do not seem to mind how deeply they plunge into a swift-running stream. The clatter they made in the river bed was an infinitely cooling sound on a hot day. Then as we loitered on through the lanes during the afternoon I had leisure to speculate on how wide of the mark is the average picture of the Cardi. We had had nothing but pleasure out of this unspoilt, pylon-free county.

By late afternoon we came to the little village of Llangeitho. No Welshman needs to be told about Llangeitho. In his mind he immediately tacks on the name of Daniel Rowland. There, in front of a chapel in the centre of the hamlet, is the statue of the most powerful preacher thrown up by the eighteenth-century Methodist Revival in Wales. Frankly it's not a good statue. Wales has produced sculptors in the past, but they didn't seem very much at home with preachers. Still, Daniel Rowland in effigy looks gaunt-cheeked, eloquent and dominating and you can believe the stories they still tell at Llangeitho of how the farmers used to come from the whole of South Wales for the meetings, camping out and taking in three sermons a day.

The sermon has collapsed in our day as an art form. We insist on them being short, staccato and sensational, but I am old enough to remember the days before television and radio; those Sundays when the cinema was unheard of and when the chapel

Llangeitho

sermon—if delivered by a master of the art—could be the high-light of the week. Then the good minister was your TV commentator, your entertainer, your philosopher, your newspaper advice column, your confessor and your spiritual guide all rolled into one. In addition the Welsh preacher had a weapon denied to his colleagues in England—he could go into the *hwyl*. The *hwyl* (pronounced 'hoo-il', with the syllables run together as nearly as possible) was a sort of chanting that the minister employed as he came to the climax of his sermon, when inspiration descended upon him and he and his audience were carried away together in a joint excitement. The voice rose and fell as his words poured forth, and in the hands of a master, with a voice that could reach the heights, the *hwyl* could be a splendid if irrational thing. Where did the practice originate? Maybe, as some experts have suggested, it goes back to the chanting of the Druids.

I'm not sure if Daniel Rowland ever employed the *hwyl*, but like every other good preacher he left nothing to chance and carefully prepared his dramatic effects. They still show you the separate entrance to the pulpit up which Rowland would go at the critical moment, and suddenly appear far above the congregation almost as the voice from on high. He was right. Serious occasions need a bit of mystery attached to them and it does not do to probe too deeply into the methods by which the mystery is produced.

I received an early lesson in this when I was a small boy from none other than Sir Edward Elgar. The great man was coming to conduct one of his works at a Swansea music festival, and father briefed us beforehand on the honour and respect due to a man of genius. In fact, we were going to sit next to Elgar as he listened to the preliminary rehearsals from the back of the hall. I was to be at hand ready to run on any errand that the great man might desire. I felt I was going to be given my first glimpse into a creative mind at work.

Sir Edward at that period of his life was rather a frightening man for a youngster to meet. With his bowler hat and thick, Kipling-type moustache he had the air of a prosperous stock-broker, a little ponderous and sparing of good tips on the Exchange. We sat in silence all through the rehearsal, then at last Sir Edward beckoned to me—revelation was at hand. He bent down and whispered, 'My boy, can you slip out and get me the afternoon edition of your local newspaper. I may have pulled off the double on the three-thirty at Goodwood.'

'The Dream of Gerontius' never sounded quite the same to me again.

I grew hardened to this unveiling of mystery as I grew older—although I still can't cure myself of always expecting the great of this world, and the famous centres of pilgrimage, to live up to the prose and poetry written around them. This has led me into some curious anticlimaxes.

On my first visit to Jerusalem I fell into the hands of a voluble Armenian guide who soon put me right about the Holy Places. He buttonholed me outside the hotel and overwhelmed me with eloquence. He handed me his card, assumed he was engaged and started off on his commentary forthwith.

'First may I ask honoured name? Thomas! You are American, Français, Deutsch, Norge? I speak all tongues. But you come from Wales? Oh ho, the Walish, I meet so many in the war, they play football and are always winning and drinking the whisky and singing. So I can now tell you the truth. My life is unhappy, for all the Holy Places are divided up stone by stone. The Greeks, the Catholics, the Maronites, the American Baptists, they all have money and we, the poor Armenians, have no great rights except the encouragement of the Walish. The others have all the prizes, and they are fighting like furies for the pilgrims to come to them. But now, on behalf of the Walish, I have made a decision, I am backing the Greek Orthodox. For why? They are most subtle. In one church they are last year disputing the rights of processing first against the Maronite Catholics. Catholics want to get at head of Christmas procession, but cunning Greeks hide lentils in their beards and drop them on the floor as they go; Catholic procession and choir skid all over the place! Thank you, Mr Thomas, *Cymru am byth*! *I'r achos*! These pieces of your great poetry your soldiers are teaching to me. Long live the Walish, may they now win the boat-race, come this way to see all that is finest in Golden Jerusalem!'

Perhaps Daniel Rowland's theory of a little mystery is correct after all. I dare not contemplate what my Armenian friend would have done at Llangeitho. The disaster would have been as complete as the one envisaged by the harassed theatre-owner, desperately trying to attract the crowds to his establishment in the suburbs, who wired to Tom Arnold to ask: 'How would *Good Night Vienna* go in Walthamstow?' He received the classic reply: 'Almost as well as *Good Night Walthamstow* would go in Vienna.'

In any case, these speculations were now driven from my mind by a splendid clatter outside the chapel. It sounded as if the Light Brigade were getting ready to charge at Balaclava. I came out to find the whole of the little village submerged in horses.

The Tregaron Pony Trekkers had ridden out to meet us and were preparing to escort us for the last five miles of the day.

A splendidly mixed-up cavalcade we looked as we trotted up the hill that took us out of the Aeron valley back into the upper waters of the Teifi. There were little girls in the regulation black peaked cap and 'jods', bouncing on the backs of prancing Welsh ponies; the matron of the local hospital defying my experience with rucksacks and carrying a first-aid kit on her back; typists from Burton-on-Trent, farmers' sons from the hills, and Mr David Jones—Dai Tregaron himself—to act as our guide. Could such a group of joyous pilgrims on horseback have assembled before the war? In those days only hunting brought horsemen together; secretaries were taboo and desk-bound heroes like myself never rode. But the advent of pony trekking has brought the horse a new world of admirers. His prestige has been restored in Central Wales, for this animal, who was about to disappear before the tractor and the Land-Rover, has been reprieved. He can earn his keep and bring money into many a small town amongst the mountains.

We thus received a royal welcome *en route*. The farmers' children were all sitting on the gates and cheering. Tika, naturally, got more than her fair share of applause and obliged with a turn of speed at the head of the procession. We came out on the top of the hill and found the whole of northern Cardiganshire spread before us. We were leaving the lush lowlands. Right across the eastern skyline lay a barrier of dark moorlands. They rolled remorselessly on to the north, rising higher and higher as they approached the wilderness of Plinlimmon. Tregaron lay at their feet, and the snipe-haunted bog of Gors Caron, the biggest tract of bogland in Wales, guarded the approach to the little town.

Dai Tregaron reined up and we paused to take in the view. 'There's your way for tomorrow,' he said, giving a wave towards that forbidding horizon, 'Wicked country. The bogs can swallow you and your horse if you don't know the tricks of them. Not much up there, a farm or two still left, but you'll have twenty-five miles of loneliness before you get to Rhayader. But don't worry; we've got the best boys in the world to show you the way.'

I grew thoughtful as we went slowly down into the Teifi valley. I knew, when we plotted this route on the map, that my sternest test was going to come between Tregaron and Rhayader. This is the endless wild mountain which people call the Desert of Wales. Here the Towy river rises in a vast, soppy, spongy bog and the treeless, trackless hills are speckled with small lakes. Each high ridge looks like the next one. When rain and mist descend, you must steer by compass or find yourself wandering in circles and coming down in a deserted valley with an extra ten miles to the nearest welcoming farm. This is country which doesn't take kindly to casual tourists. You only travel across it if you can conquer it.

I felt worried as I talked away to Dai and the Tregaron Pony Trekkers. I must be mad to set off across such an anti-horse landscape on the strength of three pleasant days in the saddle and in the sun. What if Tika sank in a bog? How would I get her out? What if I lost the way or one of our horses went lame or cast a shoe up in that lonely world of grass, bog and wind-swept hillside? Our whole expedition would founder in the Desert of Wales!

But for the moment my fears sank to the back of my mind. Here we were, entering the little square of Tregaron, with most of the inhabitants out giving us a handclap of welcome. I put on my most horsemanlike air as we passed under the statue of Henry Richard, Tregaron's pride and the Apostle of Peace. The town-hall clock showed ten to three—as it had done for the last thirty years. Before us was the pillared entrance to the Talbot Hotel. We slid gently off the backs of our horses and went in out of the evening sun to the cool, stone-flagged entrance hall. Never mind about tomorrow; we had had a memorable Cardiganshire day.

Tregaron

6

THAT night before our crossing of the Desert of Wales stays in my mind like the night Napoleon spent before Austerlitz—or perhaps, as it might turn out with more justice, the night Harold spent before Hastings. Our horses were safely out to pasture, we were snug at our ease in our inn, we were even invited to sample the wild gaieties of the Pony Trekkers' dance; Biddy, Felicity and Rowland were as relaxed as could be—but then, they didn't know the sort of country that lay ahead! I did. I'd walked across it in mist and driving rain and that experience had seemed tough enough. But what would it be like on a horse? I began to regret the gay, carefree way I had drawn our route between Tregaron and Rhayader.

Besides, all that evening I had been conscious of the presence of the dark, overwhelming shade of someone whom every travel-ler who writes about Wales has to reckon with sooner or later—old George Borrow.

This was the first time on this trip that we were crossing his track. He came tramping into the Talbot well over a hundred years before we did and spent a November night at Tregaron. He felt that Tregaron 'had the air of an Andalusian village over-hung by its sierra'—an extraordinary comparison from someone who hit Tregaron on a damp winter's evening—and the obliging local who directed him to the Talbot described it as a very good inn 'where they are always anxious to see English gentlemens'.

Borrow gave it good marks and so did we, but Borrow's approval was not lightly given. He had a pretty taste in invective when things displeased him. He must have astonished the Welsh as he strode through the land, quoting huge chunks of Welsh poetry on every occasion to farmers, solicitors and commercial travellers who were more interested in the price of fat sheep than the verses of Dafydd ap Gwilym. But he paid the Welsh the compliment of learning their language at a time when few Englishmen bothered to interest themselves in anything connected with the Principality, and when I set out to walk in his footsteps I found to my astonishment that I met family after family on his route who remembered how their grandfather or their grandmother had met the great man striding along through wind and weather, doing his twenty to thirty miles a day like a commando in training.

Only one thing worries me about his book; how did he remember the exact details and the very words spoken by the hundreds of people he met on his travels? We know he took notes, for he terrified the patrons of the pub at Cemmaes by 'dotting', as he called it—they must have thought he was a police spy. But even if he 'dotted' for hours every night, he couldn't have got down all the details of some of those conversations which run into page after page.

I, myself, try to jot down the gist of what I hear while on a tour like this one. We had to broadcast programmes and, as we travelled, I covered pages with the conversations I've recorded in this book, but none of them comes near old Borrow's reports in sheer length. In addition, for years I've had to cultivate the art of interviewing for radio and this teaches you to remember words tenaciously. You develop a technique of making certain of your starting and ending questions and of sensing the moment for asking the supplementary question that makes your interviewee really talk.

The worst people to interview are young actors or actresses, who can only talk about their 'career' and always think everyone who produced them in any obscure play or film is 'absolutely fab'.

Next at the bottom of the list are M.P.s, who twist everything sooner or later into party politics. Painters are always garrulous and composers are tongue-tied. Executive artists, conductors or leading tenors and pianists are excellent interview material, but the best of all are men and womem in their seventies who have lived a full, interesting life and are still spry and active.

And this is where I score over Borrow. I have a portable recorder and all I have to do is to play my tape back to get the exact atmosphere of an interview. One of my most curious recordings was, once again, of someone in his eighties—none other than the late Donald McGill.

I suppose I should classify him among the artists, but no Royal Academician ever made such an impact on the public. For over fifty years his scrawny landladies, his unforgiving wives bulging out of their corsets, his husbands staggering home more drunk than it is ever possible to conceive in our temperate age, have delighted the sea-side tripper.

'I've no rubber, miss,' says the schoolboy. His teacher replies, 'Then use the little boy's behind.'

This is the classic McGill joke—good honest vulgarity and, as George Orwell pointed out, devoid of any corrupt sexual import. Belly-laughs, not sniggers.

I met the artist down in Streatham when he was in his eighties—a spry, white-haired little sparrow of a man who lived 'near the business, not the studio', in a Victorian villa of many floors and a small garden in the heart of the southern suburbia of London. He was then a widower, but with a son and daughter.

I asked him, 'What do the family do when they pass a window-ful of your work?'

'Run like stags—all except my grandniece: you know, she's proud of me. She's at a most exclusive school for young ladies on the South Coast and she gets all the most fruity ones. Girls of thirteen these days know a damn sight more than I do.'

'Is your work vulgar?'

'Yes, of course it is—but not obscene, mind you. They loved it at the sea-side. I seem to go with the sea air.'

'Have you ever lived at the sea-side yourself?'

'What, Southend and that sort of thing? Good heavens, never; I can't understand what people see in them, except my postcards I'm thankful to say. Of course, Blackpool's our best-seller. We can't go wrong there. North Wales is very good too; in fact anywhere north of the Thames is first-class. But here's a funny thing, the Isle of Man wouldn't allow me to draw a clergyman; anything else—ladies with breasts like marrows, but no clergymen. And who would have thought that I'd get fined at Cleethorpes—Cleethorpes of all places. Yet they had me in court—"Wicked old white-headed granddad", that's what the headlines called me. You know, I felt quite disappointed that I couldn't live up to it. Cleethorpes! Why, when you see Cleethorpes it looks like one of my postcards, now doesn't it?'

'Did you start your career in this vein?'

'No, I gradually worked up to it. You may not believe it, but I improved the standard of the postcards. You ought to have seen them before I started! Horrible! But I did have a bit of art training, you know. South Ken. School of Art for a year, but they made me do nothing except draw from casts—I had to draw false shadows on apples and pears when I was aching to draw red-nosed men. It was enough to break your heart. You remember the great Frith—he said they made him draw a circle for a year when he longed to draw from life!'

'Frith, you say, but how about Picasso?'

'Well, I'm probably too old to see anything in him.'

'But he's over seventy himself.'

'Ah! But he's never had to earn a living drawing for tourists at the sea-side. I don't think he'd last a minute. And Cézanne now: £100,000 for a canvas with all those strange women on it—that's vulgarity, if you like!'

Not the sort of interview you could ever imagine happening to Borrow, but faithfully reproduced on the tape-recorder. Borrow might have retorted with complete justice that the best things are never said into microphones. Machines inhibit conversations. Train your mind to remember, or sneak off like Boswell and get the talk down quickly before you forget it—that's the best way. It was certainly Sir Thomas Beecham's view.

That he was completely imperturbable in front of the microphone goes without saying. He once gave an interview, to the BBC, and invited them to his flat where he was already entertaining a charming lady to Pol Roger '08 and enchanting reminiscence. He talked and the lady attacked the champagne with more energy than wisdom. It became clear from her snoring on the sofa that she had been overcome by the splendour of the occasion. Sir Thomas talked on into the microphone, giving no sign that he noticed a somewhat *pizzicato* accompaniment. The lady slid gently to the floor. Sir Thomas simply gave a sign to his butler, the admirable and unshakeable White. White murmured, 'Shall I replace the lady now, sir, or will you wait?' Sir Thomas continued his measured and eloquent discourse. He concluded, bowed to the lady on the floor, then to the BBC engineers and retired quietly and gracefully.

Next day the BBC was surprised to receive enthusiastic postcards from certain music-lovers who declared they had naturally been delighted with what Sir Thomas had said, but even more delighted to discover a facet of Sir Thomas's character that they had not suspected—namely, that he was a keen dog-lover. How charming it had been, while Sir Thomas had been talking about Sibelius, to hear the friendly and highly intelligent snuffling of his dear little pet in the background!

But I discovered Sir Thomas's real feelings when I, too, went to record him with Anna Instone in Paris on the occasion of his eightieth birthday. We had armed ourselves with a bottle of champagne and a box of his favourite Monte Cristo cigars. He received us with all his old-world formal politeness, clad in a silk dressing-gown, in dazzling form as he spoke into the microphone I held out for him. He poured out wit and epigrams with reckless generosity. His revelations about his contemporaries became more and more indiscreet. Of a certain most distinguished English composer he declared, 'He wrote his symphonies with all the wild abandon of an unmarried organist in one of our damper cathedrals, waiting for retirement.' I knew I had a first-class scoop on my hands—until I happened to glance down at my machine.

The tape had stuck. Not a word had been recorded!

I turned anxiously to explain to Sir Thomas. He was chuckling to himself with the greatest good humour. 'My dear fellow,' he said, 'I saw that your wretched appliance had stuck from the moment I began to talk, so I knew I could really let myself go. Remember all the best talk is never on, but Off the Record.' Then he turned to the embarrassed French engineer. 'Young man, cease caressing your churlish contraption and apply yourself to the wine of your own country.'

Interviewing on a tape-recorder is like fishing—the biggest and best ones always get away.

So old Borrow may have been right after all. The notebook and the retentive memory are the interviewer's best weapons; although I will continue to wonder if Borrow really remembered every one of the eloquent conversations in Welsh that he declares he held with the old farmer up at Strata Florida on his way to Tregaron. I would like to believe that this garrulous old Welshman really did end his meeting with Borrow by giving him the charming valediction: 'Farvel, Saxon gentleman!'

Just as Borrow must have done, I went out after dinner to look up towards the hills. The night was dark. The weather might be changing. I went back for an early bed, anxious about our chances tomorrow.

We were up before the dawn and I knew immediately that this was going to be a day of trial. Biddy had been down to the field to get the horses. Straight away she found that Rowland's Shannon was walking stiffly. She examined the legs with practised care. Shannon had been kicked—badly kicked. Who was the culprit? Tika was ruled out; it was inconceivable she would have wasted energy in kicking when she knew she had a long day ahead. Her motto had always been, 'Live and let live.' No-trouble Tika they called her!

Seamus or Smatcher then? But these horses and Shannon had

lived together in amity at Builth for years, why should they take it into their heads to attack Shannon, especially after a long, long day? There followed detective work worthy of trackers in the African bush. The culprits were discovered—two Welsh ponies who had come down into the field at night and taken a malicious pleasure in assaulting the newcomers. They had followed the old Punch joke: 'Here's a stranger, heave half a kick at him!'

We held an anxious council of war at dawn. Shannon had to rest, so would Rowland have to drop out? I confess I was astonished at this revelation of equine depravity. Over the last few days the horse had become a symbol of decency in my mind. I didn't exactly ennoble him like Swift in *Gulliver's Travels*, but I certainly credited him with loyalty, patience and a certain placid kindness to his fellow horses. Perhaps old Tika had misled me into believing that all horses were like her.

But here, now, were two juvenile delinquent ponies who had acted out of pure malice and mischief. Clearly the horse world was like the world of humanity—it had its thugs and master criminals as well as its honest citizens like Tika. I decided I would listen with caution to all those experts who tell you that the faults of a horse are due to the faults of its master. I had lost another illusion.

We were saved by Dai Tregaron and his friends. Rowland would borrow a stout animal who could tackle the hills. Dick Williams would meet us at Rhayader—always assuming we made the crossing—with a new mount. The expedition could set off in the growing light.

So once again the pleasures of a dawn start, of clattering through the sleeping town, of the fresh morning air blowing into our faces from the waiting hills. The sky was overcast, but there seemed no fear of serious rain. Here, at least, was one point in our favour. Perhaps the gods would be kind after all.

Our first guide was Mr Rhys Hughes. He'd been shepherding in these hills from boyhood; he knew all the lonely hill farms in the days when there was hardly a track to them. He was mounted upon a sturdy, unshod Welsh pony: 'She doesn't need shoes where we're going, it's all soft, grassy, bogs here and there, a real wilderness.' At this point his pony shied and went sideways across the road. 'Steady, *fy merch i*,' Mr Hughes reassured her. 'She's a mountain pony this one, not used to town sights. She's shying at the white lines on the road. Real country girl, she is, blushing if anyone in Tregaron looked at her. Ah, but wait until we are free of these hedges, and there isn't a tree in sight. Then you'll see her go like the mountain wind.'

With Mr Hughes was a splendid character addressed by everybody as Shanko the Shepherd. He looked the very personification of the old pastoral life as it used to be lived amongst these hills, with his tweed cap pulled over his wild mop of hair, his old macintosh held together with string and huge hob-nailed boots of the sort issued to Wellington's army at Waterloo. He and his pony formed one unit—they both looked as if they had never been separated from birth. We talked in Welsh.

'I'll watch you, Mr Thomas bach. I don't think you'd ever make a shepherd, mind you, but we'll get you across to Rhayader as if you were a parcel.' Shanko gave me a wink. 'Well, if I don't, my pony will.'

We trotted up the lane that followed the little Afon Groes deep into the hills. The world was green and fresh after the rain at night. The raindrops on the trees sparkled in the morning sun. Somewhere far off a cuckoo called.

Four miles on we climbed out of the valley on to the open hillside. The track disappeared and a vast prospect opened out before us. Is there anything quite like it in the south of Britain? Wave after wave of treeless green mountain ridges—no track in sight, you launch yourself out over this country as if you were at sea. As we topped each ridge another rose before us with no sign of a field, a house or any recognised mark of cosy living. Mr Hughes pulled in his fiery pony alongside steady-pacing Tika. 'I remember one old farmer saying to me about this part of Wales, "This is the country as God made it and between you and me I don't think He was trying very hard up here!" '

But what a wonderful exhilaration it was to ride into this green wilderness—until we came to our first boggy patch. Now, I flatter myself that I can deal with the bogs on foot. I have been brought up in the technique of 'bog-trotting', of skimming fast over shaky ground, of judging exactly how deep a bog can be by the colour of its surface. Once you come to the green section, beware. The boglands of Britain are nothing compared to the vast, sinister sheets of green treachery over which you fly in Central Africa. When you look down on the edges of Lake Bangweolo you feel as if the Earth's surface has started to fester, you can sense the sinister hum of insects settling on sinking ground.

There is nothing like this in Britain. Our boglands are small and tucked away on hill-tops, but you can't play with them, especially on horseback after rain. I had forgotten that the horse is heavier than a man on foot, and that Tika, the Welsh cob, was heavier than Mr Hughes's mountain pony.

'Walk her over the rushes,' shouted Mr Hughes. I slid off Tika's back with newly acquired ease, and led the old girl towards the path. We both of us made a splendid, squelching sound as we went through the boggy tract. You could see Tika wasn't exactly enjoying it. Just as at the beach at Aber Mawr, she hated feeling uncertain, shifting ground under her feet. 'Talk her through,' said Mr Hughes. 'You know, explain it to her. She'll understand.'

I had been a convert from my first day in the saddle to the theory of talking to your horse. Tika had grown to expect it. So once again, lost up in the green wilderness, I chatted away with Tika.

'You're all right, old girl. Easy does it, and keep going whatever you do. Keep going . . . keep going, Tika.'

And in the way the mind works, those words 'keep going' took me back clean through time to an utterly different scene; the dark banks of the Rhine near Xanten in March 1945, and the voice of a young officer giving us our final briefing as we waited to load ourselves into the armoured amphibious vehicles which rejoiced in the name of Buffaloes. I was going to record the assault of the last barrier before the heart of Nazi Germany, and with us was the piper of a famous Scottish regiment who had promised that he would 'blow the braw laddies into battle'.

I don't quite know what sort of a picture the Colonel had in mind when he placed the gallant piper alongside my engineer and myself in the leading Buffalo. Perhaps he had memories of Waterloo or the Heights of Abraham or of those splendid battle-pieces painted by Lady Butler to fill half the wall in regimental messes, with titles like 'For the Honour of Scotland' or 'The Pibroch at Spion Kop'. But there was our piper, crouched over what the Germans irreverently call the 'doodle-sak', moistening his lips as our Buffalo lurched up over the high earthen *Bund*, the embankment that guards the Rhine, and then waddled slowly down to take the water like an armoured duck.

The Rhine was an unforgettable sight, running blood-red from the glare of burning farms and whipped by the splashes of bullets. Our ears were assaulted by a continuous roar of the shells racing overhead and the engines of the Buffalo fighting the current. Over it all came the voice of our officer keeping up a running commentary to maintain morale. It had a sort of Wagnerian leitmotive: 'Keep going, men, keep going.'

A soldier behind me, whose Bren gun was sticking into my ribs, murmured, 'Where to, chum?' and added, 'Anywhere except here!'

'Keep going . . .'

We grounded on the enemy bank and slithered out of the Buffalo to cover. Our gallant piper stood up, he was the only one who risked it. 'Keep going . . .'

Bravely he set his lips to the chanter, filled the bags with air and blew. There followed the wild skirl of the pipes which immediately changed into a sad, dismal sucking sound as of dirty water running out of a bath.

The piper gave the despairing cry of an artist who sees his greatest performance ruined, 'Ma pipes, they will na' play!'

The Germans had, with unerring critical aim, put a bullet clean through his doodlesak.

The sound made by that dying doodlesak was the exact replica of the sound now coming from Tika's hoofs. It was a danger signal. Suddenly her hindquarters seemed to sink. She was well and truly into the mire. A horse stuck in the mud is a frightening sight. They lash out with their feet to find firm ground and drive themselves deeper and deeper into trouble. Shanko was at my side in a moment.

'Keep her head up. Help her on—pull a bit.'

I tried my best, but poor Tika seemed to sink deeper still. It was then that all my fears about the Desert of Wales came crowding back to me. I had pushed them to the back of my mind on the way up on to the moorlands, but here was the stark reality—these boglands were not to be trifled with. Our whole expedition was in danger of foundering in the literal sense. Shanko shouted to the rest, 'Stay out'. The procession had come to a dead halt and everyone sat still in their saddles. Everything depended on old Tika. Would she have enough strength to keep struggling and enough sense to struggle in the right way? Shanko had her head well up. I kept on encouraging her, 'Come on, old girl, you can do it.' I fairly willed her to fight her way to firmer ground.

It was now or never. If Tika failed or foundered, I knew that the wilderness would have defeated us. There would be nothing for it but to retreat in shame and abandon the expedition. 'Keep going'—this was like crossing the Rhine all over again. And then somehow or other I knew that the old girl was going to do it. She seemed to get on to firmer ground. Then, suddenly, her hindquarters came free with a super-bagpipes suck. She was out of it!

We gave a cheer. Now we knew that we would get through. Tika had put everything she knew into the battle. She was dirty, mud-splashed but triumphant as she reached the grassy verge of the bog, leaving a trail of deep holes, ruts and wallows behind. She stood trembling a little and I hurriedly felt in my pocket for some sugar. We rubbed her down with a handful of reeds and led her on for some firmer standing.

'A struggle like that can take it out of a horse,' Mr Hughes advised. 'We'll go up on to the skyline and take a breather.'

I murmured, 'Well done, old girl', into Tika's ear and we all moved up the slope in a posse. Then over the top came a troop of free-running mountain ponies, the Welsh equivalent of the Scottish red deer as the excitement and wild decoration of our hills. They both give me the feeling of something untamed, still roaming the country as their ancestors did after the retreat of glaciers at the end of the Ice Age.

We are so used to thinking of our countryside as tamed and emasculated that it takes the eye of an unsophisticated visitor to sense the wildness that lies below the smooth surface. Da Tensing, the Sherpa, was such a man. He came over to England after the Kanchenjunga expedition. He was first taken to the Savoy Hotel to be entertained. When asked what he thought of it he smiled that marvellously all-embracing Sherpa smile, and said slowly, 'In this lamasery the abbot does not appear to have his monks in good order.'

The Sherpas, however, came into their own when they came to North Wales. Immediately they felt at home—they floated over the Snowdon mountains, which must have seemed an afternoon stroll after the Himalayas. But as evening fell over Llanberis Pass they got worried. The sheep had won their hearts, every one of them was twice as fat as any goat in the Chumbu Valley, there seemed wealth untold scattered over the mountainside. But as it got darker the Sherpas got restless until one of them could stand it no longer. He asked anxiously of his host, 'But are you not now sending up the young men to gather them in?' 'No, why should we?' his host replied. 'But what a terrible risk to run. Do you not lose hundreds of them to the wolves?'

I suppose it must be five hundred years or more since the last wolf was killed in Wales. Wolves were certainly plentiful in the Middle Ages, but they had all but been exterminated by late

Tudor times. Although there is strong competition amongst the wilder parts of Wales for the honour of having the last of the wolves. Needless to say, this wilderness we were now crossing is plentifully supplied with names such as Wolf's Leap or Wolf's Cave, and when I first walked through it thirty years ago I met an old man up near the headwaters of the Towy who pointed out to me a tumble of rocks above the river and assured me that his grandfather had always told him as a boy, that he had been told by his grandfather that here the young men of the area had met to start on the hunt for the last wolf left alive in Wales. Maybe so, for folk memory is a tenacious thing, but how far back does that take us? Perhaps to the middle of the sixteenth century. Who knows!

Certainly when the mists start to cling around these endless ridges and all you hear is the croak of a raven or the far-away whistle of the kite you can almost believe that there are still wolves somewhere in the treeless wastes that stretch for thirty miles northwards to Plynlimon. The wild ponies add to the illusion.

Up they came towards us—the stallion out ahead, snorting with tossing mane and flaring nostrils and the mares in a group behind with their foals nervously close to their flanks. The stallion wheeled and pawed the ground, uncertain what to do about these curious strangers. Then he flung about and away the whole herd galloped over the brow of the hill, racing in and out of the boggy patches with the knowledge of animals born on the hills. They could have been blood brothers to the shaggy ponies painted on the walls of the Lascaux caves by the old prehistoric hunters. 'There's some nice blood there,' said Mr Hughes. 'They're mine. I've always had ponies out on the hills and we've been improving them all the time. We used to get a good price for them—just after the war, when the Americans came into the market.'

I was a little disappointed. 'So they're not wild.'

'Oh,' said Shanko, 'they're wild enough. We've got a real cowboy's act to catch them. We used to have all the boys out to see the fun when we drove them down to sell at Tregaron fair.'

'The original breed must go back a long way,' said Mr Hughes. 'Some say the Romans brought them over, but I think they were here long before that. They've been improved, of course, everybody's had a go at improving the breed with Arab stallions and all the rest of it, but our ponies are still Welsh like the ones that drew Boadicea's chariots if you like—lovely movers, all fire and spirit and can carry a heavy man like me all day over these hills.'

Now we had come up to the skyline and drew rein. The ponies were already a mile away on a far hillside to the east. A rough track came winding its way over the waste land from the south.

'The Strata Florida road,' Shanko informed me, 'it comes up out of the Towy valley away south and it will take you down into the top of the Teifi away over there.' He gave an expansive wave of his hand. 'Down where you come to the old monastery where Dafydd is buried.'

Dafydd is, of course, Dafydd ap Gwilym, the greatest of the poets of medieval Wales and maybe the greatest Wales ever produced, and it was pleasant to hear Shanko the Shepherd, pronouncing his name with such familiar reverence. I'm sure Shanko had never read a word of Dafydd's works, for to enjoy them you must know something about the complex metric system employed in Welsh poetry based on what is called *cynghanedd*, a subtle form of internal rhyming and alliteration. It comes naturally to Welshmen, and Dylan Thomas, although he never spoke Welsh and certainly never studied the 'strict metres', as they are called, has a great deal of his poetry shot through with it.

I myself grew up with it, since my father was a scholar and a most sensitive composer who was a deep student and admirer of Dafydd ap Gwilym. Father had come in touch with him first when he had gone up to Oxford and entered Exeter College with an open scholarship in mathematics. This was a family saga, an event of pride which surpassed the exploits of my grandfather and Rebecca, the glory of mother's side of the family. He had been immediately invited to join the Dafydd ap Gwilym Society, of which all distinguished Welshmen in the university were members.

I have still got the group photograph taken outside the Hall of Jesus College, a marvellous period piece, with rows of serious young men wearing bowlers and more dashing members sporting straw boaters, all with florid waistcoats and some going all the way with spats and malacca canes. Father's Oxford seems as remote in time as the Paris of Toulouse Lautrec or the New York of Major Jimmy Walker.

This was the Oxford of 'Galloper' Smith sweeping all before him at the Law School on his way to the career that would lead him to the Woolsack as Lord Birkenhead; of Sir John Simon practising his rotund oratory at the Union; of Belloc-like dons, vintage port at High Table, trams in the 'Corn' and wealthy 'hearties' who spent four years at the university because it was in good hunting country. Father used to tell the story of one of these privileged gentlemen who woke one Sunday morning after a distinctly jolly evening the night before. His scout, the admirable college servant, who knows everything, reminded him that he had to read the lesson at chapel that morning. With difficulty he got into his gown and staggered into the chapel. There came the moment when he had to walk up to the lectern, a great bronze eagle bearing the Bible. He managed to cling on to the eagle, open the book and begin, 'And Jesus said—' His eyes went out of focus and he brought them back to try again, 'And Jesus said—' He realised he was on a hopeless wicket, turned to the congregation and cried in despair, 'If only this ruddy bird would stop waggling its tail, I'd tell you what Jesus said!'

Father had no part in this 'hearty' Oxford. He had become a pillar of the Oxford Musical Union. He forgot his maths and plunged into the delights of music. His piano playing made him a figure in college and he left Oxford convinced that the only worthwhile thing to be in life was a composer. He would do for Wales what the Elgars and Vaughan Williamses were then setting out to do in England—create a national style.

It is a perilous thing to be a fine creative artist in a small country with a language that is only understood by a million people. Father never made money, but he made magnificent music and great happiness for his family. I can still hear the sound of the piano coming to me muted from Father's study as I lay half-asleep upstairs as a small boy. Father was absorbed in the task of setting some of Dafydd ap Gwilym's most complex and subtly beautiful poems. How could he get music to fit *cynghanedd*. The sounds came to me and seemed incredibly beautiful, remote, exotic—I could have wished that all life could be like this dream-world that father was building at his finger-tips on the piano. The songs were amongst the best things he ever wrote, and any mention of Dafydd ap Gwilym brings back to me a picture of my father, a cigarette at the corner of his mouth, his manuscript on the piano before him, his sensitive hands touching the keys and his mind far away from such matters as milkman's bills and school fees. Mother looked after that side of life.

There must have been moments when she wished that Dafydd ap Gwilym had never written a line of poetry. Dafydd, after all, was not exactly a model of good conduct, if the stories about him were true. He wasn't quite in the Dylan Thomas class as a Bohemian, but he had the eye of a Robert Burns for pretty women and a whiplash tongue for rival poets. The only time he ever reached peace was when he was laid to rest at the monastery of Strata Florida. This is a lonely, lovely place; there isn't much left of the abbey, just a ruined arch and the stumps of the pillars that once supported the church roof. The rooks haunt it and the hills are all around. Dafydd, I think, would be pleased that he is remembered by everybody in Welsh-speaking Wales, above all by Shanko the Shepherd.

But in Wales, and in other smaller countries, they cherish their great literary men as acts of faith. Or if they haven't got any themselves, annex anyone handy—especially if they happen to be world-famous English authors. Turkey is a case to point. I can't claim to have read deeply in modern Turkish literature; I'm sure there must be some marvellous poetry around in Istanbul and Ankara if I only knew where to look. If so, the Turks are in the same position as the Welsh with Dafydd ap Gwilym. How can we convince the world that in him we have a world-beater? We are also in the same position as the young man whom I met in my favourite Turkish city, Izmir (the Smyrna of old), who was devoted to a mysterious figure he called the Great Magnum.

I was sitting on my balcony on the upper story of the Hotel Babadan at the magic hour of six o'clock when the noise of the taxis, equipped with the world's loudest radios, was muted and the call to prayer sounded from the multitude of minarets that rise from the old city, giving it the look of a gigantic pin-cushion. The whitewashed, red-roofed houses climb the steep hills, sown with a myriad starry lights. On the roof of the apartment house across the road from us a young couple came out to enjoy the cool air that the evening brings flowing in from the sea. A string of washing was stretched between two chimneys, but the couple sat down on a double-seated swing. He held the rope in his hands and they swayed slowly, smiling at each other, floating high over the city amongst the washing. Two doves alighted on my balcony rail, with soft, grey plumage and black rings around their necks. They kept up a gentle coo-ing. It was the hour sacred in the Middle East to the indiscreet confidence.

My door opened and a worried young man appeared. I recognised him as the gentleman who had walked into my room at 5 a.m. that morning. Dramatically he had smitten himself on the forehead as I sat up in bed and then rushed out again, with a cry of anguish that went straight to the heart.

'May I speak to you, sir? I am in a position described by your author, the Great Magnum. It is because I regard the Great Magnum as your finest writer that I take courage to come to you—his works are full of these sort of happenings and because you are English you will immediately understand. This is what the Great Magnum would surely write about.'

I decided not to try to explain to a worried young man on a roof-top at Izmir the differences between Welsh and English, but who on earth was the Great Magnum? I waited for enlightenment.

'First, sir, I was not in your room last night for any naughty purpose, I am not a thief; my thoughts are, I do not know how, always running upon one lady. I am the night clerk at this hotel and therefore you have not yet seen me. But I am not what I seem to be.' (He gave me a smile compounded of dazzling white teeth and infinite self-pity.) 'I am an intellectual. I know Keats and T. S. Eliot and I propose to become a student at your

London University. But for this I need money, so that is why I am here, disguising myself as a night clerk. I save every penny.

'Now, when you are saving every penny you have no money for love. Yes, here in Izmir, for the middle classes—to which I am proud to belong—you need money for love.

'If you look across the road you will see the Apartments Meltam. These are very famous in Izmir, for here live the rich men who make money out of currants; and Mr Shabuz is a very rich man because in England you are always eating currant buns and this makes Mr Shabuz richer than ever. And his daughter, Miss Shabuz, is therefore very rich. She is the pearl of the Apartments Meltam.'

'Ah, my dear chap, I see now,' I said, 'you are perhaps engaged to Miss Shabuz.'

'That is a terrible irony, sir, worthy of the Great Magnum. Her father is rich, I am an intellectual middle-class student. He would never consent. He keeps her well guarded.'

'But how is that? Are you not all free and Western now in Turkey?'

'We are indeed. Everything is as it is in England except Mr Shabuz has not heard of all the wonderful reforms and therefore Miss Shabuz does not dance so like your modern girls. But one morning she comes with her father to the hotel, so I leave a copy of the "Ode to the Nightingale" on the desk and next day she lays a red carnation on my desk in return, and therefore I am overjoyed.'

I was also overjoyed as I listened, for clearly the fascinating language of flowers and secret signs described by Lady Mary Wortley Montagu back in the early eighteenth century has not completely died out. It must have been handed on for generations on the women's side of noble Turkish families for, after all, the seraglio as an institution was still going strong up to 1918, and many Turkish grandmothers of today—if they are into their seventies—might have languished in those elaborate birdcages of wood and marble lining the shores of the Bosphorus, where the rich Pashas kept their wives hidden from prying eyes.

It was the custom, once a week, for the ladies to drive in closed carriages, guarded by the strict wardens of the seraglio, to the pleasure grounds known by the charming name of the Sweet Waters of Asia. The gardens look a little woebegone today, with a Coca-Cola sign or two and a dusty football pitch, but sixty years back they were surrounded by cypresses and nightingales sang in scented bushes above the clear springs that ran through the grass down to the swift-flowing Bosphorus.

The harem ladies would picnic on the green sward, but the dangers of arrest did not prevent daring young men from haunting the outskirts of the Sweet Waters and endeavouring to make contact at long range with some entrancing young creature behind the backs of the guards. In the days when the Sultans still ruled with full power in old Constantinople discovery could result in the bold lover being quickly strangled with the bowstring and the erring lady ending up in a sack in the Bosphorus. The risk added savour to the silent dialogue which was carried on mainly with flowers, according to Lady Mary. Every flower or small object you picked up had a secret meaning, and you learnt this symbolic language in the seraglio. Even pieces of coal or soap, or a match, could express the passions.

A piece of soap in the lady's hand meant, 'I am sick from love.' The gentleman showed a piece of coal in return, signifying, 'May I die and all my years be yours'—steam coal obviously and not anthracite!

If you were a real expert, you purchased a bunch of flowers— the lady had already come provided—and idly flung yourself down on the grass and pretended to admire the scenery and smelt the flowers. The negro guards could not stop this conversation going on behind their backs. She, for example, would pick up a white lotus from her bunch which signified, 'Am I not pretty?'

He replies with a flower of paradise, meaning, 'You are lovelier than the houris of Korkham.'

She shows a rose: 'Do you love to look on me?'

He hurriedly picks up a lily in return: 'As the tiger lily loves to gaze on its own shadow.'

A rosebud pulled apart: 'Would you die for my sake?'

He pulls off the head of a geranium: 'I would submit my neck to the bowstring without a murmur.'

So the flower talk went on; the discreet but desperate lover opening his hand to show a pearl and a clove lying side by side: 'Fairest of the young, you are as slender as the clove. You are an unblown rose, have pity on my passion.' Happy the lover who at a distance saw the lady quietly pick up a straw to say, 'Suffer me to be your slave.'

And the red carnation so brazenly laid by Miss Shabuz on the desk of my love-dazed night receptionist? It meant, 'I have singled you out as my chosen one.' He hurriedly explained the sequel to me.

'So we exchange signs. I say with a flower, "Ah, you mock me, how can I believe all this when I have no money?"

'She says with a carnation and a rose, "Tomorrow at five o'clock go up to the empty apartment at the roof of your hotel. All will be sleeping and from my window of the Apartments Meltam I will give you undoubted and undying proofs of my love for you."

'So I rush up to this balcony at five o'clock in the morning at dawn. You will understand with what eagerness I have been waiting for this moment, with what joy I run up the stairs with my shoes in my hand, so I will not disturb the proprietor. Alas, alas, no one has told me that this room has been let for the first time—to you, sir! You are snoring. I recoil in horror. I am unable to go on to the balcony, and only a few minutes ago Miss Shabuz has come from her apartment and looked at me with a stony face and passed on. She is insulted. What a tragedy! Is this the end? I must give up my dreams and go back to T. S. Eliot. Do you not agree here is a story worthy of the Great Magnum. The Great Magnum, yes, he would have understood. It is clearly in the stars, I must go to London University and not to the Apartments Meltam. Perhaps it is better so!'

The Great Magnum? As the young man left my balcony in resigned sorrow, I knew at last to whom he referred—Somerset Maugham. Of course! Names like Maugham and my own Vaughan present an insoluble puzzle to Continental pronunciation. I have found myself introduced at a French gastronomic banquet as 'the célèbre Thomas Wagram'—although dear André Simon made the most acceptable transformation of my first name when he called me on the air 'Vineyard Vaughan-Thomas'.

Still, the Great Magnum and Dafydd ap Gwilym would both have appreciated the woes of the young man of Izmir, but what would Wordsworth have done with it? Nothing, for this sort of experience lay totally outside his grasp and interest. The world can be neatly divided into two sorts of people—those who are basically Wordsworthian, believing that Nature with a capital N is best left unaltered or at least only gently twisted to service of man, and the Magnumites, who don't mind what you do with old Nature as long as you make Man snug and comfortable. My trouble is that I am always a Wordsworthian in the country and a Magnumite in town.

Even at the top of that green ridge far above Strata Florida, sitting on Tika's back with Shanko the Shepherd at my side and the wilderness around me, I could not escape from my dilemma. For we had come to a point where the great change that is coming over the whole mountain world of Wales was dramatically illustrated. Down the track away from us to the south a jeep was drawn up, loaded with barbed wire. From here southward the wilderness was going to be fenced in. The sheep farmers had gone and the Forestry Commissioners had moved in. The whole vast area was going under trees—the dark regiments of the conifers were on their way northward to swallow up the wild, free open ranges.

I cannot blame the Forestry men. The farmers had started to retreat from the hills before the trees began their conquering march. The 1920s were the critical years. Life had become too hard in the lonely places and the young men and women started to desert the hills. As one keen Welsh agriculturist lamented to me, 'If only the cheap motor-car and television had come twenty years sooner, we'd have kept all the hills under sheep.'

The Forestry brings cash and employment into the rural fastnesses, but with it come roads and dark groves of fir trees all destined for pulp-mills, turning out the paper our cities swallow at a gigantic rate for the world of cheap magazines. To me, the Forestry represents the city's triumph over the land, the advance of the Magnumites.

Away to the north-east, however, the wilderness still lay untouched, unchanged. Shanko and Mr Hughes were disciples of Wordsworth and led us onwards away from the fences to the 'peace that lies (for a few years longer at any rate) among the lonely hills'.

So, in a fold in the vast, open ranges, near the spot where the River Towy has its source in a wide bog of treacherous soppiness and menace, we came to the deserted mountain farm of Moel Prysgau. Biddy is a good leader; she made us all unsaddle while she checked over the horses. Legs all right, no saddle sores, Tika recovered after her plunge into the morass? A breather was indicated and we sat on the ruined wall near the old farm and looked around.

Shanko and Mr Hughes would turn back here and our new guides, the brothers Tom and William Roberts, were ready and waiting for us on their ponies. They farmed in Blaen Glasffrwd— men who had lived all their lives on the hills and who knew every inch of this country. The sun was warm and gentle on the worn stones of the old yard as they talked of the life they and Shanko had led in the past. Thirty years ago Moel Prysgau was still living and sheep were the centre of the world of the Shanko, Mr Hughes and the Roberts brothers.

'Ah, boy, you wouldn't know what a shepherd's life was,' said Shanko, 'until you went gathering under Mr Edwards, Nantystalwyn. You remember how we used to be in the kitchen for a cup of tea at four o'clock in the morning, where the hearth rested on the naked rock. Aye, and you had to duck your head to dodge the sides of bacon hanging from the ceiling. We'd all ride out to the top of the bank in the dark and Mr Edwards would shout, "Start the drive, boys, as soon as there's light enough to tell a sheep from a dog."

'. . . And the dipping in the Towy Fechan. Oh, there were some pools so deep we could throw the sheep in from five feet up and they had to jump three feet to get back out of the water.

' . . . And the people at Tyddyn Fechan. The old maids lived there for thirty years and didn't speak to each other. They even walked ten miles to different chapels, one would set off to the south to go to Soar and the other walked down to Tregaron, carrying a bag of white pebbles to drop behind her so that she could find her way back in the mist. They used to communicate by notes pushed across the table.

'. . . And the old horse we used to supply to bring the minister up to Soar y Mynydd Chapel. He used to be there waiting at Llandovery station and all the minister had to do was to get on his back, drop the reins and leave it to the old horse, who would plod up on his own every inch of the way while the minister composed his sermon on the horse's back. And you could tell from the sermon what sort of a journey he'd had of it!'

The old world of pastoral solitude came back to me as they talked and made the farm of Moel Prysgau seem even more lost and lonely; even a little eerie. The roof was still on it, the windows unbroken and the door locked. But the barns and sheep-pens were open and deserted and my steps echoed as I walked into the old mangers, worn smooth by generations of Welsh ponies. Outside stood the one big tree in the whole of the wilderness, with a huge crow's nest hanging in the boughs. The crows had flapped slowly away as we came splashing into the yard across the rapid, tumbling stream.

A ghost farm with no one coming to meet you. Only a year back I had tramped through this country with a rucksack and a lightweight sleeping-bag. I had snuggled down in the barn, but I never slept a wink. I'm not a superstitious man, but something very strange was calling around that house during the night, and I never dared get out of my sleeping-bag to look. It was a fox, maybe—these hills are full of them—but the plain truth is that I never dared open the door to find out. I am a rational man when I am in the daylight in crowded places and totally irrational when alone in deserted houses at night.

It was exactly the same, sleeping in that climbers' hut at Steall at the top of Glen Nevis. In the days just after the war it was even lonelier than Moel Prysgau—an old bothie that you reached across a rickety plank suspended over the roaring Nevis stream. The great mountains shut you in and you were five miles from the nearest human settlement. A noble waterfall plunged down from the Mamore Forest before the door, and the mists came and went over the 4,000-foot spur of the Ben to the north. The night before it happened my climbing companion and I had shared the hut with a group of buoyant, tough young climbers of the Scottish Mountaineering Club. We'd had an uproarious evening around the fire with the rain banging away at the windows.

One of the lads looked across at the wall and remarked, 'That rucksack is still there.'

'Wouldn't like to touch it,' said another and told us the story. A few weeks ago a climber had disappeared on the hills; a search party had failed to find him. Some suggested he might have staged a disappearance to dodge military service; others felt he might be lost up on the wild country that stretched away towards Rannoch Moor. In any case, there, on the wall, hung his rucksack that no one was in a hurry to touch.

At dawn next day the S.M.C. party went off down the glen and we climbed through the mists on the Mamores; we came back soaking wet to dry before a blazing wood fire, then upstairs to sleep in the loft with the rain pouring outside and the gutters spouting louder than the Steall waterfall. The darkness closed down and nuzzled at the windows. We slept fitfully—and then suddenly I was awake.

There were footsteps, I could swear, sounding in the room below. Soft footsteps that went across the room to the wall where the rucksack was hanging . . . and the outside door was firmly shut. The footsteps stopped, started again and then came slowly up the stairs. I sat bolt upright and shouted, 'Who is there?'

The footsteps sounded again, going slowly down the stairs, across the room and died away. And still that front door was firmly shut! I went trembling downstairs with a flashlight, followed by my companion in fright. The spotlight picked out the rucksack on the wall. It was unmoved and the front door unopened. The rain drove hard against the window-panes. We found no footprints, no trace of any visitor. Yet I could swear there *were* footsteps.

Or were there? In the rational light of morning we made all sorts of explanations to ourselves; the rain had sounded queerly to someone half awake; there had been rats under the floor-boards; old timbers had contracted in the damp weather. Of course, it must have been the imagination building a fantasy out of ordinary sounds in a strange setting. Thus we talked in the broad daylight, but we packed and went down the glen before it grew dark again.

Now the time had come to move on. We saddled up. Shanko and Mr Hughes stood at their ponies' heads to wave to us as we rode out of Moel Prysgau and left the old house once again to silence and loneliness. The crows circled over it and finally we went out of sight over the brow of the hill.

Again mile after rolling mile of grassy ridges, featureless to the newcomer, but full of signs and tracks for the brothers Roberts. Tika had learnt her lesson. She almost anticipated Tom Roberts's warning of 'soft spot there' and picked her way in a ladylike fashion through the damp patches.

This whole country rises steadily towards the north—most of it was now well over 1,500 feet. Sheep were scattered over it; they had a long tenure here, for the monks of Strata Florida had rights of pasture over the whole of this area. The Cistercians knew how to make money out of sheep. 'They were the only ones who did,' chuckled William Roberts. 'My brother and I never learnt the trick. It's the winters that are the trouble. You can be going along nicely, saying how mild everything is and building up your flock, and then—down comes the snow. The old ewes are cunning, they try to get in the shelter of something, a wall or a rock, but on a really bad winter like 1947 you can lose half of all you possess in one week of snow. It's like the South Pole up here then.'

'You are thinking of giving up, Mr Roberts?' I said.

Both brothers reined up in astonishment. 'Give up. Oh, never, and go and live somewhere else in some crowded old town perhaps, never! Here we were born and here we stay. Money can't buy this.' Will Roberts pointed ahead.

We had come up over the last green wave of the mountain and suddenly, almost beneath our feet, a great lake stretched away for miles amongst the treeless green slopes. The sun was out and the surface of the water absolutely still. We had crossed the watershed. The Teifi and Cardiganshire lay behind us. In front was Radnorshire and the Claerwen dam. Our troubles were over.

The Claerwen is the topmost, newest and biggest of the long

series of dams that has turned this secluded corner of mid-Wales into a miniature Lake District. At the Claerwen the country is still bleak and windswept, but as you follow the valley down to the east the woodlands come down to the water's edge and the dams lie against romantic crags and seem part of the wild hillside. They built them of stone sixty years ago for the glory of Birmingham. The Claerwen, in contrast, is a clean monolithic

The Claerwen dam

slab of concrete. At the dam the road begins, and for the last six hours I had almost forgotten that such a thing as a road ever existed. Here was a hard surface again beneath our hoofs, and the freedom of the wilderness disappeared as the horses made a clatter on the roadway.

In the middle of the dam a large car had drawn up. The boot was open and a splendid array of bottles spread in profusion on a cloth on the railings of the dam. In the middle of the road stood my old friend, Alderman Kinsey Morgan, glass in hand, a speech of welcome at the ready. Kinsey belongs to the old tradition of immediate public eloquence. Every occasion, even our symbolic crossing of the border into Radnorshire, demands an oration full of references to 'our beloved Wye, washing with its limpid waters, this cherished Radnorshire of ours'. Kinsey has the presence to make every word sound like a trumpet voluntary, even when he is simply telling you what a nice day it is. His eyes twinkle behind his glasses and he carries weight in every sense of the word. The whole performance is wrapped up in old-world courtesy.

I admit I enjoy the sheer sound of words, rolled out into sentences as long as steel bars. We are a bit ashamed of this sort of eloquence today. Our statesmen talk in Pinteresque, inconsequential, clipped phrases. They would shy away from the boastful splendours of the title of Sultan Murad that I admired in Istanbul: 'By the infinite grace of the great, just and all powerful Creator and the abundance of miracles of the chief of His prophets, Emperor of powerful Emperors, refuge of sovereigns, distributor of crowns to the Kings of the Earth, Keeper of the two Very Holy Cities, Governor of the Holy City of Jerusalem, Master of Europe, Asia and Africa, High King of the Two Seas, the Shadow of God upon Earth.' Only a Communist dictator could dare give himself such titles these days!

I am wrong. There was one radio and television personality who dared to use the lapidary phrase, the ringing sentence on the air and get away with it—Gilbert Harding. Gilbert, like Dylan Thomas, was a word-intoxicated man, but he drew his inspiration from the eighteenth century. His eloquence was Johnsonian and got its effect by balancing one rolling word against another, all backed by a voice as velvety as vintage port. He got his greatest effects, however, when he was in the full flight of insult.

Now, insult is an art in itself. I don't mean vulgar abuse; any navvy can do that. Nor yet the glittering wisecrack stiletto thrust that politicians employ when they are being polite to each other. I refer to the sort of thing that the old chief petty officers of the Royal Navy used to employ to perfection, in a situation such as confronted a padre with whom I was a mess-mate on a cruiser during fleet manoeuvres in the Mediterranean.

He had to be transferred by bosun's chair to an aircraft-carrier. This involved a perilous-looking swing on the end of a rope fastened to a pulley on the deck of the carrier. A pulling party of thirty husky A.B.s supplied the motive power, and if they didn't give a steady pull the unfortunate transferee might find himself being dunked in the sea during transit.

The captain saluted the padre, who started on his crossing. The chief petty officer cast a wary eye on the way things were going and suddenly saw the rope sagging. In a voice that rose far above the roar of the waves, he shouted to his crew, 'Pull, you spavined by-blows of the Chinese-born third wife of a Port Said marine, outfitter's bastard, pull—don't you realise you've got a reverend gentleman on the rope.'

They pulled with renewed vigour and fairly shot the padre up to the aircraft-carrier, like whipping a trout out of the Wye at the end of a long rod.

Gilbert could occasionally produce the same effect. It is hard to picture it, but for a short period around 1946 he was one of the BBC's Canadian representatives. He was on a train to New York when, at the border, he was handed one of those endless immigration forms which the Americans then delighted to inflict on their visitors. Gilbert filled in the form with mounting fury: 'Can you read? Can you write? Can you speak English? Are you Caucasian?' At the end was the question, 'Is it your intention to subvert the Government of the United States?' Gilbert seized his pen and wrote in large letters, 'Sole purpose of visit.'

He was out on to the cold platform in a matter of minutes.

Yet behind it all, he was the kindest of men. After every terrible explosion as often as not an apologetic note or a bouquet of flowers would go winging its way to the victim. It was impossible not to be furious with him, for half the time you were with him, or enchanted for the other half. He was a splendid eccentric who was always his own worst enemy.

I was driving in from Toronto airport a few years back with a friendly taxi-driver. We got talking about Britain and Britishers, and how strange some of them could be in a Canadian setting. He remarked, 'Queerest guy I ever met from your country was a guy called Harding.'

'Gilbert Harding?' I asked.

'Jeeze, you know him? Here, come and sit up front.'

Apparently my friend had been employed by a taxi firm in Toronto which Gilbert used on all occasions, and the driver had got on so well with him that he was always assigned to the job when Gilbert called up. Early one morning the phone rang at the garage. Gilbert was at the other end with an imperious request, 'Send someone around immediately.'

The supervisor turned to my driver, 'Looks as if Mr Harding's cut it fine for the 8 a.m. train to Montreal. You'll just about make it.'

The driver skidded up to the door of Gilbert's Jarvis Street flat, opened it and shouted, 'Mr Harding, you've got five minutes left.' Gilbert's voice came to him from the bedroom, 'Come up, my dear fellow.' The driver raced upstairs and rushed into the room, asking, 'Where are the bags, Mr Harding? Quick, to the train.' Gilbert was sitting up in bed, propped comfortably on the pillows, a novel in hand and a smile of welcome on his face.

'Train, my dear boy, train? Who said anything about a train? I just wanted somebody to come over and make me a cup of tea.'

As the driver said, 'You've got to hand it to a guy as cool as that!'

At this point Alderman Kinsey Morgan was handing us drinks as cool as Gilbert's request to the taxi-man. Kinsey is the last person in the world to practise the art of insult. His oratory is all directed at the smoothing away of difficulties even before they arise. Our small difficulty of a meal after our long ride was immediately solved in the grand manner. Kinsey pointed down the sheer side of the dam to a snug farm placed right under the great concrete slab that held back the whole weight of the Claerwen water.

'We have everything ready, a real Welsh spread in a real Welsh farm kitchen under the shadow of this splendid symbol of power. Ladies and gentlemen, to horse!'

Carreg Cwplau

Thus we set down to celebrate our crossing of the wilderness in the bright kitchen of the sheep farm of Mr Edwards, Carreg Cwplau. The peat fire burned steadily on the open hearth, the Welsh dresser was bright with blue china, the sides of bacon hung from the beams overhead and a splendid collection of shepherd's crooks was set in a frame on the wall. Mr Edwards owns the whole sweep of the hillsides to the southwards. He must be one of the few men in southern Britain who can look out from his front door and say, 'All is mine to the distant horizon.' Five thousand of his sheep are scattered over his own mountain. Overhead, every day of his life, he's got the vast

167

Claerwen lake holding ten thousand million gallons of water. What if that 182-foot stone and concrete slab gave way?

'It doesn't worry me in the slightest,' said Mr Edwards, 'for it is one of those things that will never happen. I saw them build it, and it's become part of the mountain for me like all the rest of them. A fox ran half-way up the Caban Coch dam once, when the hounds were after him! And here's another thought— this is the only water from the mountains of Wales that eventually finds its way to the North Sea. It goes first to Birmingham, then after they've finished with it into the River Trent and thus into the Humber. Queer, isn't it, a drop of water from my hills travelling right across southern Britain!'

'Now,' said Kinsey, 'we must have you enter Rhayader in style. I'll go on ahead and bring up the pony trekkers to escort you. In fact, I'll ride with you myself. Mr Edwards can show you a route over the hills that will take you clear of every road.'

We mounted, welcomed and well fed. Mr Edwards's track led up behind the dam eastwards along the edge of the mountain world. We had glimpses of the lakes far below. There were cars and buses crawling along the roads on the water's edge to remind us that we had come out of the true wilderness, but we still had the mountain air around us and a grassy track wandering ahead, dipping down to the second of the Elan dams and then up again to the final mountain before Rhayader. The horses had rested at Carreg Cwplau. Here was the place for a final burst of speed.

Away went Biddy with Felicity and Rowland at their heels. Their horses stretched out into the gallop. In a few minutes they were away over the brow of the hill. I felt Tika getting restless. Should I, too, try the gallop.

'Come on, old girl,' I said to Tika, 'we'll show them.'

Tika began gear-changing; up into the trot safely, now into the canter. We were doing well; I even looked down and enjoyed the feeling of isolation from the roadbound tourists far beneath. 'Ah, poor conventional, purblind, car-softened fugitives from the concrete and tarmac wildernesses of suburbia,' I exulted as we gathered speed, 'what do you know of the country you think you are seeing? Here we are, riding high, over a Wales you can never understand! Larks singing overhead and old Tika going up into the gallop. This is living such as you'll never get, glued to your transistors in your mini-car mobile prisons!'

Of course, I didn't formulate the sentences with such precision, for I was now deeply concerned with staying in the saddle. Tika was also intent on proving that she, too, had not forgotten how to put her best foot forwards. We thundered after the rest. We came over the brow of the mountain world. The lush valley of the upper Wye lay below to welcome us with a pattern of fields after the free, open spaces of the now-conquered hills.

At the valley bottom Kinsey had rallied his pony trekkers. He himself was mounted on a mettlesome hunter and bounced nobly ahead of the procession like Napoleon leading his troops back to Paris after the triumphs of Austerlitz. We clattered into the main square and reined back beneath the memorial clock, which remains—in spite of the strictures of Mr John Betjeman— the pride of the little town of Rhayader. Kinsey swept off his cloth cap with a gesture that seemed to give us the freedom of the town and most of Radnorshire in perpetuity:

'Ladies and gentlemen, you have come to your journey's end for the day. Your trials are behind you, the hospitality of the Castle Inn is before you. What sense lies in wasting more time in the saddle? Bold riders across our unbeatable mountains, the champagne waits.'

We could hear the popping of the corks in the very sound of Kinsey's voice.

169

7

Our expedition regrouped at Rhayader. Biddy Williams carefully checked over every one of our horses. Even a few days on horseback had made me aware of the endless anxieties that lie at the back of the horseman's mind. Will his mount go lame, cast a shoe, develop any one of those ghastly ailments, from glanders to thrush, catalogued at the beginning of this book? And what can he do about them if the worst happens? Vets are busy people and blacksmiths are now rare birds in a mechanised countryside. The rider must carry a vast store of knowledge in his head. Non-mechanical people like myself can drive cars almost without looking inside the bonnet—we have an enormous garage industry, which depends on our ignorance, to come to our rescue. But once you buy yourself a horse you also buy yourself a cantankerous relative, a demanding friend, a chemist's shop, a library, a continual interest in the price of oats, a part share in any field that's handy, a trailer—there's no end to the extraordinary ramifications horse-ownership brings in its train.

I confess that I had been nourishing a dream as we rode up from St David's. I'd got to know Tika and established an understanding, for the first time in my life, with a horse. This was something new to me. There have been animals in my life before, but mainly on a small scale. Nothing so gigantic as a horse. Not even a dog, for I have been a city-dweller and I cannot get rid of the feeling that a dog is caged in a city. He's a countryman's friend. I have a particular delight in sheep-dogs. They seem not to be mere pets but to be colleagues, fellow workers, people in their own right. I would adore owning, or should I say going into partnership, with a sheep-dog. But in a town—no! Here I turn to the cat.

The horse—even Tika—is out. Where could I put her in London? Clearly if I decided to make an alliance with Tika I would have to acquire a field from somewhere. All right; I might move out from Hampstead to the Green Belt. And if I did that, what was the point in commuting? I had better give up broadcasting and television, maybe earn my living as a hotelier in some pleasant country hide-out. Or why stop around London? Surely it would be best to up-anchor completely and start up as a sheep farmer in Wales, perhaps on these Radnorshire hills that we were now getting ready to traverse. 'Ah, be careful, my boy,' said I to myself, 'you are running into danger.'

I smothered my overnight dream of allying myself with Tika immediately. But how could I get rid of it altogether? It stayed with me as we mounted under the memorial clock of Rhayader and set off to ride north through the rest of Radnorshire. One day, even at the end of this ride, I would consign London to perdition and settle down as a horse-riding sheep farmer amongst these high hills.

For how tempting they looked ahead of us in the early-morning sunlight; soft, strokable hills, with lost farms amongst their secret folds. We went out on to the long escarpment that bars the Wye valley to the east. The land climbs up to about 1,700 feet, but it has not got the menace and savagery of the wilderness to the west, which we had mastered the day before.

This was wonderful riding country. The forest had moved in over a great deal of it and I began to get that 'don't fence me in' feeling, especially when I looked eastwards towards the little hamlet of Abbey Cwm Hir. The new plantations were thick in that direction, but the ruins of the abbey are still there. The Cistercians again were the people who first brought the sheep to these parts but hardly a stone is left of the great church built by the monks. Today all you see of Abbey Cwm Hir are the

Abbey Cwm Hir

trees that shade the few arches that remain above ground; an inn with the strange name of The Happy Union and a signboard showing a Welshman with a leek in his hat riding a goat; and a fantastic Victorian mansion of splendid spikiness, the original seat of the Fowler family who dominated Radnorshire in the old days. Richard Fowler left his name over the whole countryside. There's a Fowler's Cave, Fowler's Horse-block, Fowler's Chair. And a rhyme which every Radnorshire child learns in his cradle:

> Alas, alas, poor Radnorshire,
> Never a park, not even a deer,
> Never a squire of five hundred a year,
> Save Richard Fowler of Abbey Cwm Hir!

We were on our way to Fowler's Chair, a great stone on the edge of the long escarpment. We had guides—Kinsey Morgan clapped his hands in the grand manner and the whole countryside assembled to greet us along the route, including the school choir of the lonely village of Bwlch-y-Sarnau, who were assembled in the middle of the road, singing Welsh folk-songs.

The road is still something you can live with in these parts—in the same way as in Ireland. You can stop and talk in the middle of it on week-days without fear of suddenly waking up in hospital. And at Bwlch-y-Sarnau, Mr and Mrs Thomas Davies were waiting with Chip, the sheep-dog.

'A working dog,' said Mr Davies proudly. 'I don't want one of those pampered cup-winners that are only good performing in Hyde Park. Chip will beat them all if we only could get them up here on his home ground.'

Chip would certainly outjump them. He raced alongside us, taking hedges and wire fences like a horse in the Grand National. So we shook ourselves free of roads and plantations and came out on to the open moorland, the Wye valley to the west, the high plateau of the Radnor Forest sealing us off from the English border to the east. There was a little dampness in the air. The sun had gone in behind a veil of thin cloud as we came up to a mound on the ridge.

'The Sounding Tump,' said Mr Davies. 'They say there's silver treasure hidden in it, and all sorts of people have had a shot at digging it out.'

Indeed, the side of the tump was pitted with small holes.

'But there's another thing about this. They say that if you stamp upon it in the right way you'll hear the tump echo with a hollow groan or else you'll get a peal of thunder.'

Rowland was the heaviest member of our party and he, therefore, dismounted and carried out the experiment. I can never resist trying all these ancient legendary challenges. I wish I could report spectacular results. The tump certainly sounded hollow, but there was no immediate flash of lightning or crash of thunder, until, as Rowland got back into the saddle, there came a low growl from the eastern sky. Of course, it was a muggy day; thunder was in the air. And a good five minutes had elapsed between Rowland's challenge and the heaven's making even a muttered grunt of protest. Scientifically, we cannot chalk up a victory to the Sounding Tump—but it had clearly done its best.

So had the grassy track ahead. This was perfect riding country, lifted high over the surrounding landscape, soft going for the horses. A mile farther on we came to Fowler's Chair—once again a landmark lived up to its name, for this natural stone *was* shaped like an armchair and a comfortable one at that. Chip and the Davieses turned back at this point. 'You've got five miles of pure riding pleasure ahead,' said Mr Davies. 'Radnorshire can give you nothing better.'

Indeed, there are very few parts of the Welsh hills that can beat it for the man on horseback.

The view was vast, inspiring. The Wye had gone and the valley of the Upper Severn had taken its place; a pattern of green fields with the silvery river winding through it. Beyond, all the mountains of Central Wales; Plynlimon, Cader Idris. the Berwyns—rolling away in glory to the north. We all said to ourselves, 'Galloping country', and away we went. Yes, even old Tika. For I now felt that I had mastered the business of changing gear on horseback. Once you are mentally attuned to the sudden change of motion that occurs between the trot and the canter you're away.

Our whole cavalcade was off in a flash; Tika, naturally, at the tail-end! Over the first skyline went Biddy and Rowland, racing all out. Tika and I were also as 'all out' as we could manage. This was the classic pleasure of riding—wind in the hair, thunder of hoofs on the soft turf . . . and then, crash! I was on the soft turf myself. Tika pulled up. The thunder of hoofs faded away in the distance. Once again I had experienced the supreme humiliation of falling off your horse.

A soft fall, agreed. All I got was a slight jolt and a few stars in the eyes, but the sense of humiliation remained. There are many worse moments in life than falling off a horse and I've experienced a good many of them, from making a fool of myself at a public speech to proposing to the wrong girl. But falling off your horse has a special feeling of personal insult about it. Maybe the speed of the accident doubles the humiliation. One moment you are riding in pride, lifted high above the surrounding countryside. No wonder the feudal knights felt that they were the lords of creation. Mere footsloggers seem vassals and serfs below you. Everyone who has to read medieval history should learn to ride, for unless you do you cannot understand that contempt for the farmer, the merchant and the priests who had to walk or go horseless through the world that runs through our history from King Authur to the Battle of Bosworth. It took gunpowder to blow the horseman off his superior social perch.

But once let the horseman fall in full career and his whole mystique disappears. The archers at Agincourt must have had a malicious if deadly pleasure in toppling the horse-proud French knights. I picked myself up and thanked my lucky stars that the rest were over the brow of the hill and could not see my public shame.

Yet, I cannot think why I, of all people, should feel ashamed of falling off a horse. After all, I have spent most of my life as a radio and television commentator, and I maintain that success in our strange profession depends on developing a face of brass. Every time you speak into a microphone or look into a camera you are in danger of public collapse.

My whole career at the BBC was punctuated by the terror of making one of those ghastly slips of the tongue which are so lovingly collected by connoisseurs. I had only been six months in the Corporation when Commander Thomas Woodroofe 'lit up' the Fleet. I had come up to London overnight to attend a meeting of the Outside Broadcasts department and found the whole of Broadcasting House in mourning. This was in the days when we were at the height of our prewar Reithian period. We were all indoctrinated with the theory that broadcasting was a sort of educational crusade conducted according to the rules of the Higher Civil Service.

Commander Woodroofe, however, had been brought up in the breezier atmosphere of the Royal Navy, where a few pink gins before battle are part of our fighting tradition. He had been assigned to cover the great fleet review at Spithead, to commerate the coronation of George VI. This was in the days when we still had battleships. As night fell every ship afloat would switch on its searchlights and one of the most glorious fireworks displays in our recent history would tear the skies apart in honour of the new King. Tommy was at the summit of his profession when he made his fateful journey to Portsmouth to return to his old ship, H.M.S. *Nelson*.

He was our first professional commentator, the man who invented so many of the techniques that all broadcasters and television commentators now take for granted. He had just done a superb description of the Coronation procession through London. 'Now,' said Sir John Reith, 'let us see what you can do for the Navy.'

Tommy, indeed, 'did' for the Navy in a way that electrified the country. As night fell he climbed up to the fighting top of the *Nelson*. But when the announcer cued over to him, he revealed an unexpected staccato utterance and a curious attachment to a single phrase—'The Fleet's lit up!' True, other phrases were freely if somewhat erratically interspersed: 'The whole scene is a mass of fairly lights! . . . It's gone . . . . There's nothing between me but sea and sky. . . .' And then again, with splendidly uncertain emphasis, 'The Fleet's lit up!'

Swiftly, on an order from the Highest Quarters, Tommy's voice was faded, leaving a stunned Britain behind him. Could this really be the Voice of the BBC? We have had many more puzzling broadcasts since then, including the memorable appearance of Mr Brendan Behan, who faced the cameras at a time, as the BBC tactfully put it, 'when he was not quite his normal self'. But this was the first time that the Voice of the BBC had spoken through a pleasant haze of pink gin.

People spoke of the 'disaster' in the hushed tones used when a family hears of an unexpected death or an unmentionable social scandal. I met Tommy coming up Portland Place, getting ready to face the music. I murmured, 'Good luck.' Tommy managed a grin, 'I'll need it', and tipping his bowler at a jauntier angle, he marched with the courage of a naval officer brought up in the Beatty tradition, to confront the biggest row that ever rocked the smooth façade of Broadcasting House. A whole string of far worse disasters has occurred since, but the Illumination of the Fleet in 1937 remains the classic.

We had announcers in those days who also added to the general gaiety by their unexpected skids in front of the microphone. Didn't the impeccable Stuart Hibbard announce that Mount Etna was in eruption with streams of molten lager flowing down the mountainside. Then there was the splendidly confidential statement put out by the BBC on the eve of the Royal Wedding, urging the public to buy the official pamphlet giving 'full biological details of the happy pair'. Every week brought new gems to the collection, from the commentator who described Princess Margaret as 'looking radiant in an off-the-hat face' to the celebrated misreading of the news-flash announcing the removal of the Stone of Scone from Westminster Abbey. The eager announcer seized the typed slip and read, 'The stone was, of course, brought from Scotland by Edward ist.' Through the glass panel he could see consternation on the producer's face and hurriedly corrected himself: 'I beg your pardon. I should, of course, have said Edward Iced.'

My own worst disaster happened at Birkenhead, when I was doing the commentary on the launching of one of our big new liners for television. The Queen Mother was performing the ceremony with her usual effortless charm and I had made careful arrangements with my producer about the points at which I would come in with my description of the scene.

'Cue into the Queen Mother,' he told me, 'then as soon as she pulls the lever for the champagne bottle, and the ship starts to move down the slipway, keep quiet—not a word. We'll have marvellous shots of the hull gathering speed under the cranes, there'll be cheering, the band playing and the tugs hooting—grand stuff for TV! Then as soon as you see her safely afloat, don't wait for my cue on headphones, come in straight away and throw the whole dictionary at the screen.'

I kept strictly to my part of the bargain. We had a splendid picture of the Queen Mother stepping on to the dais. I remained silent as she pronounced the time-honoured formula and sent the champagne crashing against the bows. Down the slipway went the hull exactly as planned. It took to the water in the midst of a vast welcoming uproar, she was safely afloat—as in I came, full blast, with my commentary.

Alas, I had reckoned without the occupational disease of all TV producers—itchy fingers! My producer, settled snugly in front of his control panel offstage, could not resist seeing what his other cameras were showing. Camera One was doing its duty by concentrating on the liner, but Camera Three showed a delightful close-up of the Queen Mother. The temptation was too strong. He forgot all his instructions to me, punched up the picture from Camera Three and filled the screen with the Queen Mother as I came in on the liner with all the fervour that I could command: 'And there she is, the whole vast bulk of her!'

After that, why should I be ashamed of falling off a horse?

In any case, the others were out of sight. My shame was unobserved and that made it no shame at all. Tika stood obediently by as I remounted. Together we put on a brave front as we cantered over the brow to join the others. 'I couldn't resist stopping to look at the view,' I explained. Which in a sense, was true, although I was careful not to add that my stop had been compulsory.

We cantered along the edge of the hills with the whole of mid-Wales spread out below us. It seemed as if we were being dragged back to the prison house when, at last, we had to turn away from the wide horizons and follow the track down for 1,500 feet into the Severn Valley.

But I wrong Llandinam to suggest that this tiny hamlet, where we emerged on to the valley floor, gives any feeling of fencing you in. This is still deep country with no trace of industry. You are all the more surprised, therefore, to see, alongside the main road at the point where it runs along the unsullied Severn, the statue of the man who could claim to be the most typical Welsh industrialist of the nineteenth century. The puzzled tourists from England stop their cars and look up at the stocky, defiant figure on his stone pedestal. He doesn't condescend to gaze out over the green hills around him. He is concentrating on the plans of a new railway, a new coal-pit and calculating every penny of the available profit. The inscription on the pedestal says with proud simplicity 'David Davies'. Llandinam was his birthplace, the railway lines of mid-Wales his springboard to fortune, and the coal-pits of the Rhondda his apotheosis.

Today his memory may be dim amongst the younger generation of South Walians, but when I first came down from Oxford I found my life tangled up with this masterful Victorian, who covered the top end of the lonely valley of the Rhondda with rows of dark miners' cottages, slashed railway lines all over South Wales and left a vast fortune to his sons and heirs— money which, in a strange way, came to fertilise an incredible variety of odd projects from running unemployed clubs and printing rare books to collecting a marvellous gallery of French Impressionist paintings.

David Davies made his impact on me when I came down from Oxford in the early thirties. These were the grim days of the Depression, and I was delighted to seek shelter within the hospitable walls of the National Library of Wales at Aberystwyth. There my first task was to catalogue the enormous mass of papers deposited by the Davies family. I sat in a vast hall lined with books that nobody came to consult, with a view of the wilderness of Plynlimon out of the far window. The National Library is a magnificent affair, created in the massive Edwardian classical style of Lutyens's New Delhi and planted on a hill in one of the most inaccessible sea-side towns of mid-Wales. North Wales refused to allow it to be built in anglicised Cardiff. South Wales placed an embargo on impoverished Bangor, so the nation's literary and manuscript treasures hang like Mahomer's coffin half-way between north and south in Aberystwyth.

Every morning I walked up the hillside and sat in front of a vast collection of letters and legal documents, spread out in silence on a beautifully polished oaken table.

I lived the scholar's life, lost in the monastic atmosphere of a library. If I had possessed the true historian's temperament I would be there to this day, digging deep into lost letters and long-unopened files. Before me I had the raw bones of the drama of the South Wales coalfield. It was as exciting, moving and tragic as any of the super-screen epics of the opening up of the West. As I turned over the leases, the solicitors' deeds, the opinion of eminent counsels and the geologists' reports, the picture opened up before me of the still untrampled, lonely valleys of the upper Rhondda, as the old travellers described them just over a hundred years ago—the salmon leaping in the clear streams, the woodlands alive with the cuckoo calling in the stillness of early summer, and far overhead the dark mountain brows flecked with sheep. David Davies was still offstage, the lad from Llandinam who had already made his first fortune out of railway construction. Under that unravished countryside of the Rhondda lay coal. And in 1864 the coal and the money of David Davies came together and the Rhondda of my youth—that astonishing mix-up of tips, mining head-gear, welfare halls, chapels, billiard saloons, pubs and endless rows of two-storied, stone built terraces stuck, in defiance of gravity, against damp hillsides—began its birth pangs.

There before me were the leases of the small hill farms with a Klondike of coal under each one of them. I could picture the first wagons arriving, loaded with the tools of the burly navvies who were to drive the railway over the sheep-walks and through the uncut woodlands; the cottages going up on the fields around the farmhouses, the river already running black with the rubble thrown out from the pit shafts as they sank down, yard after yard, through the hard rock in search of the money-spinning seams that the geologists knew were there, some seven hundred feet below.

By 1866 there was a film-maker's tension all over the valley. The coal had not been struck. David Davies was almost at the end of his financial resources. Thirty thousand pounds had been poured down his mine shafts and there was still no sign of the Rhondda Number Three seam. Davies called the men together. He told them frankly, 'Boys, I'm sorry, I cannot go on here any longer. There's some grand coal here and I believe we are close to it—but I can't go on.' He paid out the wages and when the final pay-packet was handed over, added, 'That leaves exactly half a crown in my pocket.'

'We'll have that, too,' one man shouted. David Davies shrugged his shoulder, 'Take it', and tossed him his last half-crown.

But, as always happened in a film epic, the men had been impressed by Davies's dauntless courage. They decided to give him one week's work free. The master had gone off to supervise the unfinished Whitland railway, convinced that he had lost his hard-earned fortune. Bankruptcy was staring him in the face. Then on 9 March 1866 William Thomas, the foreman of the railway, suddenly saw an excited figure making its way along the embankments and brandishing a piece of paper. It was David Davies with a telegram. 'William, I'll not take forty thousand pounds for this piece of paper. They've struck the seam at Cwmparc.'

Moses striking water from the rock in the wilderness did not produce a more spectacular result. From the seams of the Rhondda flowed the vast wealth of the Davies family and of the Rhondda in its heyday. I never saw that prosperous Rhondda. I came to the mining valleys created by David Davies when they were in ruin and despair. It was a curious twist of fortune. I soon realised that, much as I enjoyed the delights of the National

Library, I did not have the true patience and attention to detail that marks a librarian or research worker. Books and documents are perfect for the 'over fifties', but cannot hold you at hot-blooded twenty-five. I saw an advertisement for a job with the resounding title of 'Area Officer for the South Wales and Mon-

David Davies

mouthshire Council of Social Service', and within a month had deserted the academic seclusion of the National Library for the mining valleys of South Wales.

I got a shock. I had just spent six months in immagination in a world of boom, money-making and success. The Rhondda of old David Davies was a black gold-rush. My Rhondda turned out to be a waste land of deserted pits, unemployment queues, the means test and the dole. Coal had lost its magic and was starting its long decline. My job was to administer tiny Government grants to unemployed clubs. I should have found it all profoundly depressing and yet, in a curious way, I look back on this period in my life with affectionate nostalgia—as men regretted the trenches in the First World War.

South Wales in those days was a place apart. The stranger pictured it as a wilderness of slate-roofed houses leaning against coal-tips wedged into slots amongst the black mountains. Every man was supposed to be unemployed or else he sang melancholy hymns at rugby matches. Occasionally, as light relief, the funeral of Dai Jones Bookie passed the Welfare Hall (not yet paid for) and Capel Zion looked down in stern disapproval. Always the rain fell with the persistence of an endless sermon.

All true of that Rhondda of 1933—but on the surface only. The picture left out the one thing that made the whole thing bearable for me, the heart-warming comradeship of the miners. This made the Great Depression un-depressing. They knew you were sharing the anguish with them—you were their 'butty', one of 'the boys'.

So it was that I drove gaily through the Rhonddas, scattering Government grants with as lavish a hand as I dared. I rained £25 cheques on unemployed clubs to start W.E.A. classes, to set up cobblers' shops, to dig foundations for new huts and to foster a mysterious activity known as 'psychical training'—which turned out to be P.T.!

On one particularly wet and miserable day I found myself approaching the top end of one of the valleys, where the houses seemed to have been sprayed over the side of the mountain with a Flit gun, where the sheep scavenged among the garbage cans and where I had given the local unemployed club the regulation £25 grant.

The £25 was designed, in my mind, to launch a splendidly adventurous educational programme—lectures on foreign affairs, on English and Welsh literature, on Biblical criticism—in fact, on every subject which was held by the authorities in 1933 to be of vital importance to the well-being of the unemployed miner.

The chairman told me that he even had the local school-master—universally known for his interest in philosophy as Rhys the Mind—ready to start the classes as soon as the ink was dry on the cheque. I anticipated a murmur of happy intel-lectual activity as I entered the bleak lower regions of the decayed store which served as the club premises. They were deserted. I went up the rickety stairs to the second floor. No sign of life. Then on up to the third floor, where I was astonished to find the club members in a tight knot around the window, like bees swarming around their queen. The chairman spun round, gave a start, then advanced upon me with a hurriedly assumed smile of welcome.

'Mr Thomas bach, what a surprise! We were only saying yesterday that we hoped you would turn up today. In fact, the committee were unanimous about it.'

'But what's going on here, Mr Phillips?'

'Now, I'm glad you've put that very question, Mr Thomas bach. As a matter of fact—and I wouldn't conceal it from you for a moment—we've put some money on the dogs. We can see the track from the upper window here. The next race is due in five minutes, so the boys, very naturally, wanted to see how their money went.'

'But Mr Phillips, how could you have got the money to put on the dogs?'

'Mr Thomas, I'd better tell you the truth; it's your money we've put on, that twenty-five pounds you gave us.'

'Good heavens, Mr Phillips, but that's Government money!'

'Don't worry, Mr Thomas, we're on the winner. We can't go wrong. Dai Williams's brother is letting them out of the trap.'

The chairman took me by the arm across to the corner of the room, with the air of an old friend breaking the news of a sudden death in the family. He whispered, 'We had to do it, Mr Thomas bach, for to tell you the truth—no, to tell you the honest truth'—and here he lowered his voice—'we've had an unfortunate lapse.'

Mr Phillips paused, assuming that he had explained everything and that I was familiar with that great South Wales tradition, the Doctrine of the Unfortunate Lapse. But, seeing a puzzled look in my eye, he hurriedly continued, 'Well you know how it is yourself, Mr Thomas. Our treasurer—just a little confusion between red and black figures—lost his nerve. Last we heard of him was in Porthcawl, but he's sent us a most apologetic letter, poor dab, might have happened to any one of us. So you see, Mr Thomas bach, we had no option—it was the dogs or nothing with your grant. And, of course, when we get the money after the race we'll be meeting Rhys the Mind tonight, and I'll promise you one thing, we'll cascade culture around this place.'

'But what if you lose?'

The chairman gave me a wan smile, 'Well, Mr Thomas, you're one of the boys. We know you'll do your best for us. Of course, you will recommend another grant. After all, it *was* an unfortunate lapse.'

How could any feeling man refuse such an appeal? The chairman was right—it could happen to any one of us. Like a close-knit tribe, the local boys closed the ranks around an erring brother. They could console themselves with the thought that the Doctrine of the Unfortunate Lapse is universal. I have found it in full glory in Jamaica, in Ireland, in Pakistan; above all in Pakistan.

I remember a splendid, if rather exotic, example of the doctrine in action at Lahore. Now, Lahore may have been shorn of its glories since Partition in 1947, but it is still a city of ancient glamour with the airs of a capital. Every one of its conquerers has left a mark on it. The Moguls built great tombs and gardens of caged and scented air; the Sikhs added fortresses and domed temples; the British produced the most extraordinary collection of red-brick Gothic buildings to be seen outside Europe, a series of St Pancras stations 'gone native'. I should not cherish any affection for Lahore, for I first saw it at the lowest depth of its fortunes, when massacre and fire filled its streets and Muslims, Sikhs and Hindus fought around the old glories of the Citadel and Jahangir's Tomb. Like so much else in my life—from Belsen to the Congo—I keep my descents into the Inferno in the hidden corners of my mind. Should I dwell constantly on the horrors that have come my way in my reporting career, allowing them to sour my view of the essential decency of the human condition? They come back to haunt and overwhelm me at moments of unexpected recall—a strange smell, a photograph in a book, can send me back into the dark forest that surrounded Belsen, and I can see again the grim lines of barbed wire and the withered arms thrust through the cruel fences, like bare branches of a broken tree. . . . These memories must be exorcised by the commonplace. I understood the dilemma of the poor station-master in the miseries of the Partition massacres in Northern India. We saw a train come in with hardly a single passenger left alive in it. 'Oh, sir,' said the station-master in tears, 'it is hardly worth issuing tickets any more!'

So it was in Lahore. The city had been ravaged by fire and murder and yet, when the smoke and din died down, Lahore emerged again to exercise its charm, to make you forget the terror it had offered you only a few weeks before. The whole thing, you felt, had been an unfortunate lapse on a heroic scale. Our hosts of Radio Lahore, who had suffered personal tragedies in the massacres, exerted themselves to make us forget and forgive. Their hospitality was redoubled when I was joined by Louis MacNeice, the poet, and Jack Dillon, our BBC producer. Inevitably the last two names were telescoped and I gained a temporary glory from their impression that I was Dylan Thomas.

I sat on my balcony at Faletti's Hotel one hot afternoon as three earnest young men were ushered into my presence. They bowed. I bowed back, held my hands together in the approved position of welcome, and murmured 'Acha!' Tea came from nowhere, for in the great Indian subcontinent you are aware of a dark crowd of fluttering servants in the background, ready to whisk away your washing, bring in a bowl of flowers, clean your lavatory, or simply to appear with a smiling inquiry, 'Yes, sahib? I am here, sahib, always I am here.'

'Is there any hope of getting a copy of the morning's paper, Mohammed Said?'

'Oh, sir, no sir. Too much gurba is still in the city. Far better trust to God.'

'Well, I wasn't thinking of worrying the Almighty about such a trivial matter.'

'Oh, but I would, sir. Far better trust to God. He is a most capable fellow.'

As the tea was handed around the most earnest of my three visitors introduced himself, 'I am the leading young poet in Lahore in the English language. This is the second leading poet'—a spectacled young man stood up and bowed—'and this'—he pointed to my third visitor, who was trying to make himself inconspicuous with a self-deprecatory smile—'this is an ambitious young man whose poetry is not so good, but who wished to gaze on you. Mr Dylan Thomas, we bring you the homage of the poets.'

'I am afraid there is some mistake; I am a friend of Mr Thomas, but, alas, I cannot claim to be a poet.'

The leader of the deputation gave me a reproachful look, 'But in that case, why do you look so like one?'

I was, obviously, cast in the same role as the Commander-in-Chief of the Indian Army in the celebrated story which has been told in India about every C.-in-C. from Kitchener to the 'Auk'. The great man, so the story goes, was journeying by train across India, when there was the usual delay at a junction lost in the burning, featureless plains of the Ganges. The C.-in-C. got out and paced up and down in solitary state on the platform, guarded from a descreet distance by his A.D.C.

Two babu gentlemen, in dhotis and umbrellas, observed the splendid figure, consulted amongst themselves, and one of them then walked resolutely up to the C.-in-C. and tapped him on the shoulder.

'Excuse please. What time does next train leave for Bombay?'

The explosion of wrath sent the sacred cows scampering off the railway lines.

'But are you not station-master?' asked the babu.

'Of course I'm not the station-master, blast you . . . !'

The babu looked at the irate C.-in-C. with the calm born of long years of dealing with irrationally explosive administrators: 'All right, if you are not station-master—why walk so proudly?'

I ceased to walk proudly and immediately called Louis MacNeice to my rescue. Here at least was a genuine poet and one for whom they had the respect all Indians feel for the man of cultural achievement. Louis, that lone walker with the probing mind, brought the classicist's detachment to the warm chaos of India and Pakistan. His long, highly intelligent face gave him the right appearance of indrawn meditation. He was a yogi whose sacred books were Greek. India and Pakistan were his first experience of completely undisciplined life, and he enjoyed it as a don on holiday.

The deputation changed into a college tea-party. Talk, rambling and pleasant talk, is an end in itself on those hot afternoons in the Punjab when the heat of the day is dying and the mynah birds call in the trees—no need to make plans or order things. You can drift with the tide. So it seemed the most natural thing in the world that when our friends from Radio Lahore came to take us to the studio, the party should all go along together—the poets entering the estate car in careful order of precedence. And the talk continued as our car shouldered its way through crowded lanes and under overhanging balconies, decorated with woodwork cunningly carved by forgotten craftsmen.

We were pursued by the cries of the shopkeepers urging us to buy fake jewellery, sweet cakes, stationery, carpets and any old lump of cloth or metal that might be to hand. I have never solved the greatest mystery of the great subcontinent—how does the average Indian and Pakistani shopkeeper make a living? There are so many of them so close together, all selling exactly the same things.

Through the din, the donkeys and the water-carriers we entered a quarter where the ladies sat boldly on the latticed balconies.

'This' said my companion from Radio Lahore, 'is the gay part of the city; it survived every riot untouched.'

The ladies waved to him and he waved back. It was the same as it was in Kipling's day, when his Lalun had her house on the city wall—today the houses look out over gardens, for the wall has gone the way of all flesh.

'They know me here. I used to book the singers for Radio Lahore before we became Pakistan.'

'Do you mean to say the "ladies of the quarter" are invited to your studio?'

'We need them. Even today, in the Punjab, only the "professional women" practise the arts of music and poetry. The old tradition still survives of the cultivated courtesan, the sister of the remarkable women of Ancient Greece and Renaissance Rome. They had a definite status in society and were born in the quarter and into their profession. We go to book them whenever we have a concert on the air.'

(I had a momentary vision of the Head of the BBC's Variety Department ringing up Soho to fill a sudden gap in the Light Programme.)

'In the old days a man wasn't educated until he had learnt the arts from a professional. Rich men sent their sons to them to be instructed in manners.'

'Do they still do so?'

'Sometimes, but now we are free no doubt all will change. This may be the last time you will see and hear things like this. Our Minister has great plans; we will all be re-educated.' My friend sighed. 'Maybe I am too old to be re-educated; it will be a painful process. Lahore will no longer be the fountain-head of the best stories in India and Pakistan.'

189

We were now stuck in the narrow street between a wedding procession on one hand and a sweet-shop covered with flies on the other, so he told me a story—of a lady of the quarter. 'Let us call her Lalun, since that was the name of your Mr Kipling's lady. This, you understand, happened thirty years ago and Lalun was enchantingly beautiful. No one could sing or play the sitar or dance softly amongst the gold-embroidered divans of her musk-scented room as sweetly and seductively as could Lalun.

'So much beauty and youth could not go unworshipped for long. To Lalun's house came the talent of the city, the rich bunias, the poets, the newspaper editors, the pukka administrators, and with them a certain rich nabob, who owned far too much land for his own good and who poured out his wealth at her jewelled feet. He claimed the proud title of Lalun's chief lover, and for five happy years he gave her such presents, such parties, such rare pleasures, that the quarter had never seen the like before.

'Then one morning, at the end of a great and expensive feast, when the last of the guests had departed in the first of the tongas to awake, he said to Lalun, "Light of my heart, this is our last feast together. I have no more money; I have spent every rupee I had in the world in giving you pleasure. I do not regret it, for I have spent money in the best way in the world, in the worship of beauty. I have only one sorrow. My son, who is now at the Chief's College, will not go on to the University of Oxford in England. Good-bye, light of my heart."

'And he left Lalun—no, not to commit suicide, for that is not an Eastern habit except in Japan—but to take to his bed and die quietly and tactfully before his creditors could catch up with him.

'Then some weeks afterwards the sorrowing friends called to console the widow. "Of course, we must try to give your promising son his Oxford education," they agreed, "but where is the money to come from?" Unexpectedly, mysteriously, the money arrived and kept on arriving throughout the youngster's Oxford career. He returned four years later with his First, a credit to his college and to Lahore, and learnt for the first time what everyone in the city had long known—that it was Lalun who had paid for his education. Overwhelmed, he insisted that he and his mother should go to Lalun's house to thank her. "Tell him," said Lalun, when she heard of it, "that I will come after dark to see them at their house, for it is not right that a wife and a respectable woman should come to see me in the quarter."

'So in the cool of the evening, she, Lalun, the outcast rich and lowly, came to the house of the widow who was poor but proud. The two women embraced each other; the young man stammered his gratitude. When he had retired Lalun turned again to the mother. "We have done well to educate him, you and I," she smiled, "but we who know young men also know that his education is still not complete. For the memory and honour of your husband I assure you that, when he comes to the quarter, I myself will see to it that he will meet only the most refined and cultivated of all the young ladies."

'So it was arranged.'

'And the name of the young man?' I asked.

My companion murmured it softly, for it is a name that has now travelled far beyond the borders of the Punjab.

I heard that story nearly twenty years ago. I have not dared to return to Lahore since. Lalun and her sisters have no doubt left the studios, and maybe the quarter itself has given way to new, concrete tourist hotels.

Places remain in your mind in the form in which you first experience them. To go back is disappointment, and anticlimax. Thus it is that I never drive back into the Rhondda of today, with its bingo halls, new factories, advertisements of trips to the Costa Brava and chapels turned into social clubs without seeing, as on a palimpsest, the queues outside the labour exchanges, the rain falling and the boys risking all on the dog coming out of trap one. Or farther back still to the Rhondda of industrial drama that I met, before I ever put foot in the narrow valleys, in the files of the David Davies papers.

I saluted the statue as I rode by. His world was never my world. I could not make money if I tried, and in my heart of hearts I cannot really make heroes of the people that do. But there, in bronze, was that indestructible Victorian, planning to alter the sylvan, untrammelled paradise of the valleys with his railways, his coal-tips, his rows of identical cottages—he had created an environment which has stamped its mark on me and everyone of my age in South Wales.

But the landscape into which he was born has escaped his ministrations. He built his country seat at Llandinam and later Davieses also spread themselves in great houses over this landscape of clear rivers, rounded hillsides with hints of the wildness hidden behind them, and woodlands perfectly placed to frame the vistas of the valleys, fading away westward into that wilderness which we had conquered and enjoyed only yesterday. I rejoiced that this land had been spared the tips and the factory chimneys that made the Davies money. We rode through the meadowlands along the Severn with the unspoilt hills around us.

I let my legs dangle free of the stirrups. Tika would never start at anything, so I was safe in the saddle. Good horsemen, Biddy told me, have an instinctive grip which glues them suddenly to their horse almost before their mount shies at anything. My few days riding through Wales had taught me modesty about my natural gifts of horsemanship. I knew that I was a sort of intelligent sack on horseback. I had no instinctive grip. I could only risk dangling my feet out of the stirrups at the end of the day, when a horse is tired and plodding gently towards a green meadow and rest.

'Notice your horse's ears,' they tell you. Apparently the horse waves them about like a tic-tac man on a race-course when there's the danger of a stumble ahead. I was too busy keeping myself in the saddle to notice such signs. It was a daring thing for me to let go my stirrups and rely entirely upon my extremely weak knee-grip. The muscles you use to cling on to your horse seem to belong to a breed you exercise in no other sport. Until I had been gripping my saddle for three days I had no idea they existed. Afterwards I was only too aware of their presence.

I relied on my stirrups far more than I should have to keep me from falling off. I could not imagine how anyone could ride a horse without them. Yet these useful adjuncts to the saddle only reached western Europe after the time of the Romans. The Greeks never used them. You can see those serene youths in the Parthenon frieze at the British Museum riding without stirrups in a marvellously sinuous and complex rhythm of tossing horses' heads, flowing robes and hair blown back in the wind. The straight line of stirrups would have ruined a masterpiece of sculpture.

Once horsemen began to armour themselves heavily, they were bound to need stirrups. William the Conqueror, charging at Hastings, had sixty pounds' weight of chain-mail dumped on his back and needed to fix himself firmly in the saddle. It was no good King Arthur and his knights jousting without stirrups. They would have been out of their saddles at the first push of the lance. So to my infinite relief the stirrup came to stay. I would never have learned to ride bareback at my age.

But a long day's riding can tire your feet as much as walking on them. One of the pleasures of the end of the trek is this easy dangling of your feet outside the stirrups for a spell—the sign that you have done with hard work for the day. We had, once again, a perfect resting-place for the night; Maesmawr Manor, a superb halftimbered house in the black-and-white style, that penetrated up into Wales along the Severn valley from neighbouring Shropshire. The house is surrounded by the lush meadows that border the river. My last glimpse of Tika for the day was of the old girl making her way down to the water's edge and placing her hoofs slowly into the shallows, with a look of relief that took me back to an advertisement of my early childhood—a portly gentleman with his trousers rolled up to the knees, lowering his feet into a bowl of warm water and beneath the picture a phrase of compelling power—'Tizz for Tired Feet!'

I rested mine by strolling along the river bank myself. A mile away is the little village of Caersws. The guide-books are unkind about it. The Shell Guide dismisses it as a 'dull little place'. Well, architecturally it may be undistinguished, for like many of the small villages in Wales it got itself rebuilt in the last fifty years of the nineteenth century—not perhaps the best creative era in our artistic history. But who are we, to criticise, caught as we are in an overwhelming concrete and steel slab-and-box architectural jungle in one of the most insensitive building periods of all time? I looked on Caersws with more affection in the soft evening light. After all, the people of this tiny place are vigorous enough to run an Eisteddfod and a successful football team, and it is surrounded by peaceful hills with the salmon-filled Severn circling it. I know of far worse places.

It has one attraction that always holds magic for me—a Roman ruin, a real ruin not a carefully dug-up, lovingly restored, lawn-surrounded tourist attraction. I was brought up in the nineteenth century, romantic tradition about ruins. I like them to be really ruinous, ivy-covered and overgrown. When I was a small boy no one had really got to work tidying places like Caerphilly, Kidwelly and Caerleon. The dungeons were full of nettles; jackdaws nested in decaying towers and the secret passages were dark and dangerous. We supplied our own 'Son et Lumière' in our imagination as we struck matches to peer fearfully down into dank holes leading mysteriously away into the challenging gloom. If the Middle Ages were made to be ruined by the long passage of time, how much more evocative are the grass-covered mounds that now mark the passage of the Romans through our northern mists.

The camp at Caersws is far bigger than the present hamlet. It has a railway station in one corner and a farmhouse where the Roman commander issued his orders for keeping the surrounding Welsh tribes calm and contented. The outline of the walls can be traced amongst the fields. My only regret, as I followed them towards the Severn, was being alone. I not only want my ruins to be ruinous but I like to be accompanied by a learned guide— the local archaeologist who can pour out enthusiasm and information, the man who excavated a corner of the gate-house in 1912 and then covered it up again after writing an enormously long article in the *Archaeologia Cambrensis*. You have to look abroad for these pleasures now, as the Ministry of Works remorselessly restores our ruins to official order.

Thus I found my greatest archaeological pleasure recently when on a visit to Cyprus.

Cyprus is unhappy, torn by civil strife, but overwhelmingly beautiful. The clear Mediterranean sun shines on a classically taut landscape—olive trees with guarded trunks set apart in small fields, startlingly clean after the rains; blue mountains flecked with snow; the sea as wine-dark as Homer said it was— all the elements of the Aegean scene loosely thrown together. Cyprus is too big an island to distil the essence of the Greek achievement as you feel it in smaller isles like Delos and Mykonos. But the Greek world is there all right even if it has been overlain by a Byzantine and medieval skin and, today, by the plastic mac supplied by the British Army, the U.N. forces, the travel agents and developers, and the modern business Cypriots who know that money can be made out of anything— even out of political chaos.

The Cypriots on both sides are men who have read too much history. They are charming, but their minds are soaked in the past. A visiting professor admitted as much. 'Their education doesn't fit them for a realistic place in the modern world. On the Greek side it is all based upon the superiority of Greek culture; they still assume that the outside world knows all about it and appreciates it. One of my students sent in an essay on the Renaissance which began, "The Renaissance was the movement by which the world and the West turned once again to learn from the Greeks and acknowledged the debt to Byzantium".'

A British soldier put it more forcibly: 'You can't teach these bastards anything!'

But I have already confessed how absorbed I am with the past. Substitute Wales for Greece or Turkey and I am as irrationally committed to the Celtic world as any Greek Cypriot to Byzantium or Turk to the lost glories of the Ottoman Empire. So I was delighted to set out to explore the ruins of ancient Salamis about six miles along the coast from Famagusta with a splendidly eloquent archaeologist. I only wish I could have transported him bodily to Caersws.

Now, Salamis is the perfect early nineteenth-century traveller's ruin, lonely, covered with grass and shrubs, a lark singing overhead and an odd pillar or jagged piece of wall sticking up through the foliage. Ancient Rome and Athens are impressive, but the modern cities are too close—Coca-Cola flashes too triumphantly over the broken fragments of Old Time's decay. But Salamis lies on a vast plain where a dried-up river bed runs to the blue sea. Mountains in a hazy heat distance, green fennel everywhere and only a small section excavated. The amphitheatre is being slowly reconstructed, but that is about all. There is the usual forum with elegant columns, baths, headless statues, marble pavements rearranged after some great earthquake, and early Christian inscriptions scrawled on ancient stones. A perfectly placed pine tree makes a climax, framed by the line of pillars.

But for me the great pleasure was the vast, unexcavated area redolent with wild garlic, green and fragile, hiding the tumbled stone. At one spot you could trace the outline of the great basilica. Here sat the furiously quarrelling early fathers of the Church in the third and fourth centuries, debating subtle and pointless complexities of doctrine. Beyond—who knows what lies in the quiet, grassy mounds?

'Ah, you who have travelled everywhere and who have now come to this island where Venus came ashore from the foam,' said my guide, 'why is not American money poured out to uncover all these marvels?'

Mr Paleagos is the local *archéologue* who has conducted tactful excavations which have discovered the bones of St Barnabas. I deduced that he was one of those rare neutral Cypriots, a Maronite Christian perhaps, on whom the old colonial days have left a deep impress. He is a lively seventy who lives with his brisk, bird-like sister in a decaying villa outside the medieval walls of Famagusta, maintaining the good form of the vanished nineteen-twenties with invincible courage. He is surrounded by refugee Turks, squatting in rickety huts in a quarry. His garden of aloes has gone to seed; the municipality has taken his front lawn as a promenade; he is cut off from the telephone, and the nearest Greek police station is a long way down the road, but he still lives in his late nineteenth-century nest, surrounded by his collection of furniture and pictures of retired governors and Queen Marie of Roumania.

He explained to me as we stumbled over the old Greek columns of Salamis, 'Her signature has unfortunately been washed away by a leak we had in the roof, but Queen Marie was most gracious. I designed her little Greek chapel at Balchik. She quarrelled with her daughter and Queen Elena threw all her effects out into the street, including my plans, but it is nice to know nevertheless how human these great ones are. Like Sir Ronald Storrs. He was a great humanist, but perhaps not quite aloof enough to be a great Governor. When he arrived the Greeks asked, "Can we now hold Olympic Games?" All previous Governors had banned them.

'But Sir Ronald, the humanist, replied, "Of course you must have them. Did not the ancient Greeks give us the theory for our British Sports?"

'So they staged a gigantic manifestation, with Greek flags everywhere. Enthusiasm knew no bounds when Sir Ronald appeared in a white suit with a blue tie: "He is one of us, at last here is a Governor who understands how we feel as Greeks."

'But next week came the Muslim festival of Bayram. By custom the Governor, escorted by his guard of Cypriot lancers, rode off to pay his official call on the heads of the Turkish community. He wore red socks and a red tie with a crescent on it out of respect to his Turkish subjects. The Greeks went up in smoke: "What, is this man now a traitor to the sacred cause?

Down with him." Such are the difficulties that lie in wait for the cultivated man who tries to please both sides. No one understands neutrality here. We are all furious for our own side.'

'Mr Paleagos,' said I, as we sat in the sun where the Christian fathers wrangled together one thousand six hundred years ago, 'it is safer to stick to archaeology. No one can be annoyed about what you dig up here.'

'Ah, you are wrong. There are many moments when I have regretted transferring the methods of excavation into modern life, for an *archéologue* like myself cannot resist uncovering the past. I remember showing my collection to Sir Harry Luke and a very distinguished party of Cypriots. I stopped in front of one of those lovely old chests they used to make in Cyprus in which all brides kept their dowries. This particular one belonged to a beautiful Cypriot lady whose family was one of the most respected in Nicosia, but who had begun her career in the harem of Achmet Pasha in Egypt and then returned here to marry for love. I was telling this romantic story to Sir Harry when one man hurriedly left the group and has never spoken to me again. He was the grandson! And his family had always hidden this family skeleton in this beautiful chest. How dangerous it is to uncover truth. Even an archaeologist must always be careful about what he digs up!

'We are all subject to the whims of the Divine Aphrodite— even I. But if you are an archaeologist you fall in love more violently with stones. So none of us ever married. My first dear sister nearly did, but unfortunately she was killed by her doctor. Such a nice man, a Scot who was very well connected, but he drank whisky incessantly and gave her an injection of Johnny Walker instead of penicillin. Poor man, he was delightful when he didn't have delirium tremens. We Cypriots do not drink, but perhaps love is our great temptation!'

The excellent Mr Paleagos was back to the one subject that enchants all the classically educated Cypriots—Aphrodite rising from the foam near Paphos. I couldn't resist driving from Salamis back along the coast to see the spot. It's a wild, stony cove framed by white rocks, but the romantically inclined traveller is a little disconcerted to reach it through the R.A.F. camp at Episcopi. You pass such amorously intoxicating names as Isle of Man Road, the Happy Valley, El Marocco Beach Club and the fish-and-chips-and-tomato-sauce canteens for airmen and WAAFS. *O, hymen, hymen, hymenoi!*

The camp at Caersws couldn't give rise to quite such complicated reflections. Its history is obscure, and its only romantic connection concerns the little railway station tucked away in the corner. At least Caersws can boast that, at one period of its development, it had the honour of having a distinguished Welsh poet as its station-master.

When we clattered through Caersws next morning I looked across at the little station building and wondered about the efficiency of a railway line that could let a poet run a station for over thirty years—or rather stations, for he came to Caersws after a spell at two other stations on the old Cambrian line. It all looked so peaceful in the early-morning sun that it was quite clear that the railway management must have decided that the traffic potential at Caersws was such that a poet could easily find time to write epics in between trains.

The poet was John Ceiriog Hughes, and we felt our first duty for the day's ride was to turn off the main road as quickly as possible up the hill to the churchyard at Llanwnog, where Ceiriog now lies under the ancient yew trees. Llanwnog is everything that Caersws isn't. It's old and full of black-and-white timbered houses, which cluster around the churchyard. A steep tree-clad hill rises immediately behind the church. We dismounted and tethered our horses. It was pleasant to see them there, under the trees, with the morning sun dappling their sleek coats. Biddy had really worked on them. They might look a little mud-spattered at the end of the day, but they always started spotlessly.

We left them there, clamping and occasionally pawing at the ground with the surplus energy of the early morning, as we paid our tribute to Ceiriog. I felt a little difficulty in explaining to Biddy and Felicity who exactly Ceiriog was and why I wanted to start our day with a pious tribute. I couldn't even say if he was a good or bad poet. He was probably a hit-and-miss one, like a great many of the nineteenth-century Welsh bardic fraternity. When he was good, he was very, very good. His words sing quietly at the back of your mind—you can't forget them. They seem almost to have written themselves, in the

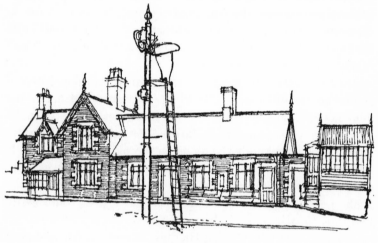

Caersws Station

same way as some of the great lyrics of Burns. But when he was bad, he became Wales's greatest master of bathos—and he had strong competition in the art of the 'unpremeditated flop' around that period!

Even the nineteenth-century bathos merchants met their match in that towering genius of bad verse, the prolific writer we christened 'The Bard of Medicine Hat'. He came into my ken through the good offices of J. D. Williams, who was the editor of our local Swansea newspaper, the *Swansea Daily Leader*. I had met his son, Emlyn, at the Grammar School, but I got to know J.D. best when I came back from Oxford and was forced to 'kick my heels' waiting for a job in the Great Depression. He was about sixty at the time; I was twenty-one. But in the way these things happen the many years that separated us seem to melt when we found we both had a passion for the mountains of Wales. He was tall, lithe, a magnificent hill-walker. I was short, stubby, but I could use a climbing-rope. We went up the Snowdonian rock faces together and I remember that it was half-way up the face of Lliwedd, as we looked out from a tiny rock-ledge that seemed suspended in air over the still surface of Llyn Llydaw and the incomparable circle of the Snowdon ridges, that he introduced me to the Bard of Medicine Hat.

He produced a slim volume from his rucksack. It had been sent to the paper for a review and obviously published at the author's expense. No doubt the verses gave the inhabitants of the cultural centre of Medicine Hat, way out on the vast prairies of Canada, great pleasure when the icy winds swept down over the winter snows that bury Alberta for five months of the year. This poem on 'The Rotarian's Picnic', for example, had a ringing message:

> Perhaps a William Shakespeare in Medicine Hat we've got,
> You never know the future of the baby in the cot!

Every year a new offering from Medicine Hat arrived at the office of the *Swansea Daily Leader* and each volume increased our pleasure in the work of this unknown master of bathos in the remote, open spaces of the Canadian West. There was his epic in five cantos, entitled 'Nora'. This described the adventures and love-affair of young Tim, a Canadian soldier sent to Europe during World War I. He was posted for training to Ireland, where he encountered love and snobbery for the first time:

> She was a servant at the Hall,
> Tim met her at the Servants' Ball.

He was instantly smitten, but when he escorted her home after the dance and, as a democratically born Canadian naturally walked up to the front door of the Hall, he found himself bounced out on his ear by the butler. In bitter, if still somewhat jaunty words, the poet records:

> The servants could not enter here,
> The door for THEM was at the REAR!

This insult settled it! Nora handed in her notice and went off to be trained as a Red Cross nurse, preparatory to following Tim straight out into the trenches. In Canto Four, she embarked on the converted liner *Celtic*, and the poet rises to heights of felicitous bathos as he describes that memorable voyage. The verses have all the staccato impact of a back-firing motor-bike exhaust-pipe.

> In secrecy, from Liverpool,
> The *Celtic* sailed, it was the rule.
> Dark was the night, the sea how calm!
> Zig-zag she sailed for fear of harm.
>
> Sudden, without warning came the blow;
> Torpedoed from the waves below,
> Amidships, 'neath the water-line
> But of the foe there was no sign!
>
> From captain and from crew, Death near,
> Arose their last but British cheer! . . .

Then came the great verse that marked the poet's final mastery of the art of sinking. It demands a certain amount of space around any reciter, since the lines describe the moment when Nora dives off the sinking ship in a maze of superbly liquid consonants and vowels.

> When Nora struck the waters blue,
> She scarcely knew quite what to do,
> But bravely for the shore she struck
> And missed the *Celtic's* sinking suck.

Talk about Tennyson, onomatopoeia and 'the murmur of innumerable bees'! Try reciting the last two lines aloud. You'll drown the audience as surely as Canto Four nearly drowned Nora.

The Bard's finest effort was undoubtedly his great philosophical verse-treatise entitled quite simply, 'Evolution'. At least, I think it was the Bard's work, but at this distance of time I find it hard to distinguish all the poets, from Wigan, Woollamaroo and the Wild West, who sent in their life work for review to the *Swansea Daily Leader*. To me, the lines have the hall-mark of the William Shakespeare of Medicine Hat. With true genius he summed up the whole of Darwin's theory of evolution in the two opening lines, thus rendering it unnecessary for the reader to peruse the remaining two thousand, five hundred and thirty-eight:

There's little difference between Man and Horse,
Not counting the external view, of course!

I looked down at old Tika. No, there wasn't much difference between her attitude and mine in this little matter of drifting through Wales. We had both reached the age of unhurried enjoyment of the little things of life. Tika had no intention of racing after anything, however tempting it might appear. She knew that sooner or later, everything drifts back to you if you can loiter purposefully.

After Llanwnog we couldn't have hurried if we had wanted to. Our way lay steeply upwards, climbing out of the trench of the Severn Valley back on to the bleak moorlands. We were launching out into a lonely, unfrequented piece of country. There is nothing obviously spectacular about it. The highest point rejoices in the inspiring name of Y Glonc! It all lies around the thousand-foot mark, the sort of land with which farmers have been struggling for the past two hundred years and no one ever made more than a living as bare as the mountain itself. It seems to me a land that has successfully dodged history. Even the few inhabitants are not at all certain what went on there in the past or what goes on in the world outside today. The names of the hills change with the seasons or with the few visitors who rent the shooting.

'What's the name of this moor?' we asked a small boy before we left the valley. 'Mynydd Palethorpe,' he replied. The famous sausage family had replaced the Welsh princes!

Small lakes lie scattered over the high ground. On one of them the black-headed gulls were breeding, keeping up a great clamour and whirling over the surface in a white cloud, dive-bombing any stranger who came too near. The last farms before the open mountain are small and tucked away in lonely folds of the hills. In one of them lived the last man in Wales who publicly declared that he often saw the local fairies, busy around the margin of the lake on their daily affairs of raising their magic cattle. The poor man instantly regretted his innocent announcement. After all, the Tylwyth Teg ('the Fair Family' as the Welsh call the fairies) had been well-known in these parts for a thousand years. His grandfather and his father before them had always left out the regulation bowl of milk which always disappeared before morning. What was more natural than that he should casually remark one day down in Caersws that the Fair Family seemed to be a little annoyed with things near Llyn Tarw.

Unfortunately, the date of his remark was 1927. His grand-father's word would never have been questioned, but our poor farmer had reached the age of the telegraph and the Sunday newspapers. The reporters descended in swarms on his farm. 'Yes, yes, the fairies are always around,' he assured them, but by the time the articles began to appear he bitterly regretted his faith in the Fair Family. Fleet Street had a high old time with the Tylwyth Teg. The farmer retired to obscurity, vexed to the heart. Nothing would persuade him to come down from his hills again; and his fairies have also hurriedly abandoned their last stronghold in Wales.

The only dangers now facing the rider over these lonely moors are the tangles of wire fences that are replacing the old stone walls. The horse and wire are natural enemies. If you are experienced, and brave enough, you can put your horse at a stone wall with a reasonable chance of getting over. But the thin, wicked-looking strand of barbed wire is altogether more dangerous. Neither you nor the horse can judge your distance from it at speed. Wired country forces you into long detours, as you look for gaps or gates. Biddy always maintained to me that Tika could jump well and was a splendid mount when it came to the hunting-field. 'Just let her hear the sound of the horn and she's off.' I couldn't picture the scene—Tika would have been a dowager duchess dancing skittishly among teenagers. I thanked my stars that there didn't seem to be a hunt about in this desolate country and concentrated on finding the gaps in the wire.

We meandered a bit along the slopes of Y Glonc and covered more ground than we had planned. We struggled through soggy patches, wondering how we would ever get on to a straight line again. We saw the slate roofs of a farm set amongst a grove of trees that looked as if they had spent their whole life battling against the wind, and rode down to try to find a more direct route through the wilderness. So it was that we came to Gors Dyfwch and found the man who had opted out.

The farm of Gors Dyfwch—the Bog of the Two Cows may be a somewhat inelegant translation—must be one of the loneliest inhabited places in Wales, and this suits the owner, Mr Ellis Jones, down to the stony ground. One by one his neighbours have abandoned the struggle and drifted away to easier jobs than cultivating a bare mountain. Mr Jones remains in the farm which his father and grandfather worked before him. What is more, he lives the exact life that they did. As for the world of television, holiday caravans, Birmingham suburbs, and Bingo, he is not only 'not with it' but defiantly against it. On his farm only Welsh is spoken. English is the traitor language through which comes the uncertainty and dreariness of mechanised living.

He has seven children. He and his wife feed them on the old Welsh recipes.

The hearth remained exactly as it used to be a hundred years ago. A forest of Welsh ham hung overhead from oak beams. A peat fire filled the kitchen with that unbeatable perfume of the open moorlands. The oven beside it added the crisp smell of newly baked bread. A vast iron pot bubbled gently, suspended over the fire. This contained the 'cawl', a stew enriched with leeks and mutton guaranteed to satisfy the appetite of the whole of the Jones family in one sitting. Mr Jones paraded them before us.

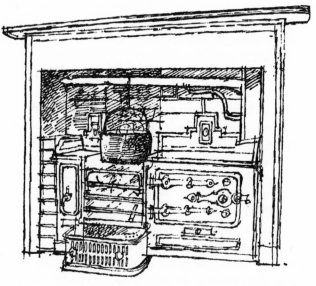

'They are all musical; we cultivate the arts here.' He waved his hand towards a composite photograph of the Welsh musicians of the past, a collection of nobly bearded men pointing to choral works in tonic sol-fa. I was touched to see that Mr Jones had pasted a snap of my father to the top of the group. 'We are are a bit out of the way for a piano, so we do our best with something more portable.'

Whereupon the children all produced mouth-organs and proceeded to give us a selection of Welsh folk-songs. 'A nest of singing birds, that's what we are,' said Mr Jones with pride, 'and I'm a bit of a poet as well. So what do we want with television and the rest of that stuff.' I looked around once more at the kitchen, which could have been lifted bodily out of Gors Dyfwch and set down untouched as an exhibit in the Welsh Folk Museum at St Athans. A wave of sympathy for Mr Jones swept over me—even a touch of envy.

There was no sign of money around Gors Dyfwch; on the contrary, everything had the air of being used again and again. 'Everything goes a long way with us.' Mr Jones smiled at me.

'Too hard a life for somebody like myself,' I said.

'Nothing is too hard if you have freedom to do what you like.'

'The children, Mr Jones?'

'It hasn't done them any harm to live simply, has it now?'

Their birdlike voices now joined in singing 'Penillion'. No, they were not unhappy or restless—as yet! But in two years' time—by the time this book is in print—who can estimate the power of Bingo and teenage adulation and the wicked wiles of the outside world. In the meantime the Jones family lived in their isolated happiness on the moors at the top of their lost valley.

'Try it yourself, Mr Thomas bach,' advised Mr Jones. 'Don't leave it too late.'

That is the problem of Opting Out. You mustn't leave it too late. The only other man I ever met, beside Mr Jones, who had also opted out did it somewhere in his early forties. This was Sir Max Beerbohm. The juxtaposition of Mr Ellis Jones and Sir Max Beerbohm may seem a little startling. It is hard to imagine the elegant Max picking his fastidious way, polished topper in hand, through the muddy farmyard at Gors Dyfwch to sit in the inglenook with Mr Jones and reminisce about Swinburne or Oxford in the nineties, while the Jones family played 'David of the White Rock' on mouth-organs offstage. Yet the incomparable Max did exactly the same thing as Mr Ellis Jones when confronted with the growing dreariness of modern life. Mr Jones wrapped himself in a dream of nineteenth-century Wales, while Max stopped the clock on some golden, Edwardian afternoon, when the fashionable world was still elegant and exclusive and small enough to be encompassed in drawings of fragile, venomous brilliance.

207

Max's Welsh mountain farm was his villa at Rapallo. I went there in 1947 to invite him to read one of his essays on the BBC. I approached the spot with some apprehension. Italy had just been through the tribulations of an election, and we had to race up from Rome overnight to keep the appointment. As we swing our car lights around one of the numerous suicidal corners of the Rapallo road, we illuminated a vast blank wall plastered with political slogans—*Viva CD. Viva Garibaldi. Viva il Papa Re*. At the foot stood a little, middle-aged, moustachioed gentleman busily filling in the one vacant space with another slogan. He had just finished it when our headlights caught him and he scuttled away into the safety of the night. He had written in flaming, defiant red paint a clarion call to the downtrodden Italian middle class, '*Viva Amore*—Long Live Love!'

We took this as a good omen as we brushed ourselves up prior to calling at the villa, for I felt sartorially inadequate in my austerity suit. Max seemed to have lived his life in such a perpetually well-dressed atmosphere that it seemed too indecent to present myself at his door in a garb whose outline had been dictated by Sir Stafford Cripps.

But it was also a desperate adventure to reach his door at all. His house, the Villino Chiara, stood on a steep hillside which gave a glorious view over the blue sea and the whole sweep of the coastline of the Italian Riviera. When Max and his wife first saw it just before World War I, it must have seemed the perfect place for the man who was proposing to opt out from the growing vulgarities of the petrol-soaked twentieth century. I could see the couple arriving by a slow-moving cab from Rapallo and deciding that the little villa on its terrace, with its vines, its small garden and summer-house perched up on the hill was the predestined and charming cell for these most elegant of hermits. What Max and Lady Beerbohm never realised was the danger implicit in their hermitage's proximity to the main trunk road between Genoa and the south. The Via Aurelia runs almost under the front windows. All may have been peaceful in 1910, but by 1947 the motor-lorries had arrived, driven by Italians who treated the Via Aurelia as if it were the Indianapolis circuit. They thundered around Max's corner in a continual imitation of the chariot race in *Ben Hur*. We parked by the gate and squeezed the BBC recording car against the wall, in imminent fear of being crushed by the next sixwheeled monster.

We walked up the stone steps and rang the bell, standing under a strangely shaped lamp which had been designed by Gordon Craig. Everything that surrounded Max seemed to link him irretrievably to his era. Even the big pine tree across the road leant—according to Max—'backwards like Swinburne when he was talking to you, don't you know'. When we were shown into the tiny library I got a strange feeling of stepping back, myself, into some spring evening just past the turn of the century, when portly King Edward was entertaining Mrs Keppel to dinner with Sir Ernest Cassel, when Mr Balfour was uncoiling his willowy length from the Front Bench of the House of Commons to give a look of infinite understanding and distaste at Mr Bonar Law, and when Max himself in spats, top-hat and an exquisitely cut overcoat complete with astrakhan collar was carefully putting on his gloves, prior to driving by the last hansom to the St James's Theatre, where he would review, writing with a silver dagger, the latest dramatic offering of Mr Jerome Klapa Jerome, *The Passing of the Third Floor Back*; a savoury *oeuvre* which, according to Max, proved that 'twaddle and vulgarity would always have the upper hand'.

The books, the pictures, the furniture, everything dated from the days before the First World War. Max had deliberately stopped his clock. In his seventies he went on living as if King Edward VII was still on the throne. He entered as we were looking at his drawing of the aged Carlyle striding unhappily along the Chelsea Embankment. The first thing I noticed was the elegance of his clothes, the negation of everything about which the long-winded Carlyle pontificated in his unread *Sartor Resartus*. 'I, too, failed to read through those uncouth, repetitive sentences,' said Max. 'I shall never understand how a man could write 622 pages on the Philosophy of Clothes and yet refuse to go to a good tailor!'

Max's English was as elegantly and carefully dressed as his person. His sentences could never be as slovenly as Carlyle's. You felt that his adjectives were wearing spats, every noun he used had a crease put in it, every verb was chosen to avoid vulgar excitement. His precise, beautifully modulated voice gave a remote quality to everything he said—as if I were listening to the voice of someone who had returned from a journey into outer space and was mildly astonished to find that the world was still going on.

This precision of speech fascinated me. When I first joined the BBC precise utterance was at a discount. The advent of the microphone was held to have revived easy, natural talk after many years of the dominance of the written and printed word. As each carefully written script arrived the devoted producers in the Talks Department struggled to make it natural. Many a a man fashioned a great reputation for himself by the expert way he was able to inject an 'er' or 'of course' or 'as you know' into an intractable slab of Statesman's Prose.

Max would have none of this. 'To "er" may be human,' he said to me, 'but to continue "er-er-ing" is hardly divine.' His voice had the quality of a beautifully played flute, every breathing pause carefully calculated, every hesitation used as a trill to embellish a particular word. 'The theatre? No, I have not, as it were, frequented the *coulisses* for some years. The last time I went to the London theatre there was a play being staged by a man who . . .'—slight pause and disarming smile—'yes, who smoked a pipe. It was hardly a play, it was a sermon. Now, the one thing that I will not suffer in a theatre is a preacher in full flight, especially if he preaches'—again a gentle smile of resignation—'. . . with a Northern accent.'

'G.B.S. ?' I interrupted slyly.

'Ah, he never preached, he simply talked on the stage as he talked to you in private. And I do not think he expected you to believe a word he said. Not so this other dramatist. This play had the title, if I remember correctly, *I Have Been Here Before.* I retired after the interval, merely remarking to the manager as I left, "And you will not see me here again." '

Max spoke about G.B.S., and indeed about Arthur Balfour, Oscar Wilde, Rufus Isaacs, and a whole host of people who existed up until 1914, as if they were still alive. After 1914, the curtain came down. But he spoke of the Edwardians with such a sense of immediacy that I kept glancing uneasily around the tiny room in case, at any moment, Henry James would ooze his bulk into the chair opposite and start an interminably contorted monologue. Max was going to record his essay on Hall Caine, but clearly we could not set up our microphones in the library. The lorries outside would have shaken the recording to pieces. Max never seemed to hear them. It was as if he had sealed off his ears as well as his mind to this vulgar twentieth century. But our engineer was only too sensitive to the noise!

We adjourned to the little summer-house at the top of the garden. Here we placed Max in his easy chair with a hot-water bottle in his lap, a vast array of travelling-rugs around his legs and a reading-desk before him, supporting a beautifully written manuscript. He sipped a glass of the local white wine and prepared to read the opening sentences.

A volley of shots erupted from over the wall outside. I rushed out into the lane, among the olive trees that overlooked the top wall of Max's garden. A splendidly equipped hunter stood before me, a *cacciatore*, complete with feathers in his hat, leggings, gun under his arm and a game basket slung over his shoulder. He was prowling through the gardens shooting at every tiny tom-tit in the district. It was as if the shooting season had opened in Tooting instead of on the Scottish moors.

'Silence,' I commanded. 'A great English writer is recording a masterpiece.'

'A masterpiece. Ah! I understand. It is that pleasant old gentleman who dresses in the style of D'Annunzio and who seldom comes out. We know him well here, but, pardon me, we did not know he was a writer. A novelist, perhaps, or a screen scenario creator?'

'England's greatest!' said I.

'In that case, I will go to shoot over Signor Begoni's garden. They say the larks are bolder over there.'

I may have committed a crime against wild life, but I was giving life for posterity to a piece of prose on which Max had worked for a year, a carefully wrought verbal jewel. The words flowed easily, eloquently, musically. He talked of his first meeting with that humourless bestseller, Hall Caine. Hall Caine is forgotten now, but as Max rolled the names of his novels appreciatively over the tongue—*The Deemster*, *The Christian*, *The Eternal City*—I could see Hall Caine before me, bearded, gloomy, tweedy . . . and a whole procession of late Victorians followed. 'Balfour was the only man I knew who did not seem to have a backbone . . . Asquith never drank seriously, don't you know; no man who could write those neat, precise letters of his could ever be regarded as a mere wine-bibber. "Squiffy", indeed! Why, all his Cabinet were afraid of him until Lloyd George came into prominence. These two men were made to hate each other. . . . Kipling? I never thought of him as a writer but rather as a photographer.

'Hall Caine was not of this class, but he had a presence, undeniably a presence. It was expected of successful men in those days. They had to dress the part. So Hall Caine wrapped himself in a cloak—was it, perhaps, a memory of Tennyson—now, *he* was distinctly a "cloaky" person. . . .'

We could have continued recording for hour after enchanted hour, but the Age of Irreverence came roaring in. We could not cut out the sounds of the Via Aurelia. The crash of the lorries changing gear seemed to bring the postwar world roaring through Max's front door. They flattened his fragile defences at six-minute intervals. Insolently, their engines proclaimed that there was now no escape. The Man who opts Out will be pursued by the mechanised furies to the loneliest ends of the earth. I had left it too late. I can only slip away now and again to escape the sound of the internal-combustion engine in some still preserved hide-out, such as Mr Ellis Jones maintained in his mountain fastness in the hills behind Caersws.

Mr Jones waved us away from his bare mountain and we drifted down the bleak valley, past abandoned farms where the hearths have so recently gone cold after a life of two hundred years. There was now an infinite sadness over this moorland and a chill wind blew from the north-west towards us, coming from the high hills whose summits came peeping up above the shivering reed-beds that formed the immediate horizon. A cold breeze on horseback is a knife inserted unfairly berween your ribs. You are a sitting target, for you cannot run or slap your chest or step out briskly, as you can do on foot, to start your circulation moving. You are perched up on your animal and the slightest chill in the air catches you defenceless. No wonder the old-style travellers in early nineteenth-century prints appear swathed in layer after layer of thick cloth. I could have done with half a dozen layers myself.

But as we followed the stream down—the Afon Gam, the crooked stream, they call it—we rode out of the wind, the sun became warm and caressing and we came, five miles farther on, into a valley where all was green, soft and summery. A chapel, a few houses, a post office and a church announced themselves as the village of Llanerfyl. We slipped out of our saddles for a few minutes' rest, and tethered the horses at the entrance to the churchyard.

Horses are not so easily parked as motor cars.-Four of them take up a lot of room. Biddy carefully checked over saddles and bridles. When you are on a long trip such as this one you cannot afford to have the slightest weak link. A frayed rein, a girth that is too tight might start some irritation on Tika's skin or annoy Seamus, and within a few hours our pleasant ride through the countryside would come to a sudden halt. Biddy's careful eye didn't miss a thing. She taught us the lesson of good horsemanship—the price of riding pleasure is eternal vigilance. We strolled through the one small street of Llanerfyl. The post office sold everything; stamps, sweets, medicine—it had the lot. And over the counter a poster in Welsh announced the great prizes to be won at the forthcoming Powys Eisteddfod.

It did my heart good to see that there were still places where the local eisteddfod was holding its own against all the siren voices of television and easy travel that are luring even the most stalwart of Welshmen away from his language and his traditions (always excepting Mr Ellis Jones on his mountain-top). When I was a youngster the small 'eisteddfodan' were one of the joys of our lives. They combined the satisfaction of taking part in a feast of culture with the thrills of a hard-fought rugby match. Things have changed in the last thirty years and the small eisteddfod has lost ground as one of the prides of the Welsh people. But in the 1920s of my youth it was still going strong.

We boys didn't bother too much about the recitations, the poetry adjudications or the tenor solos. We waited breathlessly for the inevitable Battle of the Parties. The Party, outside South Wales, conjures up pictures of grim-faced, padded-shouldered Iron Curtain massmen, automatically obeying orders from above. But in the South Wales of my youth, the Party was simply the male voice choir. Like the local rugby team, they symbolised our pride of locality, our gesture of defiance against the rows of slate-roofed cottages, the un-paid-for Welfare Halls and the coal-tips perched on rain-sodden mountains, which were the background of our lives. We gave the Party a fierce loyalty and the Party, in return, attacked the music as if they were exacting revenge at last for the defeat of Owain Glyndwr. In the battles that formed the male voice competitions, there were no holds barred. All male voice *aficionados* relish the reply of defiance given by the conductor of the losing choir to his rival after a fierce eisteddfodic contest: 'All right, I admit that you had us hands down on "Lift up thy heads, Ye gates of Brass", but in "Love, Perfect Love", we gave you Hell!'

The music sung by these choirs never seemed to exist outside Wales, but they were the life-blood of the Party. Gather two or three South Walians together and whisper 'Martyrs' or 'Crossing the Plain' or 'Nidaros' and they will immediately go into a huddle, the leader will lift his hand in authority, hum the note—and 'They're off!'

The old European joke about the English ,'one Englishman a bore, two Englishmen a club, three Englishmen the British Empire', can be changed in South Wales with perfect truth into, 'one Welshman a milk-round, two Welshmen a committee, three Welshmen a male voice choir'! And ten to one that male voice choir will start singing 'Martyrs of the Arena'. I have been told again and again that there was actually a gentleman with the improbable name of Laurent de Rille who composed this music and collaborated with a poet with the even more improbable name of Stallybrass—but frankly I don't believe these two men ever existed. To me 'Martyrs' is a musical folk ritual, part of the tradition of the mining valleys. I accepted the words, astonishing though they are, as I accepted the 'twice-times' tables I used to chant at school. But when I got a copy of 'Martyrs' a few years ago, I gazed at the poem with the wide-eyed delight I usually reserve for the productions of the Bard of Medicine Hat.

The music describes, with fruity four-part harmony, the ordeal of the Martyrs under Nero in the arena in Rome. It starts with a bold announcement by the basses, always more enterprising than the tenors in these matters:

> Great Caesar, with our dying breath,
> Thus we hail thee!

The tenors have a right to be a little wobbly on the note at this point, for they have a shrewd idea what's coming to them. And, sure enough, half-way through the piece the basses declare the arrival, contrapuntally, of the 'roaring lion and hyena, soon to be our living tomb'. No wonder the tenors go a little off the note as they sing, 'Hear ye that ringing cheer. They open now the cage.' The basses, solid, unimaginative, are a little slower in their reaction. Ah! but it's the lions who get the 'afters' in the choral epic of 'Martyrs of the Arena'; plus 'the tigers and the panthers in their rage, they come madly bounding along'. No wonder the whole chorus huddle together, forget being contrapuntal and yell (double-forte), 'Brethren, be strong!'

I could still hear the sound of the choirs practising offstage as I read through that poster in the post office at Llanerfyl, and the scene on that eisteddfod field, over thirty years ago, in the unfrequented countryside between the borders of Carmarthenshire and Cardiganshire, where the little hills have lost their ambition to become mountains and where the main products are still preachers, trout streams, and little square prewar black cars driven by officials of the Milk Marketing Boards.

I had come down to the eisteddfod in the 'chara', and the battle was due to be staged at two-thirty, in a tent by the tumbling waters of the Gwili river. All around were the deep woods, secret and warm in the morning sun. We boys got into the tent by the simple trick of appointing one of our number to get the entrance stamp put on the back of his hand. No tickets were used in those days. We slipped behind the hedge and transferred the impress of the stamp while it was still damp. The choirs set off to rehearse in the clearings in the woodlands.

But our local choir were facing those formidable songsters, the Penybont Gleemen, and everyone realised that the battle was going to turn on that vital phrase just before the end, 'and when the life-blood is pouring'. Should the choir pour its life-blood mezzo-forte or double-forte? The adjudicator was known to have strong views on this point. What were our rivals of Penybont doing? And how were we to find out, since they were rehearsing in their clearing surrounded by the defensive pickets of their supporters. It was then that Jack Rees, the wag, became serious and approached a friend and myself. 'Boys,' he said, 'are you patriots? Are you prepared to take a risk for the honour of the choir?'

'Oh, of course, Mr Rees,' we hurried to declare.

'Then will you crawl through the undergrowth and find out what Penybont are doing about the forte in bar eight after the *Tutti* before the end? Our fate depends upon it!'

Like Red Indians we slipped from the tent. We crawled through the brambles, slid on our stomachs amongst the heather and became spies for the cause of art. We came back dirty but triumphant. 'Mr Rees, it's a double-forte.' Mr Rees raised his eyes to the hills in the mood of Cromwell before Dunbar, 'Pouring out their life-blood double-forte! The Lord hath delivered them into our hands!' Indeed he had. Penybont were crushed and we returned singing like satisfied angels in the 'chara'.

I wondered if the choirs which would sing at the Powys Eisteddfod would have the same unalloyed pleasure in the musical battle as we had. Or if the various types of pleasure could be equated? Is singing in a victorious choir as intense a delight as riding your horse? I had no time for further philosophic speculation, for our breather at Llanerfyl had to be short. We still had twelve long miles to go to our resting-place for the night at Llanrhaiadr-ym-Mochnant.

I remember them as pleasant, uneventful miles. Battling over the moorlands imprints every yard of the ride on your memory. Your riding skills are at full stretch. Wire, bogs, rain, mist—any one of these hazards could stop you in your tracks or send you back to your starting-point like a bad throw at snakes and ladders. After Llanerfyl, tension went out of our riding day. Short of Tika throwing a shoe, nothing could prevent us reaching our objective by the scheduled time in the early evening.

Our route lay through side roads and lanes across the grain of the country.

We walked slowly out of one valley and trotted down into the next, in a series of switchbacks. The rivers were all filled with trout and ran fast and sparkling under low hills. We crossed the Banwy, the Vyrnwy and the tree-lined Alun. This is hummocky country, off the beaten track for tourists, foothills to the bigger mountain world ahead. For looming before us, beckoning to us from the top of every hill, was the next great riding challenge and our last before we could see a victorious end to our ride from South Wales to the north, the vast range of the Berwyns. They didn't hold quite the menace of the Desert of Wales seen from

Tregaron. The summits are much higher, up to the 2,700-foot mark, but the map showed a convenient track for horses around a flank of the long range. After the Tregaron-Rhyaader ride we knew we could tackle any mountain country which offered us the luxury of a track.

So we came down into Llanrhaiadr-ym-Mochnant with our hearts easy. The sun was warm and nothing could come between us and our final objective. Or so we thought as we clattered through the one street of Llanrhaiadr to dismount in triumph, surrounded by everyone in the village and half the farmer's sons of the surrounding area, mounted upon a glorious variety of horseflesh from mountain pony to sturdy carthorse. But now over the spur of the Berwyns the clouds began to gather. Rain tomorrow, heavy rain, To an old hand on the mountains like myself, the signs were unmistakable. Walking through heavy rain on mountain-tops is an art and an endurance test. What would it be like on horseback? Suffice to the day the pleasures thereof. I slid down off Tika's back and felt in my pocket for her reward of sugar. Tomorrow could take care of itself.

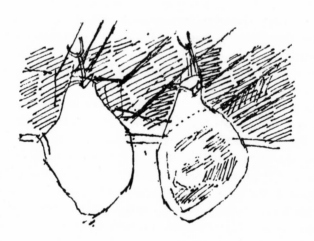

8

LLANRHAIADR-YM-MOCHNANT must look a fearful name to English eyes. Welsh orthography seems a complicated crossword of unpronounceable consonants, when, in effect, it is simpler than Russian and Greek, and the sounds it represents are far more pronounceable than French or Norwegian. Substitute 'oo' for 'w' and most of the crossword aspect disappears. To a Welsh eye the name is simple, and means, 'The village or church of the waterfall in the valley of the pig stream'. The waterfall is the glory of the place. It is easily the most impressive in Wales, but it is hidden from the village two miles away into the hills. I wish I could have been there in the days of Sir Watkins Williams Wynne when that powerful landed potentate, 'the Prince in Wales' they call him, used to dam the water upstream and then let it go with a fearful wallop to please distinguished visitors. At the start of the day we were far more interested in the prospect of a waterfall of another sort. There was sunshine, it is true, when we gathered before the old church with our guides from the local Pony Trekking Society ready to lead us on the first stage across the Berwyns, but before us, also, were the dark spurs of the main mass of the mountains. There were wisps of low cloud forming over them. The local riders showed a cheery indifference to the prospect of getting wet. 'In for a soaking today!' one of them grinned at me. 'Well, you'll always get that on the Berwyns, After all, it was here that Henry II got the soaking of his life.'

It was true. The Berwyns, those high, vast, complicated ranges, have always acted as the outer line of defence for the Welsh principalities farther west. Henry II's army came to grief on them in 1165 when he was making an all-out effort to smash the North Wales rulers. The heavens opened and fairly washed him away. The heavens looked as if they were going to repeat their washing-away act on us. It doesn't do, however, to show apprehension about the weather on horseback; it destroys the natural appearance of superiority which should surround a rider Besides, we were all armoured against the rain. Rowland and I put our trust in the mighty raincoats purchased away down south in Builth at Messrs Watts the Clothiers. I had felt at the time that these were cumbersome, overweighty, tentlike garments, but I was judging them by walker's standards. I had forgotten that the horse carries the weight. As we prepared to assault the menacing bastions of the Berwyns I needed all the weight Tika would put up with.

Our cavalcade clattered out of Llanrhaiadr and followed a narrow valley that cut deep into the hills, the valley of the Afon Twrch, running down from the distant summits and filled with the sound of the tumbling trout stream. The skies darkened above us. At Plas Maengwynedd our escort gave us our directions before leaving us—a steeplechase over the high eastern spurs of the hill and then, six miles farther on, a direct assault over the main ridge to bring us down into the valley of the Dee. We set our horses to the long climb out of the valley of the Twrch on to the first of the spurs, where the track would take us up over open moorland to about 1,500 feet. I kept swinging around in the saddle, as far as I could without falling off, to see what was happening in the skies farther west. A sinister transformation had taken place over the Berwyn summits. They had turned black, then clouds covered them and swept towards us. Great curtains of icy rain were let down over the upper peaks and—by an extraordinary freak effect—a vast, double rainbow spanned the valley before the rain reached us in a venomous roar that blotted out everything around.

After that, I didn't bother about rainbows. I concentrated on hanging on to Tika. Really heavy rain has a strangely isolating effect on a rider. The world around seems to consist entirely of water, through which your horse slops, splashes, slithers and sloshes his way forward. You tend to leave everything to him while you sit in your saddle and brood. Dreary discomfort sets in, for the rain soon begins to find out the chinks in your macintosh armour. Little runnels of icy water course down your sleeves or force their way through the high collar around your neck. The saddle seems a tin bath in which you are condemned to sit for the next hour without prospects of a warm towel.

Your head sinks on your shoulders, your horse's head sinks likewise. Our little party began to look like Meissonier's once celebrated painting of the Retreat from Moscow. The rain kept at us with almost personal vindictiveness and fairly blew us over the bleak 1,500-foot spur of the mountain between the Afon Twrch and the upper waters of the Ceiriog. I suppose I should have got off to pay tribute to the birthplace of so many celebrated Welsh poets as we came out of the clouds into the narrow Ceiriog valley. Instead, I led the party straight to the hospitable West Arms at Llanarmon, an old inn complete with a dismounting block which was a godsend to a rain-soaked rider. We got the horses into the shelter of an outhouse and presented ourselves, sopping and frozen, to the ministrations of our host, Mr Bunny. This was a Dickensian sort of arrival, with horses champing outside, and a roaring fire inside, around which we stood thawing out in clouds of steam. We should, I supposed, have been served with one of those Dickensian concoctions—a negus or a hot punch—which always seemed to be ready for Mr Pickwick and his companions in weather such as this. Instead, we drank coffee. In any case, Wales is not the natural home of negus or punch. We should have been restoring our strength with some national drink—Welsh whisky, for example. At least, Rowland should have been taking a patriotic nip of something

strong produced on the spot. As for me, I'm a temporary teetotaller when I'm on a journey of this sort. My body can't take any combination of alcohol and exercise.

We talked about this as we felt the generous warmth of Mr Bunny's roaring fire slowly soak into our chilled bones. What should we be drinking of national character as we rode through Wales? Has Wales a national drink? If not, why not? France has her wine, Scotland and Ireland have whisky. Why hasn't Wales produced something characteristic of her hills and valleys, instead of the universal beer which she shares with all the countries of northern Europe.

There was mead, of course, The ancient bards were continually singing the praises of mead in verse that became increasingly complicated in proportion to the mead consumed. But this favourite tipple of the poets seems to have been sickly stuff, with powerful after-effects. One of the earliest Welsh poems, the 'Gododdin', relates the sad story of a band of Welsh soldiers, suffering from a mead hangover, who were wiped out to a man by the Saxons. Apparently these Saxons were teetotal. How history has reversed itself!

Yet in those quiet country pubs such as the back bar of the West Arms, where discreet Welsh drinkers lift their glasses in the traditional toast of '*I'r Achos Dirwestol!*' ('All success to the Temperance Cause!'), keen patriots meet from time to time to invent some drink that could be exclusively Welsh and so remove this slur on the national honour. I once tasted a concoction called Welsh Nectar. The inventor assured me that he had obtained the recipe from an eleventh-century manuscript. The drink tasted as if the basic materials had been obtained from the eleventh century as well!

What about Welsh wine instead? No Frenchman would ever believe it, but there was a time, within middle-aged memory, when the vines grew in ordered rows on a Glamorgan hillside, when the great carts loaded with grapes creaked their way in September along the banks of the River Taff and the new wine frothed and fermented in vast vats in the very heart of Cardiff.

I must admit that the man who worked this miracle was not a Welshman but a Scot. A Celt all the same, and a romantic one at that.

James Patrick Crichton-Stuart, third Marquess of Bute, was without question one of the most gifted of our Victorian noblemen, an authority on Coptic Church symbolism and Scottish heraldry, a convert to the Roman Catholic Church, a leading investigator of psychical phenomena and the translator of Turgenev. But his greatest gift was undoubtedly the millions left to him by his father, who made a fortune out of Welsh coal.

This was in the great days of the South Wales coalfield, when the Rhondda was a black Klondyke as the rival coal-owners fought like robber barons over mining options and railway lines to the sea. The Marquess—or rather his estate—was in the thick of the fight, but clearly his heart was not in it. He was an eccentric and a dreamer and valued the coal trucks filled with 'Best Welsh', that rattled down from the valleys, only because they allowed him to give reality to his dreams.

Like all rich Victorian romantics, he fell to building, and, naturally, in the Gothic style; he demanded towers, battlements, crenellations, balustrades and all the architectural bric-a-brac of the Middle Ages—anything, one feels, to shut out the view of Victorian Cardiff. He got them in full measure from his architect, William Burges. Together they converted Cardiff Castle into a Roman fort with a Welsh Carcassonne gaily stuck on to the western wall. They then looked around for further ruins to conquer.

They found what they were looking for at Taff's Well, some five miles north of Cardiff. Here the River Taff breaks through a line of high, limestone hills in a narrow gorge. The coalfield and its industry are out of sight and the hills are steep, wooded and charming.

Perched on a crag near the gorge were the ruins of Castell Coch, the Red Castle, built by one of the Welsh princes, or an invading Norman baron, to dominate the coastal plain. There are few written records of the castle's history and that made Burges's task all the more delightful. He and his patron could give full reign to their antiquarian enthusiasm. In 1871 they cleared the site and at last there arose a romantic, turreted reconstruction which looks, for all the world, like the castles pictured on old hock labels. There was even a drawbridge that really worked—so well, indeed, that it once shot half a Sunday-school treat into the dry moat.

When the Marquess gazed with pride at his new castle he could not fail to notice how closely the site resembled the slopes of the Rhine, the Moselle and the Loire. Clearly there was only one thing wanting to make the picture perfect—a vineyard at the castle gate. When you have the Bute millions behind you it is possible to order a vineyard as the rest of us order a new car: the Marquess made his decision and Britain's biggest vineyard of modern times started to grow on this steep hillside of Wales.

I am not sure if the Marquess was a wine connoisseur. I suspect that he looked at the site, realised that it demanded a vineyard and, like a true artist, determined to place one there. He searched the pages of the Venerable Bede, William of Malmesbury and Geraldus Cambrensis for details of wine-growing in Britain in the Middle Ages. His vineyard, like his castle, was to be a grand gesture of romantic defiance against the increasing materialism of his Age.

But he didn't rely on the Venerable Bede and Holinshed for technical advice. He imported the best French machinery and invited experts over to start the experiment. In 1875 he had the slope below the castle planted with vines in rows three feet apart. The experts declared that the soil had a superficial resemblance to the soils of the Haut Médoc, but actually it was a light fibrous loam overlying limestone.

There was a long period of trial and error before it was finally decided to plant only one variety of vine, the Gamay Noir. The grapes were cultivated on the 'low stem' system as used in most of the French vineyards.

The Marquess had every right to hope that he would soon be drinking his own red wine, seated in his medieval arm-chair before a roaring fire in the guard room at Castell Coch, with the drawbridge up and a noble tome of Coptic liturgy to lend savour to the evening.

But in the world of wine you can never rely on your bottle until you have actually drunk it. Although he spent money lavishly and planted on a scale that would have made your modern British wine-growing enthusiast green with envy, he had reckoned without Welsh weather. The Castell Coch vineyard site looks perfect for the job on a sunny day in early summer.

You might imagine the grapes ripening happily and the Welsh *vignerons* singing—in four-part harmony, of course—as they tended the vines before going to choir practice in the nearby chapel. But, alas, such days are rare. As one old Welsh countryman reminded me, 'Never forget that Welsh weather is teetotal!'

Mr Pettigrew, who was in charge of the experiment, ruefully admitted, long afterwards, that 'The really experimental time for the vineyard at Castell Coch has been the worst we could have hit on for the last twenty or thirty years.'

The Marquess was unshaken. He acted on the principle that if you do something on a sufficiently large scale you are bound to succeed. He would have approved of my American general who announced, 'We don't solve our problems, we overwhelm them!' He ordered more acres to be planted. He extended the experiment to his land in Swanbridge in the Vale of Glamorgan, where he had five acres under cultivation. He even, for a brief period, had a third '*Clos*' at St Quentin's near Cowbridge.

At last he did achieve some success. In 1897 the wines were actually placed on the London market, through a well-known firm of wine merchants, Messrs Hatch, Mansfield and Co. The catalogue listed them as 'Welsh Wines; Canary Brand' and was somewhat coy about their quality, simply stating that 'Although these wines cannot yet be said to possess the delicate aroma and flavour of the best foreign wines, they are eminently wholesome and honest.' Not a very glowing encomium!

But this was a marked improvement on *Punch's* comment in 1875 when it predicted that it would take four men to drink the wine—two to hold the victim and one to pour it down his throat.

I, myself, came on the scene far too late to taste a bottle of Château Bute, but I remember that my uncle once had a bin of the 1892 in his cellar and gave me his opinion: 'It is some time since I swallowed them, my boy. The Marquess was a great authority on Coptic literature and a fine gentleman. Let us leave it at that.'

But it is only fair to say that other judges went on record with a more favourable opinion, declaring that the Bute vintages were 'luscious, golden wines, resembling first-class still champagne', and again 'with an aroma far in advance of grape wines generally manufactured in this country'.

All I can add to these pronouncements from the far-off years at the turn of the century is the information that the labels on the bottles were splendid. I remember admiring them in my uncle's cellar where he kept them as historic curiosities—they had a William Morris-Walter Crane air about them, all turrets and tangled vine leaves. Both red and white wines were made, but no distinctive names were given to wines of different natures. The labels preserved a tactful silence about the contents of the bottles and simply indicated that they came from the Bute vineyards.

The wine promise of the nineties, like so much else in that period, did not last. Welsh wines are definitely a *fin de siècle* curiosity. Soon the weather was 'at it again'. the Third Marquess died and his son carried on, but the vintages remained uncertain. In 1914 the Butes had to confess defeat. By 1920 the wines had disappeared from the slopes below the Red Castle and now only grass covers the greatest Welsh vineyard.

In the dark vaults of Cardiff Castle the vats gathered dust and the remaining bottles lay undisturbed through the Second World War. Then an expert from Messrs Harvey was called in to pronounce on the last of the Bute wines. He raised a glass to his lips and uttered the fatal word, 'Vinegar.'

The great dream of a Welsh Côte d'Or was over.

But if wine refused to become Celtic why not produce Welsh whisky? After all, whisky is a Celtic drink and Wales possesses all the right ingredients for making it—barley grown on hill pastures, clear streams flowing from peat deposits and any amount of poets to sing the praises of the product. As the Marquess of Bute was giving up the struggle in the south, a new patriot arose in the north, pledged to the task of making a whisky that would be worthy of bearing the name of Wales. He made the attempt in an area just over the mountain from the fireplace at the West Arms, where we were warming up to the discussion of the problem of the national drink.

Squire Price of Rhiwlas, near Bala, was a great Welsh eccentric in that tradition which so delighted Thomas Love Peacock. A. J. Lloyd Price, Esq., would have been the ideal host of Headlong Hall. He was a sportsman who produced such memorable volumes as *Dogs Ancient and Modern*, *Walks in Wales* and *Rabbits for Powder and Rabbits for Profit*. He was a strong supporter of cottage industries and a keen student of pedigrees, both of men and horses. In fact, at one stage of his career, he plunged heavily on the Cambridgeshire to recoup his fortunes. Rumour has it that this was the only occasion when prayers were offered up in lonely Welsh chapels for the success of a racehorse. Bendigo, with the fate of the Squire and most of Bala on his back, romped home in the race and the Squire never forgot his lucky escape.

Over the family vault in Llanfor churchyard he engraved this pious verse:

> As to my latter end I go,
> To meet my Jubilee,
> I bless the good horse Bendigo,
> Who built this tomb for me.

It may have been Bendigo's money that helped to float the great dream of Welsh whisky. Squire Price and his associates were determined to do the thing properly. They built a solid, stone-walled distillery at Ffrongoch beside the River Treweryn. They bought the best machinery and lured experts from Deeside to supervise the work.

At last the great day dawned. Welsh whisky, in a bottle decorated with a vivid label showing a lady in national costume sampling the contents with patriotic relish, was placed on the market. History does not record that the Scottish distillers were unduly worried. They have faced such competition before. Scotch—genuine Scotch—has survived all attempts to imitate its peculiar qualities.

Alas, Welsh whisky proved no exception to the rule. I do not suggest for a moment that it was as curious as the whisky entitled 'Himalayan Dew', which I once drank in India, or as nasty as the famous Japanese product 'King George V Black and Blue as served in Buckingham Palace by Queen Mary', But it did, according to one connoisseur who tasted it, possess a remarkable and unusual property—it matured backwards! It was splendid in cask and puzzling, to say the least of it, in bottle.

The Squire did his best to push it on the market, He prepared a special cask which he sent as a present to King Edward VII. The royal secretary, in a courteous acknowledgement, intimated that His Majesty was pleased to keep Welsh whisky in his cellar. There is no record of its ever coming out!

I have a picture in my mind of the gallant Squire arriving at the local inn and demanding whisky. A drop of Scotch is placed before him. 'Degenerate son of Wales!' he apostrophises the shame-faced landlord. 'How dare you serve me with this foreign concoction? I demand Welsh whisky. And if you haven't got it, sign here on the order book and I'll see that you get it—tomorrow!'

Perhaps it was his determination to popularise Welsh whisky that led the Squire to promote a special table water which could go with it. I have the advertisement for it before me, ingeniously printed on an imitation railway ticket:

Rhiwalis St Beuno,

Sparkling Diuretic Table Water,

The Nicest of all; Cheapest and the

Kidney and Liver Pacificator.

Mixes beautifully with White Wines, Lemon

or Spirits.

2/6 per dozen. Carriage paid both ways.

I am a little worried about that persuasive phrase, 'Kidney and Liver Pacificator'.

Could the Squire have designed 'Rhiwalis St Beuno' not to be taken *with* but *after* Welsh whisky?

But the First World War put an end to the Squire's dream. His distillery at Ffrongoch became a prisoner-of-war camp for, amongst other people, Michael Collins, captured after the Easter Rising of 1916. Mike Collins left no record of his opinion of Welsh whisky! In the 1930s the distillery itself was demolished and today, a few miles upstream from its site, the bulldozers have created the great dam which impounds the pure peat laden-waters of the Treweryn stream for Liverpool's new reservoir.

You may find a few bottles of Welsh whisky preserved here and there in North Wales. Bob Semple, late of the Royal White Lion Hotel, has carefully preserved some documents and legends which have gathered around the Squire's attempt to give Wales a national drink.

One day he and I will open his last bottle of Welsh whisky and raise our glasses to the next benefactor who will carry on where the Marquess and the Squire left off. After all, the old proverb says, 'Three tries for a Welshman'. Our toast, of course, could only be *I'r Achos*—to the cause!

We couldn't drink such a toast in coffee, warming and whole-some as it might be. We dried ourselves before the fire and lamented the Welsh failure to create a national drink, while out-side the rain continued to pour down as if it were washing away the last hopes of the Marquess of Bute's vineyards. Talk about wine and whisky could not postpone the evil moment of remount-ing. But we had been given a strong moral boost. The rain didn't seem quite as wet as we set up over the next spur into the top end of the side valley of the Teirw. And as a reward for our courage, the rain suddenly lifted, the clouds blew clear and in a blissful moment our whole world changed. The vast moorlands around us sparkled as the sun glittered on the raindrops. We had come out on to the trackway through the peat bogs still marked on the Ordnance Survey as 'Ffordd Saeson', the English road. This is the very spot where tradition maintains that Henry II's invading army was overwhelmed by a patriotic cloudburst.

I had a mild sympathy for anyone caught by rain in these hills, although no Welshman can feel any deep emotion about that ruthless and pathologically peripatetic Plantagenet. I could see the horses sinking into the bogs—Tika and I knew all about that—the squires trying to rescue the knights, weighed down by their rain-rusted armour. No wonder the baffled invaders declared that Merlin had returned to control anti-English weather. We trotted on, dried out and encouraged by the sparkling sun. Only two hours back I had felt that life was a damp, unending misery. Now the whole world seemed new minted, crystal clear. Biddy led us on at a trot over the mountain track leading up across the main ridge of the Berwyns. Great, uplifting views greeted us as we crossed the summit—the tops of the Berwyns miles away to our left, behind us the whole of mid-Wales, ahead the last stage of our journey to the sea. We reined up for a moment and took a breather. I confess to a sense of triumph. The Berwyns were the last barrier between us and our final objective. There were plenty of other mountains—a whole range of them in fact, the Clwydian range, which we would have to ride to reach the sea. But none of them as high as the Berwyns or as savage as the Desert of Wales. We trotted pleasantly down amongst the pine plantations into the deep trench of the valley of the Dee.

We hit it near the village of Glyndyfrdwy and got a shock. We had been so long in the lonely places, riding over moorlands and through unfrequented lanes that we had forgotten that there was such a thing as the motor-car or that the main roads of Britain have become race tracks. This road up the valley of the Dee carries most of the holiday traffic towards Snowdonia in the summer. Riding along it was like riding on the back of a circular saw—every car that passed gave an angry protesting snarl at seeing the outmoded horse usurping the place needed by the internal-combustion engine. Seamus didn't take kindly to this ordeal by noise and Felicity had to hold him in firmly. Tika, naturally, didn't flick an eyelid and plodded happily on as the cars roared by under her nose. We covered about half a mile of this petrol-soaked race-track that calls itself A5, the successor of the great highway that Telford built to speed up the Irish mail in the old coaching days. Then we turned gratefully down to cross the Dee and join the quiet, winding road that runs on the other side of the valley. We watered the horses in the Dee.

Biddy had a carefully calculated schedule for water. Like a human being, a horse must not overdrink when heated or on a hot day. And I enjoyed the moment when I rode gently with Tika into the shallows, with the sunlight filtering down through the canopy of leaves and Tika's hoofs making a soothing clicking sound as she moved to find just the right spot to sample the clear water with a satisfying sucking sound that spoke of infinite ease and satisfaction.

'Bit better than the other road,' a friendly farmer said to us, as he saw us bring the horses back out of the water. 'I never go over the other side till September.' 'Talk about perpetual

motion,' I said; 'that traffic's the nearest to it I ever saw.'
'Well, a funny thing you should talk of perpetual motion,
because they say that it was along that very stretch of road that
Edward Lloyd drove his machine. And some still say that he
had found the secret.' There and then, he told me the strange
story of the nineteenth-century engineer, Edward Lloyd, who
is buried in the churchyard at Glyndyfrdwy. Apparently this
gifted and eccentric man made a great impression on the valley
in the days when few people penetrated its quiet seclusion. He
worked in secret. No one knew quite what he was up to until,
one morning, the inhabitants were astonished to see a large
drum-like object bowling gently along the road. 'My grandfather always used to say that he saw it himself. There was no
doubt about it. The wheel went on and on and there was nothing
to show what was driving the thing along. Of course, nothing
came of it because Edward Lloyd wanted to keep the secret to
himself—died with him, I think.'

I wonder. I'm no mathematician and the whole business of
perpetual motion may be mathematically impossible, but perhaps
Edward Lloyd had found some secret that had eluded more
orthodox-minded men. The story set me thinking about the
only occasion when I met a man who claimed to have solved one
of the great natural puzzles of the world, to have succeeded when
the most brilliant scientific minds have all failed. I feel a bit
guilty about it, because I suppose I should have assisted the
discoverer to bring his remarkable break-through to the attention of the European experts. But it happened in a remote part
of the world on an extraordinary occasion and concerned a
proposition of which I had never heard before and which I still
don't understand.

It happened in the little town of Jacmel, tucked away on a wild
peninsula in Haiti, the black republic of the West Indies. I
thought about it as we turned off the road on to the mountain
track that was to take us over the next obstacle, Mynydd
Llantislio. A long, long pull up with Tika puffing a bit at the
tail-end of the procession and thus giving me plenty of time to

muse in the saddle and dream myself back into Jacmel. I had gone there to report on an Unesco project for the BBC. This was in the days before the present dictatorship in Haiti, when things were easier and life was lived in the slack, unhurried pace of the tropics. The poverty was dramatic, unbelievable, but the Haitians covered it with a veneer of French culture tinctured with Voodoo. Even the beggars had charm. A breezy old gentleman appeared at my car window in Port-au-Prince and gave me a gap-toothed smile, 'Hullo, what are you going to give me this morning?' But the prize went to a willowy youth who tapped me on the shoulder as I came out of the bank. He asked if I was a tourist. I said, 'No, *gens de radio!*' 'Then you will be interested in my literary work, monsieur?'

Out of his pocket he pulled a piece of paper and urged me to read what was written on it. It turned out to be a love-letter, packed with flowery phrases, to a young girl named Marguerite. 'You know how my deep sincerity shows in every word, every movement, every gesture. Surely you cannot be oblivious to the unhappiness that now possesses my heart and which a slight concession on your part would cure for ever. Do you remember Alfred de Musset, "A door must be either open or shut." Why do you spurn me? Besides I can assure you that my bed has good springs. *À toi, devoué,* Gérard Simon.' 'I am Gérard Simon,' he said to me. 'That is my writing and now that you know I am unhappy in love'—he came closer and whispered in my ear— 'you cannot refuse me a dollar.' I gave it to him as a tribute to an artist.

Jacmel lies about sixty miles south of the capital, but those sixty miles are hair-raising. The track wriggles through mountains and crosses a river a hundred times. Needless to say, the rains had started, the river was in flood and the road had washed away. I shut my eyes and went by plane, accompanied by a company of Haitian soldiers who carried rifles slung over one arm and their pet fighting cocks over the other. The plane brushed mountain-tops and skimmed down deep, green-choked valleys. A smart right-hand turn over a coconut grove and we were down in a soggy field. No formalities about landing. An excited crowd swarmed around the plane as if it was Lindberg landing in Paris, the baggage was hurled into the local bus by two bright-eyed boys and we set off through the long grass. The bus had rows of seats, highly painted like a dodgem at a fair and bore the pious inscription, 'La Sainte Famille'. It rattled us into Jacmel.

This was Haiti as I had always imagined it to be, where all the houses were tin-roofed, with rickety balconies and Saturday night is Voodoo night. Everybody was dozing on their verandas and children sprawled over the unsurfaced roadways. Little hotels flaunted a 1900 coquettish charm, compounded of rusting ironwork and glimpses of copper-coloured Madame presiding, half asleep, over the bar. The bus rattled past the local cinema, where a notice proclaimed to the energetic inhabitants of Jacmel that, at 8.30 p.m., they could 'assist' at that greatest of *spectacles du Cinéma, Les Miracles de l'Enfer'*. The red-and-white placard continued, *'Un film riche d'esprit et de splendeur. La Vie de Casanova n'est qu'amour, vices et volupté. Les femmes se laissent tuer pour faire sauver sa vie.'* Then the final bait in big letters, *'Une Vie Savoureuse!'*

A few days of life in Jacmel were *'savoureuse'* enough for me. A gay little garden stood in the centre of town near to a tin church, while next to the Tribunal de la Paix, a fretwork marvel imported direct from the Paris Exhibition, my own hotel, the unbeatable Excelsior, offered its hospitality to the only guest for the last week—myself! The bus pulled up with a flourish outside a door marked 'Salon de Beauté'. Madame detached herself with difficulty from her rocking-chair and floated her eighteen stone into the Salon de Reception, which was gaily decorated with adverts in five languages—pretty girls with nothing on advising you 'get Kist for a Nickel'. Over the desk was a smudged photo of the current dictator, Colonel Magloire, printed as a tribute by *'Les Amis L'Ordre'*.

Monsieur entered, every other tooth gold-filled—each time he smiled I calculated the monetary value lost to Haiti. 'Welcome, welcome to your comfortable room,' he shouted, 'but first, rum punch, eh, *mon ami*?' A little crop-haired boy, as black as coal, thrust the drinks in our hands and we clutched them as we climbed the stairs, decorated with Art Nouveau balustrades straight out of the Paris Metro. The wall-paper was a legacy of 1908. The pictures, probably bought as a job lot from a passing salesman, represented snow scenes in Alsace. Stuck in the frame of the biggest one was a simpering photo of Gaby Deslys, gnawing a string of pearls as she showed a provocative leg out of a whirl of white petticoats. Underneath Monsieur has written, *'Souvenirs d'Amour'*.

'Here you will be at home,' he promised me. 'The lavatory is on the roof, but the pigeons and the crowing of the cocks will not disturb you—this evening a high honour comes to you. Monsieur Pascal Brun will call.'

I awaited M. Brun on my balcony accompanied by a friendly cockroach who emerged from the wardrobe. I was at home among the aspidistras, the crochet-work table cloth, the elaborately bulging mahogany chair legs. The Jacmel day revealed its charm. The clouds piled up in the afternoon and emptied punctually between four o'clock and six. Then followed the magic hour before the sun disappeared. The light became mellow, the colours deepened into splendid painterly reds and greens, the scent of flowers chaliced the air. The little central garden, overlooking the curving beach filled with the citizens, the young couples hand in hand while mother kept careful watch on them from her balcony, the children playing singing games and the old men tilted back in their chairs in front of the Café de Paris deep in the complicated ritual of the card game of 'La Bette'. The Garde Haitien made eyes at the pretty, brown-skinned mulatto girls, standing in the windows of their ultra-modern concrete barracks. A new notice appeared in front of the Democratic Cinema promising a change of film at bargain prices, ' *"Romance à Trois," un film délicieux qui vous laissera quelques images de melancholie, quelques flocons d'amour!'*

Happy Jacmel, all plastered with photographs of Colonel

Magloire, with three papers appearing at irregular intervals and dreams of wealth, if only tourists would come to bathe on its fifteen miles of sand under the palms. Thrice happy to be the home of such a man as M. Pascal Brun, who, as he explained himself when he called on me at the hotel, 'both edits, owns, distributes and controls a powerful organ of public opinion, *La Nouvelle Abeille*'. *The New Bee* buzzes with news items— weddings, staggering successes of the sons of Jacmel in the Baccalauréat examination, rich jokes about the amorous misfortunes of the leading merchants, and port movements, printed under a block of a paddle steamer which might have been a blockade runner in the American Civil War. A modest note hinted that any article not signed was the work of *Notre Cher Directeur*—which meant most of the paper. *The Bee* apologised to its readers for its erratic dates of publication 'due to circumstances which are familiar to you all and which it ill becomes our dignity to adumbrate'—probably the machinations of the editor of the rival *Voix de Jacmel*, M. René Jolicoeur! M. Brun handed me two copies of *The Bee* and then gravely announced his reason for calling upon me.

'You see before you the first man who has solved the theories of Diophantus.'

Monsieur arrived with two rums. A troop of curious little boys and odd passers-by came into the room or leered in through the windows. 'It's true, M. Brun has made a great discovery. Vive M. Brun!' *'Vive Diophante!'* shouted the little boys offstage. I am certain that, like myself, they had no idea who Diophantus was or what he had propounded in his theorem, but they were there to cheer on a distinguished son of Jacmel obviously conversing with an equally distinguished scientist.

M. Brun put a pile of carefully typed manuscript on the table. 'You'll find it all there. My only regret is that I cannot get the Sorbonne to look at it. Not even your Oxford or Harvard or Yale, although naturally I would prefer the approval of the Sorbonne. All I got in return from my letter was a polite note saying it was hardly likely I had reached a solution of this proposition which has puzzled mankind for nearly eighteen hundred years. But, believe me, monsieur, I have. And I need hardly tell you of the importance of a solution of this theorem.'

I smiled and bowed in a noncommittal way. I wasn't going to reveal my ignorance. I have since discovered that Diophantus was a mathematician who lived in Alexandria around A.D. 275 and whose masterpieces included a treatise on Polygonal Numbers and a volume (since lost) with the intriguing title of *Porisms*. His name is still commemorated, according to the book of reference, by Diophantial Analysis, 'that part of algebra which treats of the finding of particular rational values for general expression in a surd form'. But did he propound a special theorem the solution of which would involve a break-through in mathematics and had M. Pascal Brun achieved this remarkable feat in isolated Jacmel, where Voodoo drums beat a lullaby every Saturday night and the local religion included ritualistic glass-eating?

'Write to me when you return and have enlisted the massive support of your great BBC and of your idealistic Unesco. Then, together, we will have revolutionised the world,' said M. Brun.

'*Vive la Révolution*,' shouted the dutiful chorus, no doubt deciding that one of Haiti's annual *coups d'état* was about to be launched. I'm afraid I did nothing to launch M. Pascal Brun's great discovery. All seemed possible in Jacmel and incredible in the atmosphere of sober London. M. Brun joined Edward Lloyd in the great gallery of might-have-beens. Besides, I can't count and the simplest mathematical problems are beyond me. Poor M. Brun! He had, once again, picked the wrong man to help him establish his reputation as the Einstein of the Caribbean.

Meditating upon Haiti had carried me high up Llantislio Mountain. We came out on to a rolling moorland, with low heather here and there and the world of North Wales below us. Instinctively our horses broke into the trot. The structure of the mountain demanded it. The mountains of Wales are divided sharply into two—those it is a pleasure to ride and those that defy you and actively attack the horse with their secret weapons of bog, rock and precipice. Llantislio was a welcoming, riding mountain. Little sheep tracks through the low heather and an easy slope leading down for miles to the north. Biddy had no need to give the order. We went up from the trot into the canter. Rowland and the rest even went into the gallop. The canter was enough for Tika and myself. We fairly floated down into the tumbled country below, past fields where the cattle stared at us and went gallumphing away in fright.

I had noticed the same effect in many parts of mountain Wales. The horse has become an unfamiliar creature to the cow, whereas the tractor and the car have been accepted as part of the natural order. Down we came into the complex of side lanes that we took to lead us through the Upper Vale of Clwyd to the welcome of Ruthin. Our nightly broadcasts had alerted the countryside. I had mentioned old Tika's habit of forming the tail-end of our procession. The crowd that lined the Castle Square gave her an ironic yet friendly cheer. She got to work on her expert trick of touching hearts for sugar as soon as we had slid out of the saddle. I added my tribute. Next morning we would ride over the Clwydian range to the sea. Nothing could stop us. I entered the Castle Inn to face the microphone with the comfortable thought that we had our objective 'in the bag'.

But next morning, waiting in the warm sun on the Square, which was empty with the loneliness of Sunday, I got the anxious feeling that never quite deserted me on these early starts of ours—would something go wrong with the horses at the very last moment? I listened anxiously for the reassuring clop–clop of hoofs in the distance. All was well, Biddy led them round the corner into the Square with all the members of the local Pony Club trotting behind her. The Square at Ruthin had not seen so many horses mustered there since before the First World War.

A large stone is carefully preserved outside the main bank in the Square. This is the Maen Huail. On it, tradition claims, King Arthur executed a troublesome and traitorous knight of that name. I was tempted to use it as a mounting-block, but that seemed almost like sacrilege. Instead, I led Tika to the kerbside and, assisted by the extra few inches of the pavement, swung easily into the saddle. With our escort of members of the Pony Club we clattered out of sleepy Ruthin towards the east. The sun was warm over the countryside. Our incredible luck with the weather still held. We had been soaked on the Berwyns, it is true, but our other days seem, as I remember them, to be bathed in perpetual sunshine. It isn't always like this in mountainous Wales!

Now we were at grips with our last mountain range. The Clwydian hills are a switchback of steep ups and downs, mounting ever higher to the climax of the 1,700-foot Moel Fammau. There's no difficulty about riding up Moel Fammau. Thousands stroll up it every Sunday, but it's got the perfect position for a viewpoint. We drew rein under the ruined tower on the summit. All North Wales was clear around us. I've rhapsodised about hill views all through this book and have now run out of adjectives. How do I convey the real excitement that always overwhelms me when I find myself hoisted high above a vast landscape, and the light clouds are dappling the valleys with patches of shade as the morning sun catches the high peaks and a lark sings overhead and our horses' hoofs sound hollow over the smooth turf—away I go into an incoherent tumble of halting phrases. But the sensation never fails to move me, this feeling of having shaken myself free of the mundane world, of ascending into a lonely place of the mind.

The summit of Moel Fammau, however, can hardly be called lonely. And in any case the highest point is occupied by a ruined tower, erected in 1810 to celebrate the Jubilee of King George the Third. The *Gentleman's Magazine* (Volume 81) fairly let itself go in its description of the scene at the laying of the foundation stone, as the official party, 'accompanied by a constellation of beautiful ladies', listened to Lord Kenyon giving the address.

'Instantly a burst of joyful acclamation made the welkin ring and the reverberation from mountain to mountain produced a most aweful and impressive sensation. The Military then fired several rounds and a *feu-de-joie*, and the music breathed forth our national pathetic air of God Save the King with enchanting effect.'

What a commentator that reporter would have made if only we could have jumped the years and got him in front of a microphone! I would have wished for a *feu-de-joie* to celebrate our own achievement. Moel Fammau was our last high summit, we were surely safe in thinking that our long ride was coming to a successful end. 'You'd better look out for broken bottles on these slopes. They can give your horse's legs a nasty cut,' our guide warned us. We rode northwards carefully, but it didn't need bottles to slow our progress. These hills are extremely steep-sided and we slid up and down them like cowboys in TV Westerns. We rode, slid and occasionally trotted for two hours along this marvellous switchback of a range. The path takes you among low heather. Ahead of you is always another steep, cone-shaped summit, and one, in especial, with the title of Pen-y-Cloddiau, where the whole summit was contoured with impressive earthworks—a sort of Welsh Maiden's Castle; an Iron Age fort which has accumulated the usual collection of legends. Rowland reminded us of the story of St Garmon, who in the early days of Christianity in Wales was wandering through these parts when he called for a night's lodgings at this very fort, which was then the stronghold of the mighty prince, Benlli. Now, whether or not the prince had had quite enough of holy men calling on him demanding free bed and breakfast is not quite certain. Wales was full of saints begging for a night's lodging at this period. But the fact remains that Benlli threw the unfortunate St Garmon out on his neck. So there was the Saint, deprived of his statutory free board, out on the bleak hillside— and it can be very bleak on this Clwydian range in winter and on a rainy night at that!

But have no fear. Celtic saints always fell on their feet. They didn't go in much for painful martyrdom. St David, St Illtud,

St Teilo—all expired gently and painlessly in the odour of sanctity. So, of course, there was a poor cowherd handy who took St Garmon in and killed his only fatted calf for him. And, lo and behold, when they woke up in the morning, there was the calf, restored to life. The Saint had given full payment for bed and breakfast.

I find these old saintly stories full of the charm of lost innocence. I long to believe in them. When I find myself in the lonely places I am half-way to belief, but whenever I get ready to take the final step some Unfortunate Lapse always seems to occur. My worst disaster took place at Les Baux in the South of France, on the occasion of the Blessing of the Lamb on the eve of Christmas. Who wouldn't want to believe implicitly in such a charming ceremony—the new-born lamb chosen from the flock and presented by the youngest shepherd to be blessed by the priest in the strange rock-cut church of this deserted city, perched on a limestone crag overlooking the limitless plain of Provence. The BBC liked the sound of it. It would make a moving item for their Christmas Day round-up, if I recorded it 'down the line' on the previous day.

I drove down through Arles, which was plastered with advertisements for the advent of 'Zappy Max' and 'Les Bulldogs Footballeurs'. We turned off the main road and drove deep into the limestone hills. At last the moon landscape of Les Baux stood before us, the desert Valley of Kings planted in the midst of France. Grotesque teeth of limestone thrust themselves out of the ground into fretted, impossible shapes, until you protested that what this landscape needed was not a painter but a good dentist. Perched on the highest group of rocks, which broaden on the southern side into a little plateau cut off by precipices, is the ruined town, a chaos of crumbling walls, empty windows and narrow, silent lanes which climb higher and higher amongst the yellowing rocks until, at last, they bring you out on to the summit château, with the whole vast plain of the Lower Rhône below you—olive groves, rice fields, the wild lakes of the Camargue.

There were no tourists. Les Baux was ours for the rehearsal.
I was profoundly moved as I sat in the deserted church of St
Vincent, cut into the solid rock. How innocent the voice of the
girl soloist sounded amongst the tombs, how strong, confident
and comforting the reply in Provençal of the aged shepherd. All
was well until next evening, when we turned up for the actual
ceremony. Half France seemed to be turning up, too, mainly in
giant Packards. Two thousand crammed into the church which
holds eight hundred. Everybody stood on the seats and flashed
cameras as the youngest shepherd entered, pulling a charmingly
decorated cart towards the altar. The lights came on with a
sizzling effect, for the Curé had sold the film rights to a company
from America named Fox Films, under the impression that it
was Twentieth Century Fox. Amidst the whirring of the
cameras, the procession of shepherds in their deep hoods came
slowly past my commentary point as I was in full emotional
flight. The last shepherd paused at my side and a deep voice
with a familiar accent murmured, 'Hullo, Mr Thomas, remember
me? I was with you at the Cymmrodorion meeting at St
James's Palace. Do you know how Wales got on against the
South Africans?'

'What on earth!' I gasped.

'Oh, these robes,' he went on. 'Well, between you and me
there aren't any real shepherds left around here. The old boy
works in the olive-oil factory and the shepherdess is from the
secondary school. But they'd sold the film rights to this American company and the producer's a nice chap. We met him in the
bistro near the Auberge de la Jeunesse, where a lot of the boys
are staying—we're on a winter bike tour around these parts.
The poor chap was so upset that there weren't any shepherds
that we volunteered to give him a helping hand.'

'So all the other shepherds . . .'

'Aye, aye, that's right. All from the Ystalefera Operatic.'

There is no doubt that there are grave difficulties placed
today in the way of simple belief. I was shaken, on the slopes
beyond Pen-y-Cloddau, to find a whole family of pleasant

sceptics waiting to waylay us. I began my career in the BBC when every word we spoke was sacrosanct. No one questioned anything heard over the radio. The Corporation leaned over backwards to tell the truth. It still does, on the whole, but has the audience changed and become infected with fashionable disbelief? As we rode down to the last of the summits that form the Clwydian switchback, the waiting committee stopped us. 'Well, we are surprised. We didn't believe you were actually riding, and we selected this spot to check up. If you came here, it would have to be on a horse.'

'But how else could we come?'

'Oh, we expected you to ride a little way, of course, but we naturally assumed that once you'd done the first section, and everyone was out of sight, you loaded the horses into horse-boxes and rode around to the last section.'

I could almost see tears of indignation forming in Tika's eyes. I saw us wallowing together through the wild bogs above Tregaron, facing the driving rain on the Berwyns, riding high over the wind-swept Presellies. A horse-box indeed! The very thought made me indignant. Besides I would not have missed one yard of those eventful miles. We smiled warily if politely at the family committee and rode on to the last few hummocks that mark the downfall of the range to the more level country towards the north and the sea. They have a strange taste in names around here, drawn from the Bible in the days of the nonconformist revival. Er Eift—Egypt—I can understand, but what Biblical stalwart decided to name the near-by farm Sodom? Perhaps reaction against the far-off memories of the old religion that still seems to hang about this lower country of limestone and small secluded valleys that marks the change over from Denbighshire into Flint.

We had only a few miles to go—after riding past the long walls that enclose Bryn Bella, where Dr Johnston visited Mrs Thrale—when we came to a curious well at the side of the road with the water spouting from a carven face of stone. The near-by cottage had the inscription, St Beuno's Well. Now, there are any amount of wells dedicated to the good saint in North Wales. We reined up to water the horses—they were about due for this, for the Clwydian range had been waterless as far as the horses were concerned—and I took the last chance of practising the Borrovian technique and of gossiping with the good folk of the house. Mrs Roberts had her young grandchild in her arms.

'Oh, the old well used to be a place of pilgrimage in the old days. I remember when people still used to come and take a bottle of the water away with them.'

'Has it any medical qualities?'

'More of a matter of faith, I think it was. Mind you, this was a well-known spot. You wouldn't think that H. M. Stanley once lived here.'

'Was that before he took the name?'

'I think it was his uncle and aunt who lived here. We've got a letter from him in the house, when he was still John Rowlands and he must have been pretty desperate. Nobody seemed to want to help him. He wrote to his indifferent relatives: "They haven't succeeded in finding me a situation at Moel Railway Station." Fancy H. M. Stanley as a station-master. It doesn't bear thinking about, does it?'

Indeed it doesn't. Stanley meeting Livingstone off the 5.30 from Prestatyn? Impossible. He wasn't the sort of man who would have stayed on a railway platform, in any case. He had that demoniacal drive that was to make him the greatest explorer ever to come out of Wales. After all, Wales hasn't produced so many—or rather those she has produced have done their exploring under other names, like Stanley, or had their work completed by other men. Such a one was poor John Evans.

John Evans is not a name which has hit the headlines, yet I was brought up on his saga as related by my Auntie Bess. Come to think of it, Auntie Bess was the nearest our family ever got to producing an explorer, or at any rate someone who ventured on a long journey into wild country. In this decade of easy travel I have found myself in any amount of semi-wild places. I have looked out towards the cruel, burning sand wastes of the still formidable Rub al Khali, the empty quarter of Arabia. I have seen the mud sky-scrapers of Shibam, wedged in the high, bare cliffs of the Hadhramaut. I have wandered with the Somali cattle tribes on the bleak borders of Abyssinia, but I have always been aware of an easy escape route offstage. The jeep would arrive from the nearest trading post or an aeroplane would whisk me back over desert, glacier or impenetrable forest to a drink and a bath at the hotel. Even in this description of our ride through Wales, I have been conscious of overstretching the sense of words like adventure, exploration or enterprise. Now that we were nearing the end of our ride I was compelled to admit that we had an easy time of it compared to the rides my Auntie Bess took as a matter of course. But then, she did her riding in the 1870s out in the West of America, when Montana had not yet become a state and the Indians were perpetually on the warpath.

Auntie Bess had indeed gone to America when the West was still wild. From the calm and peace of rural Wales in the 1870s she had suddenly been projected into the world of Sitting Bull, Chief Ram-in-the-Face and Custer's Last Stand. For forty years she had lived in Montana in the foothills of the Rockies; then, as the turbulent West subsided into respectability, she returned home, as a widow, to subside into a small house in a long suburban terrace in Swansea, within a few minutes of our home.

She became our secret family glory. No other family, we were convinced as small boys, had such a possession as Auntie Bess; she was our cinema and TV set all rolled into one. Once she started talking about the Wild West we sat at her feet and marvelled. After school and before homework we would run to 20 George Street. The way led past a shop, where the back-end bore a mystic sign whose meaning we never fathomed: 'Phillips' Fine Teas. They stand the Second Water.'

Her house was a strange structure. No one wall ever made a right-angle to the other. From some aspects it looked like the celebrated cabinet of Dr Caligari. When Swansea had begun to grow out of its architectural clothes in the full tide of mid-Victorian prosperity, the local builders ran up terraces with the ease of the little woman next door running up a new dress. They were all of a pattern, rows of two-storied houses, with a small garden in front surrounded by iron railings and a 'back', leading out into 'the Lane'. The terraces sprouted off the main roads like a skeleton of fish-bones and, from time to time, hit these main roads at an angle. Classical architects might have regarded this as an appalling difficulty, to be solved with carefully balanced columns and cunningly placed recesses. The Welsh builder knew a quicker way; he just cut up the terraces as a butcher cuts up a string of sausages.

The result was that the last house in the terrace always got the chopper. It looked square in front and lapsed into a variety of strange geometrical shapes at the back. Auntie Bess's house was a convex polygon with rhomboidal tendencies. She didn't care. '*Twt i pawb*, Wynford bach, I had to sleep in the back of a covered wagon when I first went to Montana. At least I've got a roof over my head here.' She was an invincible optimist and joined all three political parties when she came home. 'The Labour people get my vote, the Tories take me to the poll in nice cars.' 'And the Liberals, Auntie?' 'They are marvellous at running whist drives.'

So she would be waiting for us, bright-eyed, plump as a red-cheeked apple, swinging and smiling in her rocking-chair, surrounded by a marvellous collection of mining share certificates which were the chief decoration of the walls and mantelpiece. 'They are all your Uncle David left to me, and who knows, one day . . .'

We were convinced, as we looked at this gaudy gallery of hostages to unrealised fortunes, that we, too, were sitting under a silver mine. The American share-pusher of the 1880s obviously cared nothing for restraint; there was no City of London tight-lipped rectitude for him. He slapped on the colour with a free hand; his artists depicted Indians giving glittering chunks of metal to grateful prospectors, sunsets over the Rockies, while men in red shirts dug with fury in romantic creeks and gulches. The papers glowed with reds, yellows and blues, while the very names of the mines were enough to set the dullest investor dreaming—Bonanza Strike, Snake River El Dorado, Snowy Silver, the Inexhaustible, Fortunes for All Inc. Uncle David had found them irresistible. He had carved a respectable business out of the frontier chaos, a general store where he made big money by selling goods to the workers driving Big Jim Hill's Great Northern Railroad through the mountains, but every six months or so would come a tap on the door, and a group of Old Timers entered Uncle David's back office for an evening spent over maps, survey claims and Bourbon. After that, Auntie Bess prepared for financial squalls. Uncle David was on to a winner once again!

Alas for the family fortunes. All Auntie Bess's beautiful pieces of paper became worthless when the U.S.A. abandoned the dual silver-and-gold standard. 'I will never forget the morning, boys,' said Auntie Bess to us, 'when your uncle came in from the store with a heavy face, "Bess, we've ceased to be bimetallist!" '

We boys had no idea what being a bimetallist implied. We thought it was some splendidly secret religion, more exciting than Methodism; a conviction that grew to certainty when Auntie Bess recited the ringing speech of a gentleman named William Jennings Bryan, which ended with a scarifying denunciation of the New York bankers, 'You shall not crucify mankind on a cross of gold.' We pictured the prophet Bryan, with a beard like Moses and a dress like the leader of the Ku Klux Klan, riding eastwards at the head of his hordes of indignant cowboys and miners, every item of his harness made of shining silver, as he prepared to storm the defences of Wall Street.

'I mustn't blame your uncle, for I loved to listen to the talk myself. Only, after the miners left, I used to rush around to the bank with all the money lying in the house and put it into a little private account. For I remembered the advice given by our guide when I set out to join your uncle in 1872 in a covered-wagon train across the plains to the Rockies, "Always go through life as if the Indians were about to attack tomorrow." '

In Auntie Bess's stories they always were! They began with the ritualistic phrase, 'When I set out to join your uncle the railway had not got farther west than Fort Benton.' Where Fort Benton was we never discovered, but it was the magic word opening prospects of the immense, treeless prairies, the long columns of prairie schooners winding their slow way along the banks of the wide Missouri, the scout motionless on his pony scanning the far horizon for the tell-tale wisp of smoke rising in the west—Indians! The Sioux were once again on the warpath.

'We had to wait to go on until we had an escort of U.S. Cavalry. I remember how our train leader came to me and said, "Ma'am, can you fire a gun?" "No," I said, "but I can throw things quite well." "O.K.," he said, "you'll do." '

'And if the Sioux had attacked, auntie?'

'Well, I had one more chance left; I would have shouted out in Welsh to them. They might have understood.'

Then it was that I heard, from the lips of one who had actually fought her way through Indian country, the long-lived legend of the tribe of Welsh-speaking Indians that haunted the imagination of Wales from Tudor times until it received its death blow under nineteenth-century criticism and with the closing of the old Wild West. Maybe my Auntie Bess was the last one who was entitled to believe it. Her West was still wild, and somewhere, somehow, in a remote canyon of the Rockies there was still a chance that an Indian might be found who would answer a warm-hearted Welsh greeting with 'Iawn, diolch' and not with a disappointing and noncommital 'How!'

The story is linked with the equally mysterious legend of a Welsh discovery of America. According to this, around about 1170, Madoc, son of Owain Gwynedd, the ruler of North Wales, sailed away to the mysterious west and disappeared with three hundred men and ten ships into the mists of the Atlantic. Then, as the English started to explore and settle on the coast of North America reports began to appear of Indians who understood words of Welsh. One David Ingram, who had sailed with Sir John Hawkins, is reported to have heard them talking of a bird called the Pen Gwyn, which is Welsh for 'white head'. What could this be other than the penguin, in spite of the hard facts that penguins have black heads and are never seen in the northern hemisphere. By Queen Elizabeth's day the Welsh Indians had appeared in print. No one could doubt that here were the descendants of the long-lost Madoc and his men. What was more, Madoc's discovery had long predated that of Columbus. Did not this give Queen Elizabeth, with her Welsh origin, a prior claim to America far stronger than that of Spain and Portugal?

All through the seventeenth and early eighteenth centuries people appeared who claimed to have actually met and spoken Welsh to these mysterious Blackfeet-Celts. A dubious dissenting minister, by name Morgan Jones, deposed in 1686 that he had been captured by the Tuscorara tribe somewhere in the wilds of Virginia. They were about to take his scalp when he shouted for help in Welsh. A man from the Doeg tribe understood him, arranged for him to be spared and took him home, where the Doegs immediately chatted away in fluent Welsh. Morgan Jones lived with them for four months and repaid their hospitality by preaching to them three times a week. After that, it is not surprising that the Doegs hurriedly invited him to return to his own people.

Unfortunately the Welsh Indians seemed to disappear ever westwards as America became more settled. By the end of the eighteenth century the candidates for the proud title of Madoc's descendants were the Mandan Indians, who were reported to live far up the Missouri river in what is now the state of South Dakota. They had well-constructed villages and had, so it was said, whiter skin than other Indians. Keen Welsh patriots back in London wanted no further proof. This was at the beginning of the Romantic period in literature. Welsh poetry, history, antiquity were all receiving vigorous attention. The legend of Madoc sprung into new life and it seemed the most natural thing in the world for a London Welsh committee to finance an expedition to contact these lost Celts. They might become good Methodists.

In 1792 a young man from Caernarvonshire named John Evans set out with the committee's blessing to reach the Mandans. He was innocent, rash, not tactful, but he had courage, persistence and an excellent sense of map-making. Professor David Williams, the authority on John Evans's journey, declared, that 'He had in him the makings of a really great explorer.' With incredible difficulty he did succeed in reaching the Mandans and lived among them for six months. But to his intense disappointment Chief Black Cat and Chief Big White had never heard of Madoc or Wales, and although the Mandans were kind to him, their fertility rites made it clear that they would never become good Methodists. Poor Evans lost out in the disputes that followed between Spain and the U.S.A. He died early, but not before he had produced a remarkable map which came into the hands of President Jefferson. Jefferson in turn gave it to the leaders of the first expedition to complete the journey up the Missouri and over the Rockies to the Pacific. Merriweather Lewis and Clark got the fame, but they based their journey on poor John Evans's map and previous explorations. So, after all, Madoc did play a part in the discovery of America! And somehow or other, his legend still goes marching on in spite of every announcement that it has been finally killed. It reappeared after the war, up in British Columbia, where the Kootenay Indians are now the successors to the Paducas, the Doegs, the Mandans and the rest of the tribes that turned out to be such a disappointment to the London Welsh patriots. Apparently their numbers are astonishingly like the Welsh numerals and an ogham inscription has been identified at a place with the unpromising name of Spuzzum! Perhaps a lost Welsh missionary once sojourned in those parts! I think I will await further evidence before announcing that the Welsh have displaced Columbus and Lief Ericson.

But now our own expedition was reaching its climax. We hadn't had to face the hardships of an H. M. Stanley or a John Evans, but, in our mild way, we, too, had been blazing a trail. I don't think that anyone in the last hundred years had ridden our route. I'm sure that I shared the feelings of Lewis and Clark as they came over the Great Divide of the Rockies or of Stanley as he advanced with hand outstretched to meet Livingstone, when our little expedition came up over the hill beyond St Beuno's Well and caught a glimpse of the sea a mere three miles away. Half an hour's easy riding through the by-ways and we would be there!

I drifted gently along, with Tika unhurried and the sun shining over the checkered fields. The high hills were all behind us. This was the quiet, contemplative landscape that the poet Gerald Manley Hopkins came to know and wrote of it:

> Lovely the woods, waters, meadows, combes, vales,
> All the air things wear that build this world of Wales.

Thinking of these lines, I followed past Llanasia, where Hopkins stayed in the Jesuit college and struggled to learn Welsh. We had almost completed our ride through this world of Wales. We needed a finale. These last few miles had kept us in country Wales almost to the end. This is still a tableland and we could see nothing of the main road, the railway, the industry of the mouth of the Dee. The map showed it was there, but the eye couldn't believe it. We had ridden for eight days out of sight of a chimney, a factory, a pylon, an industrial town of any sort. I had almost forgotten they existed.

We came over the brow and the whole modern world poured in on us with a rush: the big Shotton steelworks away to the east, main roads, terraces, railway lines, caravan parks, pit-heads, gasworks, and on the corner where the grey sands of Dee gave place to muddy waters, the white tower of the lighthouse of the Point of Air, the most north-easterly point of Wales.

Before us was Journey's End. Tika slowed down automatically. I let her drift gently across to the roadside. Billy, Rowland and Felicity rode on until they dropped out of sight in a dip in the road. I slipped out of the saddle. The wilds were far behind us and our long journey was nearly over. I wanted to say something and I needed privacy to say it. I wanted to say 'Thank you' to old Tika. I looked at her standing so patiently on that quiet road. Eight long days I had spent in her company. When I first met her I knew nothing about the horse. I did not know much, even now, about horses in general, but I certainly knew a great deal about one particular horse—even-tempered, steady-going, utterly reliable Tika! From her back I had seen a new Wales and discovered a new world. But how do you say 'Thank you' to a horse?

Biddy and I had talked on the road about Tika's future, for this might be her last great ride. 'I might let her join the Roberts family in Towyn, on the sea in Merionethshire. They like the look of her and the children will take care of her—make a fuss over her. She'll like that. Perhaps next summer, we'll see.'

Towyn—a pleasant place for retirement, with Cader Idris in the background, the wide sands of Cardigan Bay sweeping away to the north and all the little Roberts children looking up with pride at the horse that conquered Wales. No doubt at all, Tika would like that!

I felt in my pocket and produced the inevitable lump of sugar. Tika munched it contentedly. I stroked her nose. In the end, there didn't seem to be a better way of expressing my feelings. Tika understood. I swung up again into the saddle and looked out over the steelworks and the chimneys that sprouted along the sands of Dee.

'There it is,' I said to Tika, 'the real world, the world in which most of us live. No, old girl, it isn't half as attractive as the world you have shown to me. You and I were really not born to enjoy the spreading suburbia, the pop groups, the caravan parks, the slow strangulation of the countryside. We are not Slabmen, we are natural inhabitants of the Cracks. I think we are safe for a little time yet. Together we have found a few hiding-places from the wrath to come—the moorlands are still dark and wet at the top of the Camddwr, the waves still come in on to the sea-weeded shore at Aber Mawr unsoiled by oil patches and floating paper bags, and the lanes of Montgomeryshire still defy the planners and twist themselves into leafy knots across the salmon streams of the Alun and the Banwy. When the modern world becomes too much for me I'll come back and borrow you from Towyn and ride again. You have shown me that I am a natural survivor from the Horse Age. Come up, old girl. Together we'll face it all!'

I sat firmly in the saddle in what I hoped would be the perfect horseman's posture. Tika took me slowly downhill towards the Future.

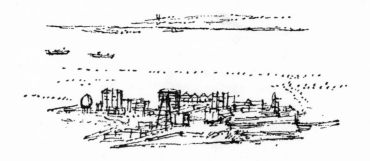